Wired for Success

The Butte, Anaconda & Pacific Railway, 1892–1985

Wired for Success

The Butte, Anaconda & Pacific Railway, 1892–1985

Charles V. Mutschler

Washington State University Press
Pullman, Washington

Washington State University Press
PO Box 645910
Pullman, WA 99164-5910
Phone: 800-354-7360
Fax: 509-335-8568
E-mail: wsupress@wsu.edu
Web site: www.wsu.edu/wsupress

Library of Congress Cataloging-in-Publication Data

Mutschler, Chas. V. (Charles Vincent), 1955–
    Wired for success : the Butte, Anaconda & Pacific Railway, 1892–1985 / Charles V. Mutschler.
        p. cm.
    Includes bibliographical references and index.
    ISBN 0-87422-252-4
    1. Butte, Anaconda, and Pacific Railway Company—History. 2. Railroads—Montana—History. 3. Copper mines and mining—Montana—History. I. Title.

TF25.B98 M88 2002

385.5'4786—dc21   2002006399

On the cover: A publicity photo, probably taken in 1915, of an electric-powered Butte, Anaconda & Pacific 50-car ore train crossing Silver Bow Creek. The original black and white photo has been cropped and colorized. *Montana Historical Society, Helena, #PAc 82-62.412.*

Table of Contents

Dedicated to the Memory of

My Father

Felix Ernest Mutschler

ACKNOWLEDGMENTS

No book is really the exclusive product of its author. Many people and organizations have assisted with this project, first as a doctoral dissertation at Washington State University, and now as a monograph. I extend my sincere thanks to my dissertation committee of Orlan J. Svingen, Richard Hume, John E. Kicza, and Jerry Gough. My colleagues at Eastern Washington University have been especially helpful. University Archivist Emeritus Jay Weston Rea, Dean of Libraries V. Louise Saylor, and her successor, Dean of Information Resources Patricia Kelley approved my educational leave, during which much of the research was conducted. Lillian Wong, in the Reference Department, and Troy Christenson and the staff of Interlibrary Loan were a great help. My assistant, Elaine Zieger-Breeding, kept the Archives operating smoothly while I was on vacation, writing and revising the manuscript.

William McCarthy, president of the Rarus Railway, successor to the Butte, Anaconda & Pacific, kindly allowed access to the company's property and records. Archivists and librarians who assisted include the following: The staff of ALCO Historic Photos, in Schenectady, New York. Jerry Hansen and the staff of the Anaconda-Deer Lodge County Historical Society. Ellen Crain and the staff of the Butte-Silver Bow Public Archives. W. Thomas White of the James J. Hill Library, St. Paul, Minnesota. Ellie Argumbau, Lory Morrow and Brian Shovers, at the Montana Historical Society in Helena. Jean Bishop, Reference Librarian, at Montana Tech in Butte. Jodi Allison Bunnell and the staff of the K. Ross Toole Archives, at the University of Montana. Richard Engemann and the staff of the Oregon Historical Society.

The California State Railroad Museum, Colorado Railroad Museum, National Model Railroad Association, and National Railway Historical Society all provided copies of pages of the *National Railway Equipment Register* from their collections. David Pfieffer of the National Archives and Records Administration assisted with records of the Interstate Commerce Commission.

Private collectors and independent researchers were equally helpful. Robert S. Blilie, Clive Carter, John B. Corns, Doug Cummings, Michael J. Denuty, Tim Diebert, Robert K. Dowler, Marshall Feehan, Eugene T. Hawk, Theodore J. Holloway, Pete Kovanda, David W. Pierson, Ray Sauvy, Philip Slocum, Bill and Jan Taylor, and Peter E. Thompson were generous with their material and time.

Several organizations have kindly permitted me to reproduce their material. ALCO Historic Photos permitted use of photographs from the American Locomotive Company collection. Anaconda-Deer Lodge County Historical Society permitted use of photographs. Butte-Silver Bow Public Archives allowed use of photographs, maps and drawings from the BA&P records held in their collection. Montana Historical Society allowed use of photographs from their collections. Simmons-Boardman Publishing Company permitted use of illustrations from the *Car Builder's Dictionary*, *Locomotive Cyclopedia of American Practice*, *Railroad Gazette*, and *Railway Age*. University of Montana, K. Ross Toole Archives, allowed use of photos by Philip C. Johnson.

Research in Montana was greatly facilitated by the generosity of Donald, Gloria, Peter, and Sarah Sprague, who allowed me to make my research headquarters in their Butte home. Judy McMillan did the final cartography for the original maps. Cary C. Collins, James Frederickson, Robert Olsen, Denise Rougon, Charles Soule, Bill and Jan Taylor, and Harry B. Treloar read and commented on the manuscript. My mother, "Bunny," proofread the galleys. I thank them all for their suggestions and comments. Glen Lindeman, chief editor of the WSU Press, has been professional and helpful in every way, as well as editor and compositor Nancy Grunewald, whose skills brought this book into its present form. It has been a pleasure to work with the entire WSU Press staff, including Jean Taylor, Sue Emory, and Jenni Lynn.

Lastly, I wish to recognize the contributions of my late father, Felix E. Mutschler, Ph.D., who began his geological career as an exploration geologist for Bear Creek Mining Company, a subsidiary of the Kennecott Copper Corporation. In 1969 he became a university professor, but remained interested in the copper industry for the rest of his life. In spite of his own prodigious work load and deteriorating health, he made time to read the original manuscript, provide geologic information about the Butte Mining District, and draft rough maps from which the final cartography was produced. This volume is dedicated to his memory with thanks and gratitude. Tap 'er light, Dad.

Charles V. Mutschler
Cheney, Washington

INTRODUCTION

*I*N THE CLOSING YEARS of the twentieth century, it has become commonplace to think of the economy of the United States as having a post-industrial base, where information and service providers are more important than traditional heavy industries such as manufacturing. During this same period, historians have turned their attention increasingly on social concepts. The lives of common people, especially those who are not members of the power elite, are often the central focus for much of modern historical scholarship. The lives of ordinary persons, however, of any race, class, or gender are shaped by economic, political, and technological issues. For this reason, a study of the Butte, Anaconda & Pacific Railway (BA&P) is of interest. Its life offers a microcosmic look at the transformation of one industry in response to technological and economic forces. Such a study tells a specific story about the economy of the United States as it moved from reliance on coal-fired steam power to electric power and internal combustion engines. It is told, moreover, against the backdrop of moving a Montana mountain of copper, the Butte Hill, to the smelter operations at Anaconda, twenty-six miles to the west.

The central subjects of *Wired for Success* are technology and corporate development. Railroads and electricity have profoundly shaped everyday life in the United States for more than a century. Transportation, energy, and communication were paramount for the development of the United States as an industrial power in the nineteenth century, and as a world military and political power in the twentieth century. These same needs must be met if the United States is to remain a global economic power in the twenty-first century.

Railroad transportation provided low-cost, dependable movement of goods and people, enabling the United States to evolve from an agrarian republic to an industrial nation in a half-century between 1850 and 1900. After the United States had become an industrial power, alternative sources of energy began to compete with coal-fired steam engines, and electricity was the first competitor to seriously challenge steam's supremacy. Efforts to apply electric power to railroads for economic reasons began after 1900, but ultimately, they never overcame the dominance of steam until electricity was combined with the internal combustion engine. Since 1960, the diesel-electric locomotive has dominated the North American railroad system, and the electric freight locomotive has become a museum piece, together with the few remaining steam locomotives. The transformation of the continent's railroad motive power over the course of a century can be observed in microcosm on the BA&P.

Inexpensive railroad transportation permitted development of industries like copper mining in the western United States. The mines in turn provided copper for electric lights, stoves, and other consumer goods at an increasing rate after 1880. Copper has proven to be particularly valuable in the sphere of communications. It is used for telephones, telephone wire, radios, and televisions. The foundation of the post-industrial, information-based economy tied to the internet is still largely dependent on copper. While overshadowed by the mystique of western mining, the role of a company-owned railroad as an integral part of the production of copper was critical to people who depended on copper for electric power to light their homes and to operate the electronic equipment of businesses and governments. Therefore, this history of a mining company railroad focuses on technology.

The Butte, Anaconda & Pacific Railway was a standard gauge common carrier railroad operating solely within the state of Montana. Incorporated in 1892, the single track main line from Butte to Anaconda opened in December, 1893. The BA&P was built to move ore from Butte to the smelter at Anaconda; freight and passenger business was of secondary importance.

The BA&P was the brainchild of Marcus Daly, whose Anaconda Copper Mining Company was the railroad's primary shipper. Daly was one of Butte's leading "copper kings," along with William A. Clark and F. Augustus Heinze. These three men were the primary antagonists in the early struggle to develop and control Butte's copper mines. An impoverished Irish immigrant, Daly began his mining career as a silver miner at Nevada's Comstock Lode during the 1860s. His hard work and intelligence were noticed by

Marcus Daly. *Montana Historical Society, Helena, #941-880*

superiors and he was soon promoted to foreman. By the 1870s he was a respected mine manager, working for Utah mine owners, who sent him to Butte. He invested his savings in a promising Butte mining claim called the Anaconda. This was the start of the Anaconda Copper Mining Company (ACM). By the time of Daly's death in 1900, the ACM was an industrial giant, comprised of mines, smelters, saw mills, coal mines, and a railroad.[1]

Known by a variety of names reflecting its corporate evolution, the ACM was the economic ruler of Butte for nearly a century. A simplified corporate genealogy is illustrated below in Table 1. Starting as a partnership comprised of Daly and his three California backers, the business was incorporated in 1891 as the Anaconda Mining Company. The Anaconda Mining Company was reorganized as the Anaconda Copper Mining Company in 1895. In 1899 a holding company, called the Amalgamated Copper Company, was created by men associated with the Standard Oil Company to consolidate their control of Montana copper mining properties. Under the aegis of Amalgamated, the copper mining companies operating in Butte were consolidated into the Anaconda Copper Mining Company in 1910. Amalgamated's operations outside Montana were then merged into the ACM before the holding company itself was disincorporated in 1915, leaving the ACM an international giant in the copper industry. The corporate name was shortened to Anaconda Company in 1955.[2] (See Table 1.)

TABLE 1. Anaconda Copper Mining Company Corporate Chronology

ANACONDA COMPANY CORPORATE CHRONOLOGY

1876	Anaconda claim located by Michael Hickey.
1876	Marcus Daly inspects the Alice claim at Butte for Walker Brothers of Salt Lake City.
1880	Marcus Daly buys the Anaconda claim.
1881	Anaconda Silver Mining Co. partnership formed by Daly, Haggin, Hearst, and Tevis.
1882	Daly convinces his partners to mine copper at Butte.
1891	Anaconda Silver Mining Co. partnership incorporates as the Anaconda Mining Company on January 16, 1891.
1895	Anaconda Mining Company re-incorporated as Anaconda Copper Mining Company (ACM) on June 18, 1895. Hearst stock marketed.
1896	Conflict for control of Butte copper mining between Daly, William Clark, and small mine owners, soon to include F. Augustus Heinze.
1899	Amalgamated Copper Company (holding company) incorporated to facilitate consolidation of Montana copper properties in hands of Standard Oil Co. executives. Amalgamated control of ACM through stock ownership.
1900	Marcus Daly dies.
1901	Clark agrees to cooperate with Amalgamated.
1906	Heinze sells his Butte mining properties to Amalgamated.
1910	Clark sells his Butte mining properties to Amalgamated.
1915	Butte copper mining consolidated as ACM, and Amalgamated dissolved.
1955	Anaconda Copper Mining Company renamed Anaconda Company.
1976	Atlantic Richfield Co., a major petroleum company, buys Anaconda Company.
1980	Atlantic Richfield closes Anaconda's Montana properties, offers them for sale.

William A. Clark came to Montana with the rush of goldseekers in the 1860s. Ambitious, hard-working, and mercenary, Clark soon discovered that "mining the miners" was more profitable than digging for gold himself. Starting as a shopkeeper who plowed his profits into more goods and then banking, he was an established banker by the time Butte's silver boom began

William A. Clark, 1898. *Montana Historical Society, Helena, #941-722*

in the 1870s. Banking profits invested in Butte mines earned even greater returns for him. Clark was the leading economic and political power in Butte by the late 1870s, and he resented Daly, who held antagonistic political views. The two became bitter rivals. During the 1880s and 1890s, Clark appeared to be a serious challenger to the Anaconda Company. But beginning in 1901, Clark chose to cooperate with Anaconda's owners in return for their support of his election to the United States Senate in 1900. He sold his Butte mining properties to his erstwhile competitors in 1910.[3]

F. Auguste Heinze, from "Fight of the Copper Kings" by C.P. Connolly, *McClures Magazine*, May 1907, p. 318. *Photo courtesy of Montana Historical Society, Helena.*

Heinze was the last of the copper kings to arrive in Butte. His attempts to control a significant share of Butte's copper mines started in the 1890s, and concluded in 1906 when he forced other Butte mine owners to buy him out at inflated prices. The purchase of Heinze's Butte mines, along with Clark's non-combative stance after 1901, effectively completed the consolidation of the vast majority of Butte's copper mining under control of the Anaconda Company.[4]

Marcus Daly, the driving force behind the Anaconda Copper Mining Company, was responsible for the birth of the Butte, Anaconda & Pacific Railway. Typical of industry-financed short lines, most of its traffic consisted of hauling the parent company's ore and mining supplies.

Daly believed in using the best equipment available. Supplied largely with new equipment, the BA&P began operations in 1892 well prepared for efficiently hauling ore from the Butte mines to the smelter in Anaconda. During its first twenty years, the company kept pace with new technology, buying modern rolling stock. For example, when all-steel hopper cars came on the scene in the late 1890s, the BA&P enthusiastically replaced its old wooden cars with a fleet of steel cars. Electrification was perceived as the railroad's crowning technological achievement in 1914. Electrification was an economic blessing, allowing the company to move heavier ore trains from mines to smelter than had been possible with steam locomotives. Although a few steam locomotives were retained, they were largely used for switching.

The BA&P came under electrification between 1912 and 1915 within the context of the competition between two electrical manufacturers striving to sell electric motors to industrial users. One of the companies, Westinghouse, advocated the use of single-phase alternating current for railroad locomotives and other large motors. Its rival, General Electric (GE), promoted Thomas A. Edison's theories for the use of high voltage direct current. It was General Electric that persuaded the BA&P to become a proving ground for its designs. By 1915 the BA&P appeared to be a textbook example of modern railroading.

Although the company continued to experiment with innovative ways to improve service, it had reached its high-water mark by 1915. Gradually, the BA&P retreated into its role as a local transportation subsidiary of the copper company, with little reason to modernize its aging fleet of freight cars and locomotives. Although several efforts were made to modernize the physical plant and rolling stock, the majority of the equipment remaining at the end of operations had become so obsolete that it no longer met the interchange requirements for use on the nation's common carriers.[5]

The BA&P terminated over a half-century of electric operation in 1967. Main-line electrification had not swept steam locomotives from the nation's rails, it turned out. Diesel-electric locomotives replaced steam power in the fifteen years after World War II, and most electrics as well. On the BA&P the last steam locomotives were retired in the early 1950s, replaced by new diesel-electrics from the Electro-Motive Division of General Motors. About fifteen years later, the BA&P dieselized completely, retiring its entire fleet of electric locomotives. Although modernization of the railroad proceeded more rapidly in the 1970s, the closure of the ACM mining and smelting operations at Butte and Anaconda in 1980 resulted in a more drastic change. In 1985 the BA&P was sold to some former BA&P officials, who renamed it the Rarus Railway, after one of Heinze's key mines during the battle for Butte's mineral wealth. The Rarus Railway is more of a typical short line than its predecessor. Fewer trains run, the staff is much smaller, and the railroad is not owned by the mining company. Rarus operates a small number of older, second-hand diesel-electric locomotives, and has relatively few freight cars used in interchange service.

The casual observer of the Rarus Railway would probably not guess the wealth of history and technological advancement that took place on this twenty-six-mile line. Generally, one would not realize that its predecessor, the Butte, Anaconda & Pacific, enjoyed a few years in the early 1900s as one of the most technologically advanced railroads in the world. The story of the BA&P deserves to be told, as it reflects the shift of American industry from steam to electricity in the twentieth century.

Notes

1. *New York Times*, November 13, 1900, p. 2; Michael Malone, *The Battle for Butte: Mining and Politics on the Northern Frontier, 1864–1906*, (Helena, Montana: Montana State Historical Society, 1995).

2. *New York Times*, April 26, 1899, p. 1; Ibid., April 27, 1899, p. 14; Ibid., June 18, 1899, p. 12. See also, Thomas R. Navin, *Copper Mining and Management*, (Tucson, Arizona: University of Arizona Press, 1978), pp. 202–219. Charles K. Hyde, *Copper for America: The United States Copper Industry from Colonial Times to the 1990's*, (Tucson, Arizona: University of Arizona Press, 1998) pp. 80–110. K. Ross Toole, "A History of The Anaconda Copper Mining Company: A Study of the Relationships Between a State and Its People and a Corporation, 1880–1950," (Ph.D. dissertation, University of California at Los Angeles, 1954). Malone, *The Battle for Butte* gives a good historical overview of the relationship between the company and Montana's political affairs, and the creation of the Amalgamated Copper Company. Isaac F. Marcosson,

Anaconda (New York: Dodd, Mead & Co., 1957), is the official corporate history of the company.

3. *New York Times*, April 16, 1901, p. 16; Ibid., May 15, 1910, p. 9; December 14, 1910, p. 11; Ibid., March 3, 1925, p. 1; Ibid., March 8, 1925, p. 4. Also see: Malone, *The Battle For Butte*.

4. *New York Times*, February 14, 1906, Ibid., p. 1; February 15, 1906, p. 14; Ibid., February 18, p. 7; Ibid., November 5, 1914, p. 11. Sara McNelis, "The Life of F. Augustus Heinze," MA thesis, Montana State University, 1947, is an uncritical, highly favorable biography of Heinze.

5. Interchange service means that the cars meet both the legal and industry mandated requirements to be safely exchanged, or interchanged, from one railroad to another. See: United States Department of Transportation, Federal Railroad Administration, *United States Safety Appliance Standards and Power Brake Requirements*, Washington, D.C.: U.S. Government Printing Office, September, 1977.

Chapter One

THE RICHEST HILL ON EARTH, 1860–1900

In the copper area the slopes are gridironed by railway tracks leading to the different mines, and great mine buildings, tall smokestacks, and steel hoist frames mark the course of the greater veins.[1]

*B*UTTE'S RESIDENTS CALL IT "the richest hill on earth," and for decades it was the economic engine of Montana. The mines were mostly spread across the hillsides north and east of the city's business district. Houses crowded around gallows frames and ore bins. At the peak of activity, the Butte Hill resembled an oversized model railroad layout, with a maze of trackage serving the mines in and around the city. Ore trains rumbled through back yards, and wound around hills on the margin of city streets. For over eighty years, from 1894 until 1980, the locomotives of the Butte, Anaconda & Pacific Railway (BA&P) hauled ore from the Butte Hill to the Anaconda smelter. The BA&P was a creature of the mines. To a great extent, the history of the Montana operations of the Anaconda Copper Mining Company is coupled to the history of the railroad it owned. Therefore, an overview of mining development in the Butte region will be helpful to place the railroad in context.

Mining development in Butte progressed through three distinct periods associated with three different metals: gold, silver, and finally, copper. Initially gold brought miners to the Silver Bow Valley. After the gold rush, silver became the mainstay of the district's economy. Copper moved into the preeminent place in Montana's economy as reliance on electricity for industrial and domestic applications increased rapidly in the 1880s and on through the 1920s. Copper mining and refining in the United States underwent significant changes during those years. Those changes, and others which followed during the rest of the century, in turn shaped the operations of both the Anaconda company and its railroad.

Butte today is still a mining town, though the economy is shifting toward increasing dependence on tourism, export business through a Pacific-rim jet port, and service-economy businesses. At Anaconda the concentrator and smelter which comprised the Washoe Works were razed during the 1980s, except for the stack.

Tourists with cameras instead of miners with lunch buckets pass through the gate of Anselmo Mine on the Butte Hill, now a museum, where the last BA&P boxcab and a single example of the 50-ton ore cars—once synonymous with the railroad and Butte—are on display in the now-silent mine yard. Below the statue of Our Lady of the Rockies, the Continental pit, operated by Montana Resources, has obliterated the suburb of Meaderville and Butte's amusement park, Columbia Gardens. Long-closed deep mines like the Rarus have also vanished into the voids left by the old Berkeley pit and the present day Continental pit. The enormous open-pit mine continues to grow, helping to supply the nation's demand for copper, silver, gold, and other metals. These are extracted from low grade ore which would have been deemed worthless when William A. Clark, Marcus Daly, and F. Augustus Heinze were fighting to control "the richest hill on earth." Much has changed in a century. Copper mining today would be almost unrecognizable to the miners of Daly's Butte. And yet one thing remains the same— the ore still starts its journey toward becoming finished copper by riding out of Butte over the rails once owned by the BA&P.

Butte is located just west of the Continental Divide, bordered on the south by the Highland Mountains, and on the west by a low plateau separating the town from the Deer Lodge Valley. Silver Bow Creek cuts through this plateau on its course running westerly and then north to the Deer Lodge Valley and the Clark Fork River.[2]

Approximately twenty miles west of Butte, where Warm Springs Creek enters the Deer Lodge Valley, is the town of Anaconda. Anaconda was created by Marcus Daly to be the primary processing point for ores from the Butte mines of the Anaconda Copper Mining Company.

Butte has an average elevation of 5,490 feet above sea level, almost a thousand feet lower than Homestake Pass where Interstate 90 and the former Northern Pacific cross the Continental Divide.[3] The city is located within the Boulder batholith, a 2,450 square-mile granite intrusive mass about 80 to 75 million years old. Quartz monzonite and granodiorite compose the major part of the batholith, which includes rocks ranging in composition from gabbro to granite.[4] The Butte Quartz Monzonite is the host rock for most of the ore bodies lying under and adjacent to the city.[5] The Butte ore deposits formed between 76 and 59 million years ago.[6] Along the bottom of the rugged western slope of the Continental Divide, and at the foot of the Butte Hill along Silver Bow Creek, are alluvial deposits caused by erosion of the surrounding mountains.[7]

While most of the nation was preoccupied with the military campaigns of the Civil War, prospectors found placer gold along several creeks in southwestern Montana. Rich discoveries were made at Alder Gulch in Virginia City, and at Last Chance Gulch in Helena during 1863. These resulted in a rush to Montana Territory, and a general search for other placer deposits. In the spring of 1864, a passing traveler noticed gold in some gravel in the location of Butte's present-day Main Street, but he did not work the site. Actual mining in the Butte area began in the summer. In the winter of 1865, the Summit Valley mining district was officially created, and claims were staked along Buffalo, Missoula, Town, and Parrot gulches above Silver Bow Creek.[8] As the population of the mining camp grew, the community took on the name of Butte in 1866, named after the distinctive Big Butte, a landmark to the west of town. By 1900 the mining district was "now universally known as Butte," sharing the name of the city.[9]

A period of placer gold production followed the initial discovery. Working these claims was difficult, as the gold-bearing gravel was on hillsides and in the normally dry gulches north of Silver Bow Creek. Because the claims lacked sufficient water to work them, the gravel had to be hauled by pack animal or wagon to Silver Bow Creek to separate the gold. Transporting ore from mine to processing location, and its related costs, were thus a concern to Butte miners from the beginning. An effort to develop a technological solution to the problem was sought by constructing ditches to bring water to the gravel deposits in the arid gulches. By 1867 three ditches were supplying water

for washing gold-bearing gravel in the gulches, making the haul to Silver Bow Creek no longer necessary.[10] The community of Rocker along Silver Bow Creek is a reflection of the history of the area's early mining heritage, drawing its name from a commonly used placer mining tool.[11]

An additional reason for Butte's relatively short life as a placer camp was the extremely small grain size of the gold—fine dust—valued at only ten to fourteen dollars per troy ounce because it was mixed with silver.[12] Although the placers around Butte produced over $1,500,000 in gold dust during the initial three-year period of exploitation, the deposits were not as rich as other Montana placers. Placer mining peaked in 1867, and with it, the town's population. As placer gold production diminished, Butte's population dwindled from an early high in 1868 to virtually ghost town status in 1875.[13] Although gold production was soon eclipsed by silver and then copper, the district contained gravels which continued to be worked for gold until the start of World War I. Total placer production between 1864 and 1914 was approximately 363,000 troy ounces of gold.[14]

Quartz veins were located soon after the initial placer discovery. The first lode claim to be located was the Asteroid, which was staked by William Farlin in 1864. This claim later became known as the Travona. Although gold may occur in quartz veins, the Travona, like most of the other early lode claims in Butte, was developed as a silver mine. In the late 1860s a small amount of high grade silver ore from the Mountain Chief mine was shipped to Newark, New Jersey, for reduction by way of Fort Benton, Montana, and the Missouri River.[15] The value of most ore would not afford such high freight costs.

Initially, miners in Butte tried to work the veins for gold because gold was easier to mill than silver ore with the existing technology of the early 1860s. Gold ore was broken up, and the gold removed from the waste rock by the process of amalgamation with mercury. When the crushed ore was mixed with mercury, only the gold adhered to the mercury, resulting in an amalgam of gold and mercury. When the amalgam was heated in a retort, the mercury evaporated off, leaving metallic gold.[16]

Butte's silver ores could not be treated effectively with this method. The blue-black stained quartz veins containing high silver content proved unprofitable to mine until the technologically more sophisticated techniques developed at Nevada's Comstock Lode became common practice. At Butte, the silver-bearing ore was not susceptible to the older process of crushing and amalgamation with mercury. Miners called these ores which resisted amalgamation "refractory."[17] Efforts to process refractory ores began with simple trial and error methodology, which gradually led to increased dependence on science and technology.[18] The coupling of science and technology to mine and process ores was later applied to copper production in Butte.

Discovery of a particularly rich vein of silver ore in the Travona in 1865 sparked the initial efforts to produce silver in Butte. Farlin's first attempt to mill silver ore in 1866 with an arrastra failed. An arrastra is a simple crushing system, used widely in Mexico and South America, as well as in the early days of the California gold rush, which uses animal power to drag boulders around in a circular pit to crush ore sufficiently to allow amalgamation of the metal. A pivot post is placed upright in the center of a circular crushing floor surrounded by a masonry wall. A cross-beam extends from the pivot post to the outside of the crushing floor, to which draft animals are hitched for operational power. Boulders are chained to the cross-beam within the area of the crushing floor to break up the gold-bearing ore. A relatively simple and inexpensive technology, the arrastra was adequate for mines processing relatively small quantities of ore.[19] For mines in remote regions, ore crushing with arrastras represented a minimalist technology not requiring extensive transportation systems to support it. There was no heavy machinery to be hauled overland; aside from the chain and a relatively small amount of iron for hardware, there was no manufactured equipment to haul to the mill site. Everything else needed could be produced from locally available materials.

Butte's complex silver ores did not lend themselves to milling with an arrastra, because the silver was not in a native form that would amalgamate with mercury. Farlin, like most of his contemporaries, did not understand the nature of Butte's silver ores.[20] Because Farlin believed that amalgamation did not occur because the arrastra could not reduce the silver ore to a fine enough powder to amalgamate well, he had a ten-stamp mill hauled in, hoping that finer crushing of the ore would permit amalgamation. In a stamp mill, the ore is placed in metal mortars called "batteries," where it is broken into a fine powder by metal stamps. The stamps were iron (later, steel) castings on steel rods, which were actuated by cams on a revolving horizontal shaft. Powdered ore was then processed by amalgamation. Mercury was sometimes placed in the batteries, or the precious metal was separated by washing the powdered ore through riffles comparable to those in sluice boxes. In such an instance, the metal, being heavier than the waste rock, accumulated in the riffles, and the waste was washed out to a tailings pond.[21]

The stamp mill was more efficient than the arrastra, but required a more advanced technology to support it. The stamps and mortars were castings, and the shafts and machinery of the mill required more iron or steel parts than the simple arrastra. If water-operated, the mill required a steady supply of water year round; if steam-operated, the mill required fuel in addition to water. Access to a blacksmith at the least, and preferably the services of machinists and a foundry, were necessary to support a stamp mill operation.

Although the silver ore from the Travona was pulverized more efficiently by the stamps than by grinding in an arrastra, the results were still not economically viable. The silver would not readily amalgamate with mercury, so Farlin's initial experiments to profitably mine Butte's silver failed.[22]

After these failed experiments, Farlin concentrated on gold production at the Travona for the next nine years, until 1875, when he applied smelting techniques to silver ore from his mine. A ten-stamp mill and a furnace were constructed near the mine. Silver ore was processed in the new plant by chloridization and roasting before amalgamation. Only a very small amount of silver bullion was produced before Farlin chose to sell out to William A. Clark in 1876.

Clark is credited with operating the first commercially successful plant treating Butte's silver ores, starting in 1876. Clark's operation was a contract firm, processing ores from mines throughout the district, and not just from his own. Although the prices charged were moderate for the time and place, at $25.00 to $30.00 per ton, it was judged steep enough so that some of the other mines began building their own mills.[23]

Clark was one of the fortunate few who was in the proverbial right place at the right time.[24] He sought profitable silver mines, and ventured into the profitable copper business following Daly's lead.[25] Like Daly and Heinze, the junior member of Butte's "copper kings,"[26] Clark built an empire of mines and railroads to serve them.[27] Shrewd investments in Butte's mines made Clark a millionaire, and yet, unsatisfied, he craved public respect and the honors of a political life. Clark's public image and political career were marred by the bribery and other blatantly corrupt practices he employed. Clark is actually more renowned for his political machinations than for the significant role he played in developing western copper properties or the consolidation of Butte's mineral wealth in the hands of the Anaconda Copper Mining Company.[28]

Lode mining in Butte involved sinking shafts to access rich veins and ore bodies. The method required to process silver, and later copper ores, was only one element of the increasingly technological nature of mining in the west. Shafts, stopes, and drifts all required copious quantities of timber to support them and prevent cave-ins. Here Butte's mines benefited from techniques pioneered earlier in Nevada's Comstock Lode. The Comstock's large stopes had been made possible by the development of a system of timbering to support the roof and prevent caving when large blocks of ore were removed. This was the square set system, developed by Philip Deidesheimer late in 1860. Timbers were cut to uniform sizes, and assembled into uniform rectangular box-shaped units underground. Four timbers were laid down as horizontal sills, a foundation upon which four uprights posts were placed, one in

Timbering to shore up a Butte mine. *Butte-Silver Bow Public Archives, #223*

each corner. Four horizontal caps rested on these, with the entire assembly outlining a cube. The caps on one layer of square sets served as the base for the next layer, and uniform size allowed systematic expansion of the timbering as the ore was removed from the stope.[29] At Butte the use of square sets allowed for the development of the mines, but it required ready access to large quantities of timber. Transportation was thus doubly crucial for the miners of Butte. Not only did concentrates, bullion, or matte have to be shipped out, but great loads of large, heavy timbers had to be received by the mines.[30] The arrival of the railroad in 1881 greatly facilitated the receipt of timbers for the mines.

As the development of silver mines in Butte continued in the 1870s and 1880s, the consolidation of ownership into the hands of a few capitalists accelerated. This process, called rationalization, was the normal sequence of events in the mining regions throughout the west during the nineteenth and early twentieth centuries.[31] The initial prospectors typically lacked the finances necessary to develop their claims, and either

Miners preparing to extend a drift. *Butte-Silver Bow Public Archives, #224*

sold out to moneyed interests or sought financial backing from men who could enable them to develop their claims into paying mines. As capitalists took control of a mining district, efforts to rationalize ownership to minimize expensive competition frequently followed, and smaller firms were acquired by larger corporations, resulting in fewer companies operating within the district. This process played out in Butte after it became primarily a copper-producing district. Eventually all the mines came under the sole ownership of the corporation begun by Marcus Daly, the Anaconda Copper Mining Company (ACM).

Marcus Daly arrived in Butte in the spring of 1876, representing the Walker Brothers, Utah bankers from Salt Lake City who had capitalized in mining properties. The Walkers had become interested in the Butte district when some high grade silver ore was shipped to them from the Acquisition claim. They sent Daly to inspect the mining district, and to report on its potential. Daly, an Irish immigrant who had started as a common miner in the Comstock district, Nevada, had rapidly advanced to become a foreman, and then a respected mine manager. His experience and practical knowledge made him a sought-after expert in the 1870s. Academically trained mining engineers and geologists were still enough of a rarity in the United States that a man like Daly, who had learned through experience on the job, was held in high regard by mine developers.[32] Daly was a man of simple tastes in his personal life, but firmly believed in buying the best equipment and hiring the best talent in the business realm. Marcus Daly became the driving force behind the initial development of the Anaconda Copper Mining Company, and its subsidiary, the Butte, Anaconda & Pacific Railway, but died in 1900, prior to the final consolidation of the mining industry in Butte.[33]

Daly was so impressed by the Alice claim that he took a $5,000 bond on the property for the Walkers. Improvement work on the Alice began that summer, and continued for the next decade. Initially a mill was constructed with second-hand machinery in 1877. In response to the refractory nature of Butte's silver ores, a roaster was added to the mill, and the Washoe process of treating silver was successfully undertaken.[34] The Washoe process involves roasting the ore in a reverberatory furnace to reduce the sulfur content before the ore is smelted. Other mines soon adopted the same technology, and by 1887 five mills were processing about 400 tons of silver ore a day. Another 100 tons of ore were shipped to smelters daily, for a total daily output of approximately 500 tons, with an average yield of $25 in silver and gold per ton of ore.[35]

Transportation improvements had made this possible by 1887. After the railroad arrived in 1881, miners enjoyed lower fares than traveling by stage. Moreover, supplies and equipment for the mines cost less to ship to Butte by rail than by wagon.[36] High grade ore, concentrates, or bullion were also easily shipped out of the district.

The silver bonanza ended suddenly across the West in 1893, when two of the largest markets for western silver collapsed simultaneously. The mint of India stopped buying silver, and the United States repealed the Sherman Silver Purchase Act. The blow was catastrophic for silver mining camps. Fortunately for Butte, the mining companies were able to shift their primary production to copper, for which there was a burgeoning demand due to the need for electric wire.

Copper was discovered almost at the beginning of mining in Butte, but initially the copper deposits were significant mainly because of their lucrative silver and gold content. Until the crash of the silver market, copper was simply regarded as a marketable by-product from the precious metals mined in Butte.[37]

Prior to 1880, copper mining in the United States had been concentrated in two areas: Michigan and Arizona Territory. Michigan mines, especially those of the Calumet & Hancock Company, were the most productive in the country at that time. After 1880, demand for copper in the United States, spurred by increasing electrical needs, exceeded the output of the Michigan mines, further encouraging the development of copper mining in the western territories by astute mine owners.[38] Development of copper properties advanced steadily in Arizona during the 1870s and 1880s, despite transportation hindrances. When copper became a major interest at Butte, Arizona was already an important copper producing region. Largely due to Daly and his associates, and the richness of copper deposits encountered in some of the Butte mines, Montana surpassed Michigan's copper production in 1887. For the next three years, Montana produced more copper than Michigan or Arizona, then dropped below Michigan in 1891. In 1892 Montana regained the lead, remaining the nation's largest copper producing state until 1910, when it was surpassed by Arizona Territory.[39]

The Gagnon, Original, Park, and Parrott claims were all located in Butte in 1864, and by 1872 Clark began buying claims which would become important copper producers in a few years.[40] Clark's initial improvement work was done on four claims, including the Colusa and the Original. The lower grade ore Clark sought to exploit contained not only the silver and gold which were his primary interests, but significant amounts of copper as well.

Daly was the first of the mine owners to see a copper-clad future for Butte, but, like Clark, he arrived at it by way of silver mining. The Alice Mine, which the Walker Brothers purchased in 1876 on Daly's advice, provided his financial stake for entry into the world of mining capitalism. The Alice produced handsomely, and the Walkers, out of gratitude, gave Daly a share in the property. By selling his share in the Alice, Daly raised enough capital to purchase a promising claim for himself—the Anaconda, which he bought for $45,000.[41] Financially unable to develop the property by himself, Daly nonetheless had personal connections to financial backers. He enlisted the aid of three California investors in order to raise the capital required to develop the Anaconda, initially as a silver mine.

Daly's Anaconda Mine investors were James Ben Ali Haggin,[42] George Hearst,[43] and Lloyd Tevis[44] of San Francisco—all highly successful investors in mining and banking circles. The trio had obtained spectacular returns from the largest gold mine in the United States, the Homestake Mine at Lead, South Dakota.[45] When Daly approached them in 1881 to back his Anaconda silver mine, the Californians were receptive, especially Hearst, who recognized Daly's past record as a successful manager of developing silver mines in Nevada and Utah. The Anaconda seemed to be a reasonable investment, given the geologic evidence and Daly's reputation. Daly's agreement with his supporters gave him a 25 percent share of the company, as compensation for his initial work buying the claim and beginning its development. In return for his mining expertise and a relatively small cash investment for the purchase and beginning development of the mine, Daly was to receive a larger share of the company than his dollar contribution represented. The other three put up the majority of the capital for development, anticipating returns when the Anaconda became a major silver producer.[46] Daly was appointed to stay in Montana to manage the property, while the other members of the syndicate would remain in California.

The Anaconda (indicated by the single smokestack) and Neversweat (beneath the seven stacks) mines on the Butte Hill, above uptown Butte, circa 1900. *World Museum of Mining, #5541*

The mine began operating as the Anaconda Silver Mining Company. Daly leased the Dexter mill in Butte to treat ore from the Anaconda until he could build his own mill. During 1881 approximately 8,000 tons of ore from the Anaconda were processed by this mill, with a return averaging 30 ounces of silver per ton.

Daly is generally credited with being one of the first of the Butte mine owners to view copper as a primary commodity instead of as a marketable by-product from silver mining. He ordered exploratory work in the Anaconda, including deepening the shaft and running drifts at 100-foot levels to ascertain the extent of the ore body. In less than a year of exploration, the Anaconda encountered the copper sulfide ore that became Butte's true wealth. A vein of chalcocite, a high-grade copper mineral assaying nearly 40 percent copper, changed Daly's focus.[47] By 1882 Daly had recognized that the Anaconda might have greater potential as a copper mine than as a silver producer, because so many chalcocite veins had been encountered. (See Table 2.)

During 1882, the Daly-Haggin-Hearst-Tevis syndicate rapidly expanded its ownership of mining claims near the Anaconda. The St. Lawrence and Neversweat were purchased outright, along with adjoining portions of other claims.[48] This decision to consolidate the ownership of the principal claims surrounding the Anaconda followed the decision to develop the Anaconda as a copper mine. From this decision came the need to reinvest the profits from the Anaconda to develop the extensive plant required for treating the chalcocite copper ores that had been encountered. This would require a concentrator and a smelter. As the Anaconda owners plowed their profits into larger and more sophisticated plants, their acquisition of additional mining properties in the Butte district continued.

Consolidation of the various mining claims under several groups of owners was well under way by 1881, and continued throughout the rest of the century. During this period, the nation's industrial base gradually moved from reliance on steam powered machinery toward more modern electric power. The increasing demand for electric motors and lighting in the United States helped drive up the demand for copper, just as Butte's mine owners recognized the potential mineral bonanza under their feet. Daly was

TABLE 2. Lode Production of the Butte District, 1880–1991.

BUTTE MINING DISTRICT, MONTANA			
Product	Short Tons	Troy Ounces	Notes
Copper (Cu)	11,611,840		1
Molybdenum (Mo)	>37,478		2
Gold (Au)		2,779,195	2
Silver (Ag)		692,741,480	1
Lead (Pb)	659,180		1
Zinc (Zn)	3,802,970		1
Manganese (Mn)	1,851,394		2
Cadmium (Cd)	2,153		2
Bismuth (Bi)	2,021		2
Selinium (Se)	158		2
Tellurium (Te)	119		2
Sulfuric Acid (H_2SO_4)	954,105		2
Arsenic (As) Compounds	159,117		3
Ore Treated	1,171,709,400		1,4

Notes
1. Long, 1995
2. Miller, 1973
3. Myer et al., 1968
4. Ray Tillman, MRA, to Felix E. Mutschler, Personal communication on March 4, 1998.
5. Koschman and Bergandahl, 1968

Material provided by Felix E. Mutschler, Ph.D.

not the first man to recognize Butte's copper future, but he was the first to initiate large scale production of the red metal in Montana. Across the western half of North America—from the blistering deserts of Arizona to the frigid, glacier-clad mountains of Alaska—copper production increased. Even so, between 1892 and 1910, no other place in the nation could match the output of Butte.

The Lewisohn brothers were successful New York City businessmen selling various commodities, including coffee and copper. They took an interest in the Montana copper prospects, hiring mining geologist Charles Meader to investigate the Butte district for them in 1878. Meader was favorably impressed, and he purchased several claims for the Lewisohns, including the East Colusa and West Colusa. In 1879, Meader and the Lewisohns incorporated the Montana Copper Company.[49] Two other firms controlled by the Lewisohns were formed in 1887 and 1888, the Boston & Montana Consolidated Copper and Silver Mining Company (B&M), and the Butte & Boston Consolidated Mining Company (B&B).[50] Both of these concerns controlled mines in the Butte mining district. The Lewisohns acquired smelters in Butte, but the B&M built a large smelter at Great Falls, and eventually became the dominant Lewisohn company operating in Montana.

F. Augustus Heinze, a dapper dynamo of a man, was the "underdog" who took on the larger copper companies, ultimately forcing them to buy him out at inflated prices. Heinze and his brothers were the well-educated sons of a successful German immigrant businessman in New York City. F. Augustus Heinze studied mining engineering and geology at Columbia University and Freiberg, then went west to seek his fortune, arriving in Butte in 1889. Heinze was the best trained of the Butte copper kings, having graduated from two of the most renowned mining engineering and geology programs in the world. In contrast, Daly had learned geology as a miner and mine manager, but had no schooling. Clark's brief crash course in geology at Columbia helped him somewhat, but by no means did he emerge as a mining engineer. Both Clark and Daly remained skeptical of college-trained men.

Employed by the Boston & Montana as a mining engineer, Heinze convinced his family to invest heavily in his plan to operate a custom smelting business in Butte. After arranging financing, he and his brothers formed the Montana Ore Purchasing Company (MOP) in 1893. Although primarily intended as a smelting business, MOP was obligated to obtain ore in sufficient quantities to operate efficiently. At first, this was accomplished through the lease of various small mines. But by 1895, MOP had been so successful that it was able to buy the Rarus Mine, one of Butte's largest. Heinze left Butte briefly, engaging in a short period of mining and railroad development in Canada before returning to Montana.[51] Upon his return, the battle for Butte was fairly joined. Filing lawsuits against the larger firms, claiming that the ore bodies in their mines apexed on his claims, Heinze had efficiently positioned himself to be a major irritant to the planned consolidation of Butte's copper properties under a single ownership. Despite his public claims of confidence in his cause, Heinze was not the financial equal to the interests opposing him. He sold out to Amalgamated, only after inflating the price for his Butte properties. In effect, Amalgamated (later Anaconda) had neutralized all serious competition in the Montana copper industry.

While the so-called "war of the copper kings" was getting headlines, the copper industry itself was beginning to experience change. Butte's mines were all underground, or "deep" mines, as were those in Michigan, the site of the first copper bonanza in the United States. Copper production in the United States during the nineteenth century was dependent on underground mining of medium to high grade ores. Daniel C. Jackling changed all of that when he proposed the exploitation of large, low-grade "porphyry" copper deposits using open pit mining.[52] Jackling's mine, opened in 1907, became the Bingham Pit in Utah, and changed the way the world mined copper. Other open pit operations followed in the southwestern states. Conversion of some of the Arizona mines from underground to open pit operations occurred after World War I; similar changes did not happen at Butte until 1955.[53]

Smelting became an important element of Butte's growth during the 1870s. Clark was the driving force behind the first smelter erected to serve the mines. As he was sinking the shaft on the Original claim, Clark had 150 tons of high-grade silver ore shipped to Colorado for smelting in 1877. The Boston & Colorado smelter, located in Black Hawk, Colorado, was a technological leader in smelting in the United States. Clark's shipment interested the Boston & Colorado management, resulting in the incorporation of the Colorado & Montana Company in 1878, which built a smelter at Butte that began operating in the summer of 1879. That first smelter was capable of processing twelve tons of ore every twenty-four hours.[54] The finished product was a silver and copper matte sent to the Argo smelter in Denver for further refining.[55] Thus, Clark got in on the ground floor of an advantageous situation, profiting doubly from the mines which produced the ore and from the smelter.

Large-scale smelting depended on inexpensive transportation of large quantities of fuel and other supplies, including minerals for use as flux. Use of charcoal as a fuel allowed the initial smelters at Butte to operate profitably. However, the cost of wagon freight and the gradually increasing distance to the charcoal supply eventually made coal a preferable fuel—if it could be moved by rail.

Clark's smelting success bred imitators, but with an important difference: copper, not silver, was becoming the primary objective. As a result, other smelters were built in Butte or its immediate environs in the early 1880s. The Montana Copper Company built the Colusa smelter in 1880. The Colusa smelter was fired with charcoal and was placed in operation (called "blown-in" or "in blast") in 1881,[56] followed shortly thereafter by the Parrott smelter.[57] The Parrott smelter, in 1883, was first to pioneer the adaptation of the principles of the Bessemer converter for use in copper smelting.[58] Sale of the Colusa smelter to the Boston & Montana was consummated in 1888, and the new owners operated it as their Upper Works in Butte for five years. Although the Colusa smelter was close to the mines, minimizing the distance the ore had to be shipped, the combination of a more modern plant at Great Falls, approximately 120 miles northeast of Butte, and low railroad freight costs caused B&M to close the smaller plant in 1893.[59] The larger works at Anaconda and Great Falls came after rail transportation facilitated the transportation of large quantities of ore, fuel, and flux over greater distances.

Great Falls became the location of the Boston & Montana company smelter in 1890. Subsequent expansion of the plant after 1890 included the addition of blast furnaces, anode casting equipment, and, in 1892, an electrolytic copper refinery. By 1901 this latter operation included 312 electrolytic tanks. Modernization and expansion of the Great Falls smelter and electrolytic refinery allowed Boston & Montana to consolidate its smelting and refining functions in a single location, ultimately leading to the closure of several smaller smelters at Butte which had come under B&M control.[60] The B&M plant at Great Falls passed to Anaconda in 1899 as part of the general consolidation of Montana copper mining properties undertaken by a newly formed holding company, the Amalgamated Copper Company.

Daly's Anaconda Silver Mining Company did not move immediately into smelting, but when it did, it was part of a deliberate, careful decision to enter the copper business on a very large scale. After 1882, when the company changed its primary focus to copper, silver and gold were considered highly desirable by-products of copper production from the Anaconda properties. The silver and gold output financed the conversion of the Anaconda plant from silver production and the construction of the smelter at Anaconda. Daly first leased the Dexter Mill in 1881, and had 8,000 tons of oxidized silver ore treated there that year. No immediate work to build a smelter was undertaken, but copper production in the Anaconda accelerated. Daly then persuaded his backers to enter the copper business on a large scale. Although there was some initial resistance, especially from Tevis, the proposal was agreed to. Since no facilities existed locally to treat copper ore, Daly had some of the richest ore processed outside of Montana. Commencing in 1882, high grade copper ore, averaging 45% copper, was shipped to Swansea, Wales, for smelting. Copper smelting in Wales was technologically superior to smelting in the U.S. until the mid-1880s, when American smelters began using either the Welsh design of reverberatory furnace, or blast furnaces.[61] Between 1882 and 1884, 37,000 tons of high grade ore were shipped to Swansea.[62]

By 1883 Daly was preparing to apply Welsh copper smelting practices in Montana. A site on Warm Springs Creek was selected for a smelter, and work began in 1883. The location was in the Deer Lodge Valley twenty-six miles west of Butte, on the north side of the creek.[63] Anaconda, as the place was named, had abundant water, necessary for the operation of the concentrator and smelter.[64] This facility was designed with a 500-ton-per-day capacity. Ore was first concentrated, then smelted to produce a copper matte which was sent to Swansea, Wales, or to the eastern U.S. for final refining until 1891.[65]

The process of extracting copper from ore at Anaconda followed four steps. These started with milling, progressed to concentrating, followed by smelting, and lastly, refining. Ore from Butte arrived at Anaconda by rail, and was unloaded at the concentrator. In the milling process, it was pulverized into a powder. A primary crusher broke the ore into small pieces, which were fed, along with water, into a mill—a large, cylindrical drum in which steel balls ground the ore into a fine, flour-like powder. The pulverized rock and water mixture created by milling was then ready for concentrating.[66]

Concentration was first accomplished using gravity. Slurry from the mill was placed on slightly inclined tables that were mechanically agitated as a trickle of water flowed over the concentrating table. The agitation and water film caused the relatively light, worthless rock particles to float free from the heavy, copper-bearing minerals and wash away, to be discarded as waste. The heavy minerals which remained on the concentrating table were called concentrates. After 1915 Anaconda used flotation, a more efficient concentrating technique in which the metals adhered to bubbles in an oily foam, which rose to the surface of the concentrating vat. Skimming the bubbles captured the concentrates, which were then sent to the smelter.[67]

Smelting is the heating of material to melt metals, and separate them by gravity. At Anaconda the concentrates were roasted first, to reduce the amount of sulfur contained, producing a copper-bearing flour-like substance called calcine. A reverberatory furnace was then "charged" with the calcine (roasted concentrates), and limestone for a flux. When smelting in a reverberatory furnace, the charge of copper ore was placed on a shallow hearth, with the fuel kept apart from the ore. Flames from the burning coal entered the furnace from one side, and swept over the charge, which was melted by heat radiated back from the roof of the furnace as well as from the flames over-sweeping the hearth itself.[68] Molten copper sank, and the waste, or slag, was drawn off of the top. Copper matte (a combination of copper, iron, and sulfur) produced by the reverberatory furnace was poured into a converter, which used a forced air stream to cause the remaining iron and sulfur to separate from the matte, leaving 98% pure copper.[69]

The product of the converter, called blister copper, still contained impurities, including precious metals such as gold and silver, which could be removed by electrolytic refining. The rough-cast copper anodes were suspended in an acid bath, and by the process of electrolysis, pure copper collected on a starter sheet suspended next to it. All the impurities, including gold and silver, fell to the bottom of the bath, and could be collected and refined later.[70]

The Anaconda Company's first smelter soon proved inadequate for the volume of ore that could be mined by the firm. Planning for expansion began almost as soon as the first matte was produced. The first smelter at Anaconda came to be called the Upper Works when it was supplemented in 1888 by an additional plant, a mile downstream, called the Lower Works. Like the Upper Works, the new plant was located on the north side of Warm Springs Creek, adjacent to the town of Anaconda. As mining fast outpaced the smelting capacity of the company, a third smelter was built. This was the Washoe smelter, completed in 1902, east of Anaconda, on the south side of the creek.[71]

Since the copper produced by smelting still contained some impurities, they had to be removed by a final refining process. The earliest method, fire refining, worked only with high and medium grade sulfide ores, and with native copper. The fire refining process had been perfected in Europe, and most U.S. copper was shipped to Europe for final refining until late in the nineteenth century.[72] An electrolytic refining process was developed in the 1870s, but electric technology was in its infancy, and it was not until the development of more efficient and reliable electric generators in the late 1880s that the process gained wider acceptance. In a move that made Anaconda a vertically integrated company controlling all aspects of copper production from mine to refining and sales, the company built the first electrolytic refinery in the western United States at Anaconda, bringing it into operation in 1891. This pioneering plant operated for eight years before being closed as part of the consolidation of plant functions undertaken in 1899. Although only a year newer, the former B&M electrolytic refinery at Great Falls had the advantage of being located on the Missouri River, a major source of hydroelectric power. Until its closure in 1980, the Anaconda works shipped blister copper to Great Falls for electrolytic refining.[73]

After copper became the primary metal mined in Butte, consolidation of the mines and smelter ownership began, culminating in the ACM monopoly created under the aegis of the Amalgamated Copper Company. In copper, as in railroads, oil, and steel, "rationalization," or consolidation of facilities to eliminate competition, was viewed as the logical outcome of Gilded Age capitalism. The process of rationalization was turbulent in Butte, where the economic and political goals of Clark, Daly, and Heinze clashed bitterly with each other. Finally, Amalgamated consolidated the majority of the Montana copper properties under a single management, a process completed in 1915 by the ACM.[74]

Mining consolidation moved toward a diminishing number of large corporate mine owners after 1880. In 1897, after Heinze arrived, there were eight large corporations mining on the Butte Hill. Some had their

A mining crew poses for a group portrait, prior to 1900. In the upper right appears one of the BA&P's Rogers Patent Ballast Cars. *Butte-Silver Bow Public Archives, #76*

own smelters, some did not. The largest was the Anaconda Copper Mining Company, which owned a dozen major mines: the Anaconda, Bell, Diamond, Green Mountain, Ground Squirrel, High Ore, Mountain Consolidated (the name was soon abbreviated to "Mountain Con"), Modoc, Neversweat, Ramsdell-Parrott, St. Lawrence, and Wake-up-Jim. The ore from these mines was shipped by rail to the company's concentrator and smelter in Anaconda.[75] Next largest was the Boston & Montana, which operated three major mines in Butte: the Colusa, Mountain View, and Parrott. Ore was shipped by rail to Great Falls to be smelted. The Parrott Company, operating the Parrott and Moscow mines, operated its own smelter in the Gaylord district outside of Butte.

After 1895, a number of Standard Oil Company executives, headed by Henry H. Rogers, became interested in copper.[76] Rogers and his associates were among the second-level managers of Standard Oil and were seeking to form a copper empire comparable to John D. Rockefeller's Standard Oil. Informally called the "Standard Oil Gang," the Rogers group began purchasing Anaconda stock. In 1899 they formed a holding company called the Amalgamated Copper Company

to facilitate their plans. Daly bought into Amalgamated, becoming its first president. However, his health failed that summer, and, despite visits to European doctors and spas, he lost the battle against Bright's disease, a chronic kidney disease. Daly died in New York at age 59, on November 12, 1900.[77] Control of the Anaconda Copper Mining company passed into the hands of the new trust, which then proceeded to end the chaotic state of affairs in Butte within the next decade. Having established itself as the power behind the ACM, Amalgamated secured Clark's cooperation in 1901 by agreeing not to contest his political aspirations. This left only Heinze opposing the trust. Heinze could not successfully oppose the economic power of his opponents for long, and he sold out in 1906. Finally, Clark sold his Butte copper properties to Amalgamated in 1910. All of the mining operations were consolidated into the Anaconda Copper Mining company, and Amalgamated itself was then dissolved in 1915, leaving the ACM the surviving corporate entity.[78]

Although the final consolidation of Butte's major mines was not consummated until a decade later, the process was well under way at the time of Daly's death. Under his management, the one-time promising Montana silver mine called the Anaconda had become one of the most powerful copper conglomerates in the United States. In the process, Daly's company acquired mines, built smelters, sawmills, and an electrolytic refinery. To connect the mines and smelters he also created an essential component of this industrial empire: The Butte, Anaconda & Pacific Railway.

NOTES

1. Walter H. Weed, *Geology and Ore Deposits of the Butte District*, U.S. Geological Survey Professional Paper No. 74, (Washington, D.C.: GPO, 1903), p. 17.

2. Walter H. Weed, "Ore Deposits At Butte, Montana," in: *Contributions to Economic Geology, 1902*, U.S. Geological Society Bulletin No. 213, (Washington, D.C.: GPO, 1903), p. 171.

3. Marius R. Campbell et al., *Guidebook of the Western United States: Northern Pacific Route*. (Washington, D.C.: GPO, 1916,), pp. 105-109.

4. Harry W. Smedes, Montis R. Klepper and Robert I. Tilling, "The Boulder Batholith, Montana," in: Richard N. Miller (Ed.), *Guidebook for the Butte Field Meeting of the Society of Economic Geologists* (Butte, Montana: Anaconda Company, 1978), pp. E1 - E2.

5. Robert I. Tilling, "The Boulder Batholith, Montana: Product of Two Contemporaneous but Chemically and Isotopically Distinct Magma Series," in: Richard N. Miller (Ed.) *Guidebook for the Butte Field Meeting of the Society of Economic Geologists* (Butte, Montana: Anaconda Company, 1978), p. C3.

6. Mark W. Martin, J. H. Dilles, and J. M. Proffett. "U-Pb Geochronologic Constraints for the Butte Porphyry System," *Geologic Society of America Abstracts with Programs,* Vol. 31 (1999), No. 7, p. A-380.

7. Campbell, Sheet No. 16 [between pp. 112 and 113.]

8. Weed, *Geology*, p. 18. Weed notes that the mining district subsequently became commonly known as the Butte District, and uses the term throughout his work, indicating that by 1912 the name Butte District had replaced Summit Valley District throughout the mining community and the U.S. Geological Survey.

9. Weed, "Ore Deposits," p. 171; Roberta C. Cheney, *Names on the Face of Montana* (Missoula, Montana: University of Montana, 1971), p. 31.

10. Weed, *Geology*, p. 18.

11. Cheney, p. 191.

12. Weed, *Geology*, p. 18.

13. Ibid. The pattern of progressing from initially working placer deposits to lode mining within a mining district is well documented in the western United States. Eliot Lord, *Comstock Mining and Miners*, U.S. Geological Survey Monograph No. 4 (Washington, D.C., GPO, 1883), notes this sequence of events in his history of Nevada's Comstock Lode. Once the mineral deposits were exhausted, mining camps were promptly abandoned. The Census of the United States gives Butte's population as 400 in 1860, 241 in 1870, and 3,363 in 1880.

14. A. H. Koschmann and M. H. Bergendahl, *Principal Gold-Producing Districts of the United States* (Washington, D.C.: GPO, 1968) (U.S. Geological Survey Professional Paper No. 610), p. 169. Placing Butte's placer gold output in perspective, placers of the Nome, Alaska, district produced over 3,600,000 million troy ounces of gold between 1897 and 1959. Koschmann and Bergendahl, p. 18. Calaveras County, California placers produced an estimated 3,000,000 troy ounces of gold from 1849 through 1959. Koschmann and Bergendahl, p. 59.

15. Weed, *Geology*, p. 18.

16. Lord, pp. 80-81; Albert H. Fay, *A Glossary of the Mining and Metal Industry*, U.S. Bureau of Mines Bulletin No. 95, (Washington, D.C.: GPO, 1920), pp. 30, 566.

17. George F. Becker, *Geology of the Comstock Lode and the Washoe District,* U.S. Geological Survey Monograph No. 3, (Washington, D.C.: GPO, 1882), p. 6. Also see Rodman W. Paul, *Mining Frontiers of the Far West, 1848-1880* (New York: Holt, Rinehart & Winston, 1963), p. 118.

18. Lord, pp. 81-121. Lord explains that the "Washoe Process" developed by Comstock miners was actually a refinement of a technique which had been used in New Spain, as documented by Francisco Zavier de Gamboa. Fay, p. 731.

19. Lord, pp. 80-81; Fay, p. 44.

20. Weed, *Geology*, p. 18.

21. Lord, pp. 80-81; Fay, pp. 643-644.

22. Weed, *Geology*, p. 18.

23. Ibid.

24. William Andrews Clark (1839-1925) was one of the first capitalists to invest heavily in Butte's mines. Clark was a Missouri school teacher who joined the Colorado mining rush in 1859, then went to Montana seeking gold in 1863. He found the role of merchant more prosperous than that of miner, and soon became wealthy. He entered the banking business, and began buying Butte mining properties in 1872. He was Daly's chief rival for the control of Butte copper production until Daly died. New York *Times*, March 3, 1925, pp. 1, 7; *Dictionary of American Biography* (New York: Charles Scribner's Sons, 1930), Vol. 4, pp. 144-146. Michael Malone's *The Battle for Butte* gives a good overview of Clark's activities in Montana, including an evenhanded account of the dirty political campaigns in which Clark willingly participated. Richard H. Peterson, *The Bonanza Kings: The Social Origins and Business Behavior of Western Mining Entrepreneurs, 1870-1900* (Norman, Oklahoma: University of Oklahoma Press, 1991), places the business practices and social background of Clark, Daly, and many of the other Butte mine owners in a wider perspective.

25. Marcus Daly (1841-1900) was a poor Irish immigrant who worked his way up from being a laborer in a Nevada silver mine to being president and manager of the Anaconda Copper Mining Company by the time of his death. The BA&P was Daly's brainchild. New York *Times*, November 13, 1900, p. 2; *Dictionary of American Biography* (New York: Charles

Scribner's Sons, 1930), Vol. 5, pp. 45-46; Malone's *The Battle for Butte* provides ample coverage of his Anaconda years; Peterson's *The Bonanza Kings* places Daly in a larger context.

26. F.[rederick] Augustus Heinze (1869-1914) was college educated as a mining engineer in the United States and in Germany. Using his technical knowledge, he made his Montana Ore Purchasing Company a successful competitor in Butte's mining district. By making shrewd purchases and initiating aggressive litigation against competitors, he was able to force the Anaconda interests to buy him out. New York *Times,* September 5, 1914, p. 11; *Dictionary of American Biography* (New York: Charles Scribner's Sons, 1932), Vol. 8, pp. 507-508.

27. William A. Clark's career after leaving Butte involved the United Verde copper properties at Jerome, Arizona, and railroads in Arizona, California, Nevada and Utah. New York *Times,* February 18, 1906, p. 7; Ibid., May 15, 1910, p. 9. Malone briefly outlines the mining activities in the conclusion of *The Battle for Butte.* Brief sketches of Clark's railroading activities are contained in David F. Myrick, *Railroads of Nevada and Eastern California,* Vol. 2, (Berkeley, California: Howell North Books, 1963) and Russell Wahmann, *Narrow Gauge to Jerome: The United Verde & Pacific Railway* (Boulder, Colorado: Pruett Publishing, 1988). Clarkdale, Arizona, three miles northeast of Jerome, was named in Clark's honor. Wahmann, p. 9.

28. New York *Times,* March 3, 1925, pp. 1, 7. Malone, *The Battle For Butte,* gives a good brief synopsis of Clark's background, and his life after he ceased being involved in Butte affairs. The focus of Malone's book is the consolidation of ownership of the Butte Hill in the hands of the Anaconda Copper Mining Company (ACM), and is the best single-volume treatment of the subject available, starting with the first placer claims, moving through Amalgamated and the so-called Standard Oil Gang to the unification of control of Butte's mining properties by ACM.

29. Lord, pp. 89-90.

30. Fay, pp. 175-176, defines concentrates as the product of the concentrating process. Concentration is the removal of waste rock material from ore by mechanical means. Bullion is uncoined gold or silver, generally cast in bars of unrefined metal. Fay, pp. 114-115. Matte is crude metal, combined with sulfur, resulting from the smelting of sulfide ores of copper, lead, or nickel. Copper matte requires additional refining to purify the metal. Fay, pp. 423-424. The necessity of rail transportation for Butte is mentioned in: U.S. Geological Survey, *Mineral Resources of the United States,* 1882, (Washington, D.C.: GPO, 1883), p. 225.

31. Lord alludes to this in his history of the Comstock Lode. Paul, pp. 93-94, 111, 120. Alfred D. Chandler, Jr. discusses this in *Strategy and Structure: Chapters in the History of the Industrial Enterprise* (Cambridge, Massachusetts: MIT Press, 1962).

32. New York *Times,* November 13, 1900, p. 2; Spence, pp. 18-19.

33. Daly left a relatively small body of personal papers, having given his wife and legal counsel instructions to destroy most of his personal papers after his death. Much of the study of Daly thus has been confined to interviews with persons who knew him, or secondary sources. K. Ross Toole remarked on this in his studies. Daly's personal reasons for making the decisions he did relative to the BA&P, as with everything else in his life, are obscured by the intentional destruction of his personal papers after his death. K. Ross Toole, "Marcus Daly: A Study of Business in Politics" (Missoula, Montana: University of Montana, MA Thesis, 1948), pp. i-iv.

34. Fay, pp. 573-574.

35. Weed, *Geology,* pp. 19, 74.

36. Weed, *Geology,* pp. 20, 74; Merrill D. Beal, *Intermountain Railroads: Standard and Narrow Gauge* (Caldwell, Idaho: Caxton Printers, 1962), pp. 87-88.

37. U.S. Geological Survey, *Mineral Resources,* 1882, p. 224.

38. U.S. Geological Survey, *Mineral Resources,* 1882, p. 216. Thomas R. Navin, *Copper Mining and Management* (Tucson, Arizona: University of Arizona Press, 1978), pp. 10–12. Navin argues that western copper developers like Daly and Clark were not as forward-looking as it appears, but that they were fortunate in being able to profit from the electrical boom when it began; later, in the 1890s, they built on early good fortune by aggressively promoting the use of copper, thereby enriching themselves. Hyde, chapters 4 and 5, are good as an overview of the industry in Arizona and Montana.

39. U.S. Geological Survey, *Mineral Resources,* 1882–1911 production figures. The five-month closure of the Anaconda smelter during the rate disagreement with the Montana Union Railway occurred in 1891.

40. Weed, *Geology,* pp. 19–20. Fay, p. 405. The term "locate" is used by the mining industry to mean marking the boundaries and establishing right of possession to a mining claim. Slang terminology is "staking a claim," indicating that the person is marking the boundaries of a mining claim with survey stakes.

41. New York *Times,* November 13, 1900, p. 2; Navin, p. 202.

42. James Ben Ali Haggin (1827-1914) was Lloyd Tevis's law partner. The two of them invested in mining enterprises, often associated with George Hearst. Haggin became one of Daly's Anaconda partners along with Hearst and Tevis, and supported Daly more willingly than Tevis and Hearst. New York *Times,* September 13, 1914, Section II, p. 9; *Dictionary of American Biography* (New York: Charles Scribner's Sons, 1932), Vol. 8, pp. 83–84.

43. George Hearst (1820–1891) was a prospector who made good in the California gold rush, and became associated with J.B. Haggin and Lloyd Tevis, then Marcus Daly. He bought the San Francisco *Examiner* in 1880, and later served in the U.S. Senate. His son, William Randolph Hearst, made a career of the newspaper business. New York *Times,* March 1, 1891, p. 1; *Dictionary of American Biography* (New York: Charles Scribner's Sons, 1932), Vol. 8, pp. 487–488.

44. Lloyd Tevis (1824–1899) was J. B. Haggin's law partner, and was president of Wells Fargo & Co. for twenty years. He and Haggin joined George Hearst in mining investments in the west, including Anaconda. New York *Times,* July 25, 1899, p. 7; *Dictionary of American Biography,* (New York: Charles Scribner's Sons, 1936), Vol. 18, pp. 384-385.

45. The correct pronunciation of the town of Lead, South Dakota is "leed," rather than "led." Rodman Paul gives a good overview of Hearst and his associates who became involved in the Homestake gold mine in *Mining Frontiers of the Far West.* The Homestake mine and its paternalistic management is the subject of: Joseph Cash, *Working the Homestake* (Ames, Iowa: Iowa State University Press, 1973) which places the mine owners in a larger historical context.

46. New York *Times,* November 13, 1900, p. 2.

47. U.S. Geological Survey, *Mineral Resources,* 1882, p. 224. Chalcocite is also referred to as "copper glance" in some of the early literature.

48. Malone, *The Battle for Butte,* p. 29.

49. New York *Times,* July 23, 1887, p. 1; Ibid., January 20, 1888, p. 2. Malone, *The Battle for Butte,* pp. 22-23.

50. New York *Times,* March 6, 1902, p. 5; U.S. Geological Survey, *Mineral Resources,* 1887, p. 216; Malone, *The Battle for Butte,* pp. 48-49.

51. New York *Times,* September 5, 1914, p. 11; Heinze's role in railroad development in British Columbia is amply discussed in Barrie Sandford, *McCulloch's Wonder: The Story of the Kettle Valley Railway* (West Vancouver, B.C.: Whitecap Books, 1977). His mining and smelting activities in Canada are briefly discussed in John Fahey's *Inland Empire: D.C. Corbin and Spokane,* (Seattle, Washington: University of Washington Press, 1965), and also in Fahey's *Shaping Spokane: Jay P. Graves and His Times* (Seattle, Washington: University of Washington Press, 1994).

52. Jackling was the first to begin open-pit mining of porphyry copper ore, but there were others thinking along similar lines almost simultaneously. In 1906 the Nevada Consolidated Copper Company (Kennecott) decided to use open pit methods to work their Copper Flat property near Ely, Nevada. Actual work began in 1908, a year after work began at Bingham Canyon, Utah. See Arthur C. Spencer, *The Geology and Ore Deposits of Ely, Nevada,* U.S. Geological Survey Professional Paper No. 96, (Washington, D.C.: GPO, 1917), p. 153; Navin, p. 31.

53. Richard N. Miller, "Production History of the Butte District and Geological Function, Past and Present," in: Richard N. Miller, (Ed.) *Guidebook for the Butte Field Meeting of the Society of Economic Geologists* (Butte, Montana: Anaconda Company, 1973), p. F-5; BA&P Records, (All citations to BA&P Records are for the body of material held by the Butte-Silver Bow Public Archives, Butte, Montana) Administrative Correspondence, "East Anaconda Tipple," F. W. Bellinger to Mitchell, January 14, 1952, I-5-4.

54. H. O. Hofman, "Notes on the Metallurgy of Copper in Montana," *Transactions of the American Institute of Mining Engineers,* Vol. 34 (1904), pp. 259-260; Malone, *The Battle for Butte,* p. 22.

55. U.S. Geological Survey, *Mineral Resources,* 1882, p. 224; Hofman, pp. 259-260. T. A. Rikard, *A History of American Mining* (New York: McGraw Hill, 1932), pp. 350-351.

56. Fay, p. 88.

57. U.S. Geological Survey, *Mineral Resources,* 1881, p. 233; Hofman, pp. 260-262.

58. U.S. Geological Survey, *Mineral Resources,* 1883-1884, p. 338; Hofman, p. 261.

59. Hofman, p 260.

60. Ibid., pp. 267-269.

61. Navin, p. 52.

62. Weed, *Geology,* pp. 20, 74.

63. Hofman, pp. 265-267. Rikard, p. 353.

64. Water requirements for concentrating ore were between 3,000 and 5,000 gallons of water per ton of ore, according to Charles W. Goodale, "The Concentration of Ores in the Butte District, Montana," *Transactions of the American Institute of Mining Engineers,* Vol. 26 (1896), p. 608; Cheney, pp. 5-6.

65. Goodale, pp. 608-609; Hofman, p. 266. Rikard, p. 353.

66. Goodale, pp. 609-613; Hofman, pp. 265-267.

67. Navin, pp. 45-47.

68. Fay, p. 560.

69. Hofman, p. 261. The first successful application of the Bessemer process to copper was by a French metallurgist named Manhes; the first Manhes converters used in the United States were at the Parrott mine's smelter in Butte in 1883. Fay, pp. 180, 418.

70. Hofman, pp. 308-316. Navin, pp. 61-63.

71. Hofman, pp. 265-267.

72. Navin, pp. 61-62.

73. Hofman, pp. 266, 308-315.

74. New York *Times,* April 26, 1899, p. 1; Ibid., June 18, 1899; Ibid., April 16, 1901, p. 16; February 14, 1906, p.1; Ibid., May 15, 1910, p. 9. See Alfred D. Chandler, Jr., *Strategy and Structure: Chapters in the History of the Industrial Enterprise* for a conceptual overview of the argument that consolidation is a continuing business trend. Scholarship on the pattern of business consolidation in oil, steel, and railroads leans heavily toward biographies of corporate leaders, such as John D. Rockefeller, Andrew Carnegie, and James J. Hill. A recent global examination of the oil industry which considers these trends is Daniel Yergin, *The Prize: the Epic Quest for Oil, Money and Power* (New York: Simon and Schuster, 1991). Less has been written about copper mining. Navin's *Copper Mining and Management* provides the essentials of the corporate consolidation, but focuses largely on an overview of the technological aspects of copper production in the United States through the early 1970s. Malone, *The Battle For Butte* is probably the best single-volume study of the personalities, finance, and politics leading to the formation of the ACM as a monopoly controlling Montana copper. A scholarly history of the ACM from 1900 to 1985 would be a welcome complement to Malone's book.

75. Samuel F. Emmons, and George W. Tower, *Geological Atlas of the United States.* U.S. Geological Survey Special Folio No. 38. (Washington, D.C.: GPO, 1897), p. 5.

76. Henry H. Rogers was one of the second tier of Standard Oil executives. He was primarily involved in oil, copper, and railroad companies. New York *Times,* May 20, 1909, pp. 1-2, 8.

77. New York *Times,* April 26, 1899, p. 1; Ibid., June 18, 1899, p. 12; Ibid., November 13, 1900, p. 2.

78. New York *Times,* April 26, 1899, p. 1; Ibid., June 18, 1899; Ibid., April 16, 1901, p. 16; February 14, 1906, p.1; Ibid., May 15, 1910, p. 9; Ibid., April 14, 1915; Ibid., June 8, 1915, p. 17.

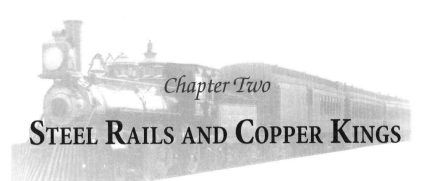

Chapter Two

STEEL RAILS AND COPPER KINGS

There probably hasn't been a warmer celebration in the history of the community than that night when Butte welcomed its first regular passenger train over the shimmering narrow gauge rails of the Utah & Northern Railroad.[1]

*B*UTTE ORES WERE RICH, but only the richest ore could be economically exploited until the camp had inexpensive transportation. Placer gold production was economically viable, even with primitive transportation, since placer mining did not require the movement of bulk commodities. Initial development as a silver camp was possible without railroads, but development of copper mining required the low-cost, high-volume carrying capacity of railroad transportation. Butte's copper mines demanded heavy equipment, coal, and immense quantities of timber. They produced a large tonnage of ore which had to be moved to mills and smelters for processing. The smelters in turn produced copper matte to be shipped to refineries and finally to factories which produced finished copper products.

Butte, like many other mining regions in the West, was not a primary destination of large transcontinental railroads. If anything, the mining town was merely a way station on the route to the port cities of the Pacific Northwest. During the corporate chess game of late nineteenth century railroad development, Butte was just another place claiming to have traffic potential.

The Union Pacific (UP) became concerned about protecting its western connections after 1870. The UP was dependent on a connection in Utah with the Central Pacific for all its transcontinental business, making it vulnerable to potential competitors who could build their own lines all the way to Pacific ports. One such imminent threat was the Northern Pacific (NP), expanding westward across Montana toward Washington Territory. Consequently, the UP began running lines into Idaho and Montana as part of a plan to build its own line to the Pacific.[2] Both railroads began serving Butte in the early 1880s, and both recognized that a traffic pooling arrangement for Butte's business served their corporate ends better than competing with each other.

Butte finally received competitive railroad service when the Great Northern (GN), in the form of its Montana Central (MC) subsidiary, reached the city in 1888, and all three transcontinental roads sought a share of the expanding business.[3] A final transcontinental railroad arrived in 1908, as the Chicago, Milwaukee & St. Paul (CM&StP, also known as "the Milwaukee") built its extension to the Pacific coast. Butte's copper industry was well served by railroads after 1883, though only the Milwaukee intentionally placed Butte directly on its main line.[4]

The transcontinental railroads benefited from the traffic Butte's burgeoning copper industry created, but Butte's largest shippers were soon unhappy with the service. Pooling agreements kept freight rates up, instead of reducing them. Service was not dependable enough to meet the ACM's needs. Daly's efforts to obtain better service at lower rates failed. Finally, in 1892 the Anaconda Mining Company ordered the building of the BA&P to haul its ore to the smelter.

When the Montana gold rush started in 1863, transportation to and from the gold camps was an arduous undertaking. Travel to Montana was initially on foot or horseback, followed by stagecoach.[5]

Although President Abraham Lincoln had signed the Pacific Railroad Act in 1862, the nation's energies were focused on the Civil War, not on developing railroads to cross the sparsely settled western territories. The closest long-haul railroad was either in Iowa or Sacramento, California.[6] When Montana gold was discovered in 1863, the Central Pacific was just taking delivery of its first locomotive at Sacramento, and the Union Pacific had yet to lay a length of rail at Omaha, Nebraska.[7] One could reach the diggings at Alder Gulch, 60 miles southeast of Butte, by coming over the Oregon Trail to what is now southern Idaho, then

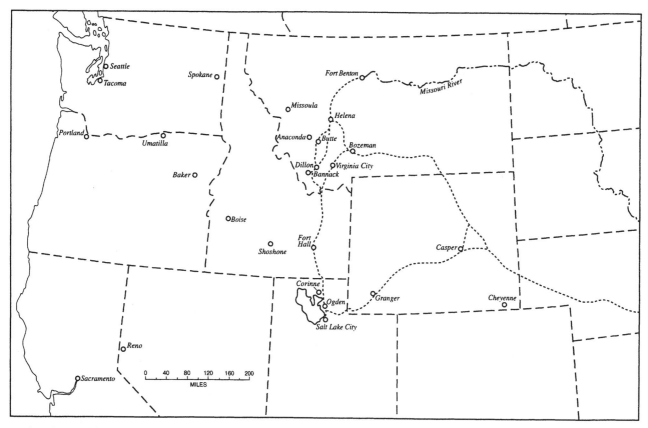

Trails and navigable river routes from the East to Montana gold fields, 1865.

traveling north to reach Alder Gulch and the nearby town of Virginia City.

Wagon freighters worked primarily from the east and south to supply Montana's placer gold camps.[8] Freight wagons required a large outlay in their own right, and carried a relatively small cargo. The typical Studebaker freight wagon of the period weighed 4,000 to 5,000 pounds (2 to 2.5 tons), and had a capacity of 8,000 to 12,000 pounds (4 to 6 tons). Teams of oxen or mules were generally used to pull freight wagons. The tonnage carried was often determined by the size of the team available. A team of eight oxen might pull a pair of wagons weighing two tons each, with a load of twelve tons of freight. A twenty-mule team was rated to be approximately equivalent to eight oxen.[9] Utah farmers helped encourage the freighting business serving Montana from the south, while simultaneously a small but growing white population in the Salt Lake basin was trying to market their agricultural surpluses. After 1863 the demand for foodstuffs rose in Montana mining communities, offering a relatively nearby and profitable market for farm products. Teamsters extended service between Utah and Montana, and some Utah farmers entered the freighting business in competition with the teamsters.[10]

Two routes from the east were used to reach Montana's gold camps. The Bozeman Trail, which opened in 1864, was a relatively direct wagon route from the North Platte River in Nebraska to Virginia City and Bannack, Montana. Although the Bozeman Trail appeared to be the fastest way to reach Montana's mining camps from the east, it was considered to be dangerous. In northern Wyoming and eastern Montana territories the trail crossed the hunting ground of Indian tribes who resisted encroachment upon their lands. Civil War military priorities did not include extensive protection of civilian freighters. Tribal resistance increased from 1866 through 1868, forcing closure of the route.[11] It was, consequently, not a practical means of supplying Butte, or shipping either bullion or ore.

The second route to the placer camps was a wagon trail from Fort Benton, Montana. Fort Benton, approximately 160 miles northeast of Butte, was the head of navigation on the Missouri River. However, even with shallow-draft vessels, the river was navigable as far upstream as Fort Benton only four to six weeks of the year. Steamboat transportation proved to be inadequate for the needs of the growing mining camp. The Missouri River was simply too shallow for extensive boat service into its upper reaches. Often boat owners were able to complete only a single round trip between St. Louis, Missouri, and Fort Benton before the water level dropped too low to permit navigation. In 1864, for example, only two boats were able to reach Fort Benton, and only four landed there in 1865. The following year proved to be a much better year for navigation, with thirty-one steamboats arriving in Fort Benton.[12]

The short navigational season was only part of the problem with this route. Once a boat delivered its cargo to Fort Benton, there were still several hundred miles of wagon haul necessary. A stamp mill such as the one Farlin used in Butte cost between $360 and $420 a ton to bring up river from St. Louis to Fort Benton. Then it had to be hauled another 200 miles by wagon, at $.05 to $.08 per pound, or $100 to $160 per ton for the remainder of the trip.[13] The total cost from St. Louis to Helena or Butte was between $460 and $580 a ton. A rate-war between rival steamboat companies in 1868 brought the rate from St. Louis to Fort Benton down to $160.00 per ton, and a further reduction of rates occurred in 1869, when the boats slightly underbid the rates for a combination of rail and wagon freight from St. Louis to Helena or Butte via the Union Pacific Railroad to Corinne or Ogden.[14] Freight costs on outbound ore would be equally high—far in excess of what most ore was worth. Silver mining would be viable only if silver ore could be processed locally, and bullion or silver-copper matte shipped out.

Competitive pricing by river boats and teamsters in the face of the new Union Pacific Railroad competition only delayed the inevitable advance of rails into Montana. During the 1870s, while Farlin, Clark, and others struggled to adopt the metallurgical techniques learned in Nevada's Comstock and in the smelters of Colorado to Butte's refractory silver ores, railroads inched closer to Montana with each passing year. Most of the mines in Butte continued to be worked for silver through the 1870s, although the district's copper potential had been recognized as early as 1878.[15] At that time, however, U.S. copper smelting was in its infancy, and the closest smelters which could successfully process Butte's sulfide ores were in Swansea, Wales. Shipping copper ore to Wales clearly was not economically viable in the 1870s. Butte's copper deposits would never pose a threat to Michigan's copper mines without the convenient and inexpensive shipping a railroad could provide.

Interest in developing the trans-Mississippi West increased after the Civil War. Federal subsidies aided railroad construction for two railroads destined to be important to Butte: the Union Pacific and the Northern Pacific. The Union Pacific had done little construction until 1865, but after Appomattox the railroad was pushed to completion in four years. The 1869 completion of the nation's first transcontinental railroad at Promontory, Utah, where the Union Pacific joined the Central Pacific, proved immediately beneficial to Montana. The Union Pacific was far to the south of the placer diggings of Alder Gulch and Bannack, but regular stage and wagon service was instituted to link these communities with the railroad at Ogden or Corinne, Utah. The two communities vied to serve as the railhead for wagon freight to Montana; Ogden had the advantage of being a larger city, but Corinne, approximately 25 miles northwest of Ogden, had the advantage of being that much closer to the mines. Although the wagon haul from Corinne was longer than that from Fort Benton, Montana, the railroad was open throughout the year, unlike the Missouri River. An additional benefit was that the railroad route and the wagon trail connecting Corinne with Butte and Helena did not pass through lands occupied by powerful, angry Indian tribes.[16]

Throughout the 1870s the incomplete Northern Pacific line was not a viable route to Montana's mines. Construction stopped at Bismark, Dakota Territory, after the collapse of its financial agent, Jay Cooke & Co. in the Panic of 1873, and did not resume until 1879.[17] When the NP resumed construction across Montana, it was at a disadvantage competing for Butte's business, because its main line was not completed. The UP, on the other hand, was aggressively building feeders off its main track, such as the Utah & Northern and the Oregon Short Line, which were much closer to Butte.

As early as 1870, Butte's mining men had hoped for a railroad connection. Throughout the 1870s and early 1880s a number of efforts were made to secure financial subsidies for railroad construction from the county and territorial governments. The issue wound up pitting eastern and western counties against each other, and fiscal conservatives against those who hoped to profit personally from railroad construction and service to their communities. The Union Pacific and Northern Pacific each lobbied Montanans to favor their companies by granting them land or credit. Bills to permit public aid to railroads failed in the territorial legislature, and both the NP and UP resumed construction of their own accord after 1879.[18]

The Utah & Northern (U&N) which was the first railroad to directly serve Butte, reached the mining camp on December 26, 1881.[19] The U&N was built at

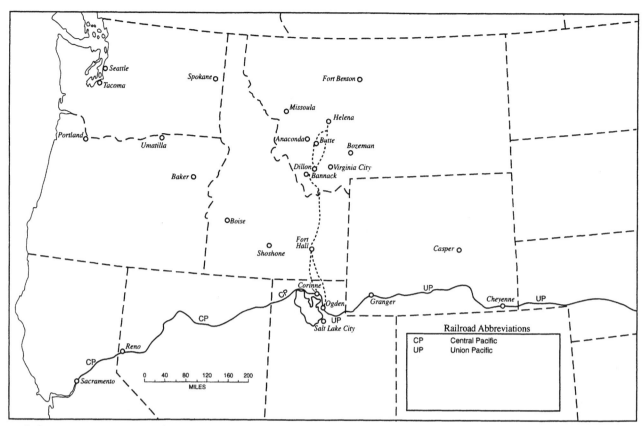

Trails from western Montana to the Union Pacific Railroad, 1869.

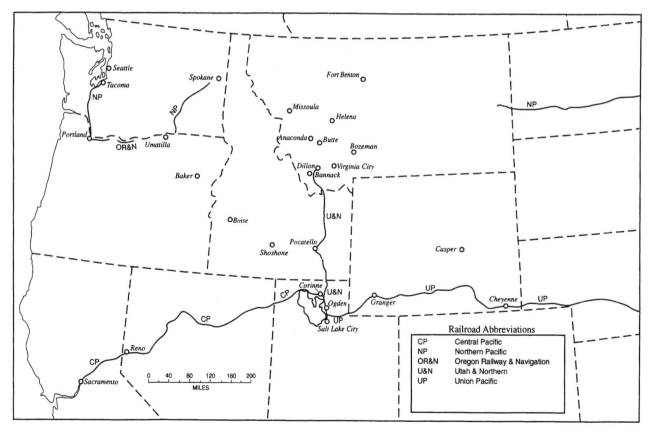

Railroad routes to Butte, Montana, 1881.

the end of the so-called "narrow gauge fever" that had briefly swept the United States in the 1870s and 1880s.[20] Based on the premise that the smaller equipment would allow lower construction costs, narrow gauge railroads were promoted as the inexpensive answer to the transportation needs of remote or marginally lucrative parts of the world.[21] The idea had its roots in the slate hauling railways of Wales. An energetic Englishman, Robert Fairlie, boosted the concept for all he was worth, and found ready converts on the outer fringes of the industrializing Western world. One of the places the narrow gauge idea was particularly well received was in the United States, where the rapidly industrializing nation still had large expanses of land with sparse white settlement.[22]

In 1871 leading Utah businessmen had proposed to build a narrow gauge railroad north from Ogden. The line would funnel the freight to and from the Montana mines through Utah communities, thereby enabling Salt Lake City to retain its economic dominance of the region. The Church of Jesus Christ of Latter Day Saints (Mormons) encouraged its membership to support railroads. With Brigham Young's blessing, and his son's assistance, the Utah Northern was chartered to build from Ogden, Utah, to Soda Springs, Idaho.[23] Initial efforts to finance Utah Northern construction failed locally. Union Pacific management recognized the potential value of the line as a feeder, and by 1877 the U&N was a UP subsidiary.

Construction of the Utah Northern (U&N)[24] began at Brigham City, Utah, on August 26, 1871. Much of the grading was done by farmers in northern Utah, and a year later rail and equipment began arriving. Trains reached the Idaho border at Franklin in April, 1874, seventy-seven miles north of Ogden. This gave Ogden a distinct advantage over Corinne as a supply center for Idaho and Montana points. Ambitious Helena businessmen agitated to make their city the northern terminus of the U&N.[25] Butte, meanwhile, was just coming into its second wind as a silver camp as the rails reached Idaho. Two years later, track was extended to Battle Creek, ninety miles north of Ogden, which then became the railhead for Montana freight.[26]

Original surveys for the Montana extension of the U&N plotted the route through Soda Springs, and then north toward Helena, skirting the eastern border of the Fort Hall Indian Reservation. While this plan simplified right-of-way acquisition, it did not offer as direct a route to Butte. An alternative proposal was to run the line across the Fort Hall Indian Reservation, then over Monida Pass to obtain an easier access to Butte, which was considered a silver plum worth picking. Strategically, the latter plan to extend the line north and west would give the U&N a monopoly on the Butte traffic, as well as deterring the projected Northern Pacific (NP) from the rich mining areas of western Montana Territory. Pursuant to this rationale, and in haste to reach the silver mines of Butte, the U&N was built directly across the Fort Hall Indian Reservation without first waiting for the legal niceties of obtaining a right-of-way. The legalities were eventually sorted out to the railroad's satisfaction. The federal government granted the U&N a legal right-of-way across the reservation and later paid the Shoshone and Bannack tribes—about a year after trains were running to Montana.[27]

Once the U&N reached Dillon, Montana, in 1880, mining in Butte accelerated. Reducing the distance of wagon haul had cut the cost of shipping ore to distant smelters. For the richest copper sulfide ores, it was finally possible to ship ore profitably from Butte to Swansea, Wales, for smelting. The Anaconda's partners counted on even lower transportation costs when the railroad was completed to Butte. Low freight costs and construction of their own smelter would permit Anaconda's Butte copper to compete with other U.S. copper producers. Efficient, inexpensive transportation was the key that unlocked the door to expansive copper production in Butte.

Union Pacific interest in Butte was part of a larger corporate strategy. Along with assuming control of the U&N in 1877, the UP orchestrated the construction of a new standard-gauge line from western Wyoming across Idaho on its way to Portland, Oregon.[28] Called the Oregon Short Line (OSL), it crossed the U&N at Pocatello, Idaho, in 1881. By the time the narrow-gauge U&N reached Butte, the standard gauge OSL had made Pocatello, rather than Ogden, the logical transfer point for Montana-bound freight. Despite involving two gauges of track and a freight transfer at Pocatello, the new railroad was a blessing for Montana mine owners, for it permitted access to Wyoming coal deposits. Coal was a more efficient smelter fuel than charcoal, and also served as the nation's preferred fuel for industrial and domestic purposes. Coal-fired boilers provided energy for the steam engines that hoisted ore from the mines and pumped water from them. Households relied on coal for heating, and cooked on coal- or wood-burning ranges. Even as new uses for electricity increased the national demand for copper in the 1880s, American industry and domestic life remained fueled by coal.

For the Anaconda syndicate, the initial coal supplies for its Montana operations were located along

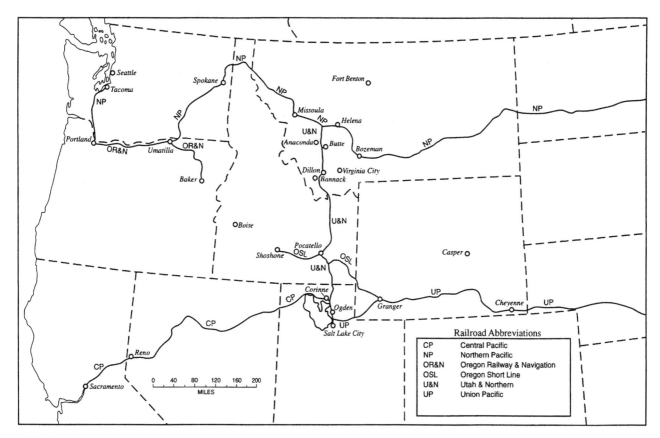

Railroad routes to Butte, Montana, 1883.

the UP in southwestern Wyoming. Although Montana itself contained extensive coal deposits, without effective transportation, this coal was not competitive with that mined farther away near a railroad. Since the only rails to Butte in 1882 led to Wyoming, that was the logical source of coal for the ACM in its early years.

Realizing that buying coal from the UP or any other company cost Anaconda and himself money, Daly instigated the development of Anaconda's own coal mines at Diamondfield, Wyoming. Diamondfield, located along the UP main line in western Wyoming, provided fuel for the smelter, plus a profit from coal mining to ACM partners.[29]

Soon other railroads, serving other coal fields, entered the coal market, further ensuring competitive rates for mining operations. GN's Montana Central subsidiary served the Sand Coulee coal mines near Great Falls, Montana, and in eastern Montana there were coal mines along the NP. Thus the ACM had access to coal from several different mines, which provided the copper company with some leverage over railroads and coal companies. If the UP pushed the freight rate too high on Wyoming coal, then ACM could seek a better rate from the NP or GN for Montana coal.

By now, an industry maxim had been established: Shipping by rail was vastly superior to wagon freighting. With rail transport, fewer men did more work with machines at a lower cost. Although the journey involved transferring freight from standard-gauge cars to the narrow-gauge U&N at Ogden, or at Pocatello, it was still vastly more efficient. The typical freight wagon of the period weighed 2 or $2^{1}/_{2}$ tons, and could carry up to 4 tons.[30] The narrow-gauge U&N freight cars, though smaller than their standard-gauge counterparts, generally had a capacity of between 10 and 20 tons.[31] Standard-gauge freight equipment in use on the UP in the 1880s had a capacity of 20 to 30 tons.[32] A mill and smelter processing 100 tons of ore per day would need eight to ten teams and teamsters, with sixteen to twenty wagons to move the ore. In addition, additional teams and wagons would be required to move coal or charcoal, limestone, and other supplies. In contrast, a short freight train of five to ten U&N cars could haul the 100 tons of ore in a single trip, with a five-man crew.[33]

After the U&N reached Butte, many of the mine owners were satisfied that their transportation needs had been met. Coal, timbers, and machinery all arrived in Butte, and the finished product of the Colorado &

Montana Smelter departed. For Daly and his partners, however, another rail link was still needed: one that would connect the Anaconda Mine to the new concentrating mill and smelter being planned on the north bank of Warm Springs Creek, twenty-five miles away. ACM's copper smelter was to employ the most modern Welsh technology and save the company the time and cost of shipping ore to Wales for smelting. Daly chose the site at Warm Springs Creek because concentrating and smelting the ore would require more water than was obtainable at Butte. Daly was planning big. Ore wagons and ox teams were not going to be sufficient to meet the transportation needs of the smelter he envisioned: no small plant like the Colorado & Montana works, but a huge, integrated works that would process a train-load of ore a day, every day. Designed to handle 500 tons of copper ore every twenty-four hours, the Anaconda smelter would require the movement of 50 ten-ton cars, or 25 twenty-ton cars per day just for the ore moving to the smelter.[34] Coal, limestone for flux, and other supplies would also come in carload lots. For the partners owning the Anaconda Mine, getting the U&N to extend its line to the smelter site was critical.

Daly had the confidence of his partners, but the UP management remained skeptical, suspecting that the entire Anaconda venture might fail if copper prices fell. Although the UP pushed the U&N north from Silver Bow to Garrison in 1882, a branch to the new town of Anaconda was not viewed with any urgency. Anaconda did not get its railroad connection until July, 1884.

After Daly had convinced his partners to go into copper production, planning for the smelter at Anaconda began. Acquisition of land and of water rights commenced in November 1882. Water to mill 500 tons of ore per day, and an ability to obtain more water to permit expansion of the concentrator and smelter, were as important as obtaining the large tract of land required. Extensive real estate and water rights along Warm Springs Creek had been secured by June, 1883.[35] Construction of a concentrator and smelter began immediately, but was hampered by the lack of direct railroad access. Stuart was the nearest station on the U&N, eight miles east of the rising town and smelter. Everything had to be hauled by wagon from the railroad, adding to the cost of the smelter and the town of Anaconda, which had been laid out across the creek from the smelter site.[36]

Wagon freight and stages served Anaconda for a year until the Montana Railway, a locally chartered company, finally laid track to the town.[37] The eight-

mile-long line, which was initially operated as a branch of the U&N, left the U&N main line at Stuart and crossed the broad valley floor to Anaconda. Passenger traffic began between Butte and Anaconda on July 15, 1884. Though no mention is made of freight trains, undoubtedly freight began moving by rail to the Anaconda smelter as soon as the rails were spiked down and minimal ballasting was completed.[38] When the smelter, later called the Upper Works, was completed in the fall, the railroad was in place to move the ore there. In September the fires were lit, and the furnaces "blown in," or charged with concentrates and flux to be smelted. General smelting operations commenced in October.[39]

Although tremendously more efficient than wagon freight, the narrow gauge U&N was not the ideal railroad connection for the burgeoning Anaconda Company. The break in gauge presented a serious problem for movement of bulk commodities such as coal, which originated on the standard-gauge UP. Labor costs and time were saved by using the Ramsey transfer at Pocatello, which allowed cars of one gauge to be re-equipped with trucks for the other gauge.[40] Standard-gauge cars of Wyoming coal went through the transfer at Pocatello, and continued their journey to Anaconda on narrow-gauge trucks. On the return trip, the cars regained their original running gear at Pocatello for the trip east to the mines. Although it was less labor intensive than shoveling coal from one car to another, it was an added expense that an entirely standard-gauge route would eliminate. After the Northern Pacific became transcontinental in 1883, the prospect of standard-gauge competition for Butte's business was implicit to UP officials and Butte business leaders alike. Recognizing the threat of all-standard-gauge competition from the NP, the UP chose to convert the U&N to standard gauge. The portion from Pocatello to Garrison was widened on July 24, 1887, giving the Anaconda smelter and Butte's mines direct access to the rest of the nation.[41]

Montana had a relatively small non-Indian population in 1880, and both the UP and the NP sought to discourage competition for that market. By building the U&N north from Silver Bow to Garrison in 1882, the UP effectively kept the NP out of Butte, since NP's remaining options would have required expensive construction and heavy grades. NP, on the other hand, reached Helena first, capturing that traffic. Eventually both companies came to a pooling agreement to permit either of them access to Butte or Helena.

Butte businessmen welcomed the first railroad to arrive, envisioning economic prosperity and growth riding into town on the steamcars. Similar to other western communities, Butte soon discovered that railroads were not an unmitigated blessing. For although the U&N brought necessary transportation, it also held a monopoly on that transportation. This situation had not been foreseen, since in 1882 Butte's business community anticipated competition in the near future, arriving on the standard gauge rails of the Northern Pacific. Indeed, at one time the NP had been expected to be the first railroad to serve Montana. After six years of inactivity after the collapse of its underwriter in 1873, the NP had resumed construction between Minnesota and Kalama, Washington Territory in 1879. Unfortunately for Butte, however, the NP chose to locate its main line through Helena. Running track through Helena required fewer expensive cuts, fills, tunnels, and bridges than a line by way of Butte.[42] When the NP construction crews built west from Helena in 1883, they met the U&N at Garrison, where the narrow gauge stopped the year before. Soon afterwards, the NP was completed when its east and west ends of track met at Gold Creek, Montana, a few miles to the west.[43]

With trains running from St. Paul to Puget Sound, NP began looking for ways to develop the region it crossed. Butte, which had seemed inconsequential when the surveyors were locating the route in 1871, was booming by 1883. The initial NP solution was to arrange a pooling agreement with the U&N to share the Butte and Helena business between the two railroads. News of this arrangement brought dismay to the residents of the two cities. Seven years would pass before a competitive line would run through Butte.

NP management soon came to regret their decision to bypass Butte, and ordered surveys of possible routes to place the burgeoning copper camp on its transcontinental line. NP's pooling arrangement with the U&N between Garrison and Butte was not working very well; the change in gauge proved to be a considerable inconvenience for the standard-gauge NP. Even after the U&N track was converted to standard gauge in 1887, disagreement between NP and UP made a direct NP line to Butte desirable. Within five years of the NP's completion, another railroad began to serve Butte. The newcomer was the Montana Central (MC, a subsidiary of the Great Northern), which in 1888 connected Butte with Helena. Direct competition from this third company finally goaded the NP management to place Butte securely on their own line.

After considering several alternatives, and building seventy-five miles of redundant line paralleling the MC, NP chose to lay track east from Butte, across the

Continental Divide at Homestake Pass, to join the original main line at Logan, seventy miles away. Action began in June 1889 and regular train operations commenced in June 1890.[44] The westernmost portion of track, from Butte to Garrison, used the former U&N line, which NP eventually wrested from UP control.[45] Because the grades were easier on the line through Helena, transcontinental freight traffic continued using the original line. Most passenger trains and the local freights serving the mines and smelters were soon routed via Butte.[46]

The NP proved to be ACM's primary timber provider, an important commodity for the mines. Before coal was available, Daly had considered the possibility of firing the smelter with charcoal or wood.[47] But after the coal issue was settled, the primary need for wood was for mine stulls and square-set timbering for the mines, which used 15,000,000 board feet of timber a year by the 1890s.[48] Working through lumbermen such as Andrew B. Hammond and E. L. Bonner, the ACM obtained control of extensive timber holdings to supply its needs. The result was the ACM lumber department sawmill at Bonner, east of Missoula on the NP main line. Purchase of land from the NP land grant was legal, but logging federal land was not. Through subterfuge or outright timber theft, federal lands as well as legally purchased property were logged to supply the ACM lumber department's big sawmill at Bonner. Daly's timber machinations in western Montana are representative of the problems that typified much of the Gilded Age. Federal land policies had been written to facilitate the advance of an agrarian republic of yeoman farmers, as envisioned by Thomas Jefferson. But those land-use policies were proving inadequate to confront the challenges created by the growth of industrial capitalism, even possibly encouraging dishonesty on the part of railroad companies and industrialists like Daly.[49]

Even while he negotiated with the NP for timber lands and hauling, ACM's manager tirelessly sought better service and lower freight rates for his company. Daly never hesitated to entertain the idea of using the services of another railroad, in the hope of playing the different railroad companies against each other, thereby forcing them to keep rates low.[50]

In 1886 Butte found itself in the midst of a strategic chess game played by transcontinental railroad barons. The NP and the UP were not the only players interested in the Northwest by this time. James J. Hill planned to extend his St. Paul, Minneapolis & Manitoba (popularly called "the Manitoba," and soon to become the Great Northern) from the Dakotas to a

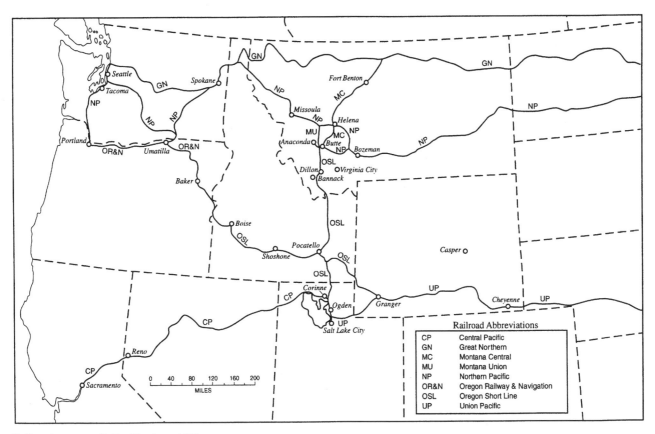

Railroad routes to Butte, Montana, 1893.

western port city on Puget Sound.[51] Hill recognized that a regional railroad like the Manitoba would be doomed to become a tributary to the larger systems unless it became a transcontinental line itself. More importantly, the northwestern states were still growing, and he believed they could profitably support another transcontinental railroad. Butte, with its expanding copper industry, could be a good source of freight revenue to help finance construction of the Great Northern (GN). As early as 1886 Hill encouraged Daly to consider routing his copper east over the new system.[52] In the next decade, Hill proved to be a good business associate, assisting Daly in building the BA&P.

Hill desired to balance construction costs and traffic potential, with an eye to efficient operation. At the same time, he sought to avoid exposing his expansion plans to his competition, the NP, until absolutely necessary. In January of 1886, Charles A. Broadwater and associated Montana businessmen chartered the Montana Central Railway to build lines in Montana connecting Great Falls and Helena with the Manitoba (later GN), which had reached Minot, North Dakota. Although Montanans appeared to be the initiators, the Montana Central was a Hill road from the start. Construction of the Manitoba and the MC moved west rapidly, reaching Great Falls and Helena in 1887. The

following year, MC rails arrived in Butte.[53] Curvature and grades between Helena and Butte were kept to a minimum through expensive construction such as the 6,145 foot-long tunnel east of Boulder. Initially, Hill had considered a transcontinental route through Butte. But in 1889, when he began to consolidate his railroads into the GN, he decided to build the main line directly west from Havre instead of south to Butte and then west. Hill chose transcontinental operational economics over local convenience, since the Havre route reduced the distance between St. Paul and Seattle when the GN became transcontinental in 1893.

One reason for early consideration of a GN transcontinental route via Butte may have been the issue of obtaining a right-of-way through the Blackfeet Indian Reserve to the west of Havre. Hill's efforts to obtain this right-of-way were stymied in 1886, doubtless due to NP lobbying of key members of Congress. A subsequent effort succeeded in early 1887, when President Grover Cleveland signed the bill authorizing a 150-foot-wide right-of-way not only through the Indian Reserve, but also through military reservations along the route. The route for the main line west of Havre was clear of legal obstacles by 1888. Therefore, it is unlikely that by 1889 Hill would have seriously considered running the GN main line via Butte.[54]

Although bypassed for the GN main line, Butte had new access via the Montana Central to the important coal reserves at Sand Coulee, near Great Falls. The railroad also offered the ACM another route east for its copper matte. Furthermore, the GN cemented a tight relationship with the ACM between 1886–93, through the construction of the Butte, Anaconda & Pacific in 1892–93.

By 1890 Butte enjoyed direct service from two transcontinental railroads, the NP and GN. A third, the UP, had connections with Butte through the shortline Montana Union (MU) which UP owned jointly with the NP. Anaconda, however, was served by only one railroad, the Montana Union (MU), which connected Butte, Silver Bow, Anaconda, and Garrison. Since the MU was the only railroad connecting the mines with the smelter, the lack of competition was detrimental to the ACM.

The MU was incorporated in 1886 to facilitate the pooling of traffic between Butte and Garrison on an equitable basis between NP and UP. The U&N (a UP line) conveyed its narrow-gauge trackage between Butte and Garrison to the new MU on August 1, 1886.[55]

By all accounts, the MU should have been a mutually beneficial terminal railroad, serving Butte and Anaconda. Both the UP, which junctioned with the MU at Silver Bow, and the NP, connecting at Garrison, appeared to be equally dependent on the good services of the MU to handle their trains over the final few miles to Butte or Anaconda. However, the two transcontinental railroads soon disputed not only the division of traffic, but virtually every aspect of the management and operation of this vital piece of trackage. Converting the MU to standard gauge was immediately pursued by the NP, which recognized that narrow gauge was an impediment to the shipment of timbers to the ACM mines from Bonner and other locations along its line. However, a standard-gauge MU would put the UP at a competitive disadvantage until the U&N had also been widened. Preparation for the conversion took a year, and when the UP converted the U&N to standard gauge from Pocatello to Silver Bow in 1887, the MU was converted at the same time.

Management of the MU from the outset caused problems for the mining company, because the NP and UP each attempted to gain the greatest share of MU revenue at the expense of its partner. Where this proved impossible, rates were raised by MU managers (frequently replaced) to increase the share of revenue for the two parent companies. It annoyed Daly and the ACM no end when the MU increased freight rates, or began assessing switching charges for spotting cars during loading or unloading.[56] Moreover, service was hampered by numerous derailments. The derailment problem was possibly due to increased use of larger, heavier cars and locomotives, and to deferred track maintenance as both parent companies pursued maximizing their individual profits from the MU. Another probable factor was the hasty conversion of the MU from narrow to standard gauge. Newspaper accounts comment about the frequency of derailments on the Montana Union, suggesting that standard-gauging was done at the least cost possible, simply putting in longer ties, and re-gauging the rails, without upgrading the roadbed.[57]

The number of derailments had been reduced by 1890, but Daly was still unhappy about the periodic shortage of cars for ore loading.[58] Car shortages, or delays in the delivery of coal, flux, and ore were not trivial matters, because any of these could require shutting down the smelter—an expensive and time-consuming process.

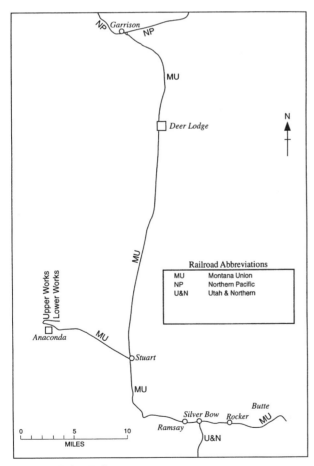

Montana Union Railway, 1887.

Dependable train service was essential to the operation of the ACM's smelter. Relatively low freight rates were also vital. When, on February 1, 1891, MU raised the rate from $.40 per ton to $.60 per ton for the 25-mile trip to Anaconda, it proved to be the last straw for ACM. Daly and James Ben Ali Haggin protested. Haggin claimed ACM had a contract for the lower rate that would not expire until March 15, 1891. Reaching an impasse with the MU, Daly ordered the shutdown of the mines and smelter, and suspended ore shipments beginning March 20, 1891.[59] The mines and smelter were closed for six months while Daly and Haggin argued with railroad executives. On October 21, 1891, Haggin wired Daly from New York: "Start the works as soon as you can. I have agreed with the railroad. J. B. Haggin." Men began reporting to work at the smelter and some of the mines the next day.[60] Five days later, on October 26th, 60 cars of ore were sent from Butte to Anaconda over the Montana Union.[61] The ACM was back in production, but the days of reliance on the MU were numbered. The fight with the railroad had ended only because ACM had decided to build its own railroad to haul its ore.

As for the fate of the MU, both NP and UP ultimately went into receivership. The NP, which was the first to recover its financial footing, was able to obtain

control of the MU in 1898, through a 999-year lease of the property. As it turned out, NP used the former MU track from Garrison to Butte, and UP ran trains from Silver Bow to Butte under a trackage rights agreement with NP.[62, 63]

Eventually a fourth transcontinental railroad came to town, the only one to include Butte on its main line. This was the Chicago, Milwaukee & St. Paul (CM&StP, CMStP&P, or often just called "the Milwaukee"),[64] owned by investors connected to the so-called "Standard Oil Gang," which controlled the Anaconda Copper Mining Co. Although it was the last railroad to reach Butte, the CM&StP had the closest technological ties to the BA&P.[65]

In 1905 the CM&StP was a prosperous midwestern regional railroad. Believing that its solvency depended on secure routes to western ports, the Milwaukee chose to extend its line to Puget Sound in Washington. The work was completed in 1909. The final northern transcontinental railroad to be built, the CM&StP was also the most expensive to construct, and the first to be abandoned. Was it one railroad too many for the limited traffic, or was the CM&StP badly managed? Both arguments have merit, and there is probably some

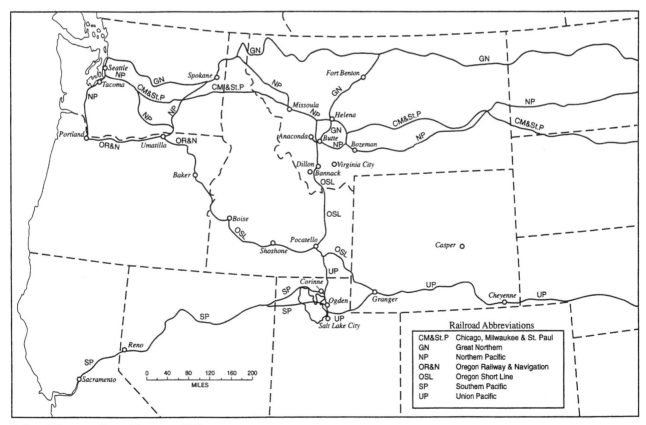

Railroad Routes to Butte, Montana, 1910.

justification to both complaints.[66] However, the fact that the CM&StP attempted long distance electrification following the prototype of the BA&P clearly helped push the carrier into economic collapse, an issue to be examined at length later.

To bring its track into Butte the CM&StP crossed the Continental Divide at Pipestone Pass, east of Butte—a route which had been rejected by the NP. Because the most convenient route through Butte had been taken by other railroads, the CM&StP skirted its south side, then crossed over the NP track to follow the BA&P and NP through Silver Bow canyon. At Colorado Junction, located in southwest Butte, the CM&StP connected with the BA&P, which gave the new railroad access to Butte's business district. Soon after completing its transcontinental line, the CM&StP erected a stylish passenger station east of Colorado Junction. Far more elaborate than the NP or BA&P

stations, the CM&StP station included a clock tower and other architectural embellishments. After completion, the BA&P began sharing the station for its own passenger traffic, using two tracks on the north side of the building adjoining its own right-of-way.

The CM&StP arrived nearly fifteen years after the ACM had already entered the railroad business for itself. The greatest benefit the CM&StP offered the ACM was to increase competition for ACM's long-haul freight. No nearby coal deposits were located on the Milwaukee to compete with the Sand Coulee mines on the GN, or the coal mines on the NP in eastern Montana, or the southern Wyoming coal fields on the UP. However, the CM&StP did compete with the NP for the timber traffic from the ACM lumber department mill at Bonner, and with the GN for ore, limestone, and blister copper anodes bound for Great Falls.

NOTES

1. Montana *Standard,* June 13, 1954.

2. Julius Grodinsky, *Transcontinental Railway Strategy, 1869–1893: A Study of Businessmen* (Philadelphia: University of Pennsylvania Press, 1962), pp. 134–44, 157, 235–36.

3. Albro Martin, *James J. Hill and the Opening of the Northwest* (New York: Oxford University Press, 1976), pp. 335–38, 348.

4. August Derleth, *The Milwaukee Road: Its First Hundred Years* (New York: Creative Age Press, 1948), pp. 158–88. Derleth wrote a very friendly history, with company cooperation. The corporate chronology is correct, but the book is short on analysis of management and decision making.

5. W. Turrentine Jackson, "Wells Fargo Stage Coaching in Montana: Trials and Triumphs," *Montana: The Magazine of Western History,* 29:2 (April, 1979), pp. 38–53, offers an overview of one well-known company's operations during the early territorial period.

6. The portage railroads on the Columbia River were not intended to operate for any distance, and were merely navigational aids to transport passengers and freight around rapids that the steamboats could not negotiate safely. The first steam locomotive in the Northwest was placed in service on the Oregon Portage Railroad at the Cascades in 1862. Sternwheelers on the Columbia River had another two decades before railroad transportation threatened their freight and passenger monopoly. Carlos Schwantes, *Railroad Signatures Across the Pacific Northwest* (Seattle, Washington: University of Washington Press, 1993), pp. 39–42.

7. David Haward Bain, *Empire Express: Building the First Transcontinental Railroad* (New York: Viking Penguin, 1999), pp. 143, 227. Lynne R. Mayer and Kenneth E. Vose, *Makin' Tracks* (New York: Praeger, 1975), pp. 16, 18–19, 64.

8. Efforts to supply Montana points from Portland, Oregon were less practical before the Northern Pacific railroad was completed. The military wagon road built under the direction of Captain John Mullan from Walla Walla to Fort Benton missed the southern Montana placer camps. In addition, there was

the expense of wagon transportation from the Columbia River to Walla Walla before starting on the Mullan Road. Efforts to provide competitive freight service by a series of steamboats and wagon portages using the Columbia River, and then the Clark Fork, were also attempted. Hubert H. Bancroft, *Works of Hubert Howe Bancroft, Vol. 31, History of Washington, Idaho and Montana* (San Francisco, California: The History Company, 1890), p. 729.

9. Frances and Dorothy Wood, *I Hauled These Mountains In Here* (Caldwell, Idaho: Caxton Printers, 1977), pp. 54–56, 158–59, 204.

10. Beal, pp. 1–3.

11. Susan Badger Doyle, "Indian Perspectives of the Bozeman Trail," *Montana: The Magazine of Western History,* 40:1 (Winter, 1990), pp. 56–67. Bancroft, *Works,* Vol. 31, pp. 695–700.

12. Bancroft, *Works,* Vol. 31, pp. 728–29.

13. Ibid.

14. Ibid., Vol. 31, pp. 733–34.

15. New York *Times,* April 26, 1899, p. 12; Ibid., Ibid., February 16, 1901, p. 11; Ibid., March 6, 1902, p.9. See also, Malone, *The Battle for Butte,* pp. 22–23.

16. Robert G. Athearn, *Union Pacific Country* (Chicago: Rand, McNally & Company, 1971), pp. 204–05. Athearn argues the Union Pacific lessened the need for the military in the west by reducing the need to station troops along the Bozeman Trail. The sporadic nature of freighting traffic along the Bozeman trail route due to Indian resistance in 1866 is mentioned in: Bancroft, *Works,* Vol. 31, pp. 730–31, 734.

17. Eugene V. Smalley, *History of the Northern Pacific Railroad* (New York: G.P. Putnam's Sons, 1883), pp. 205–10, 216–17, 230–31; Robin W. Winks, *Frederick Billings: A Life* (New York: Oxford University Press, 1991), pp. 208, 220–28.

18. Bancroft, *Works,* Vol. 31, pp. 677–87. See also Rex Meyers, "Montana: A State and Its Relationship with Railroads, 1854–1970," (Los Angeles: University of California at Los Angeles,

1972), Ph.D. dissertation, for an extended study of the political aspect of the railroad subsidy bills in the territorial legislature during this period.

19. Mallory H. Ferrell, "Utah & Northern: The Narrow Gauge that Opened a Frontier," *Colorado Rail Annual* No. 15, p. 47; Malone, *Battle for Butte*, pp. 23–24. Merril D. Beal, *Intermountain Railroads: Standard and Narrow Gauge* (Caldwell: Caxton Printers, 1962), pp. 86–87, gives the date of Butte's first train arriving as December 21, 1881. Probably the first construction train arrived on the 21st, and a few days were required to complete enough yard track to allow regular service to begin on the 26th.

20. Gauge is the distance between the rail heads. The standard track gauge throughout Europe and North America is 56.5 inches (four feet, eight and one-half inches). Wider track gauges exist elsewhere, and were used in North America, especially in the southern United States, before 1870.

21. George W. Hilton, *American Narrow Gauge Railroads* (Stanford, California: Stanford University Press, 1990). The definitive overview of the rise and fall of the narrow gauge in North America. An economist, Professor Hilton concludes that the entire concept was fatally flawed from the outset because the labor cost of operating the railroad was the same for either gauge, but the standard gauge hauled more freight for the same cost in employee time.

22. Robert F. Fairlie, *Railways or No Railways* (London: Effingham Wilson, 1872; repr., Canton, Ohio: Railhead Publications, n.d.)

23. Beal, pp. 4–8.

24. In 1877 the Utah Northern was reorganized after the Union Pacific took control of it as the Utah & Northern. For simplicity, the Utah & Northern (U&N) reporting marks will be used for both corporations, and the entire narrow gauge railroad from Ogden, Utah, to Montana. Beal, pp. 34–42; Ferrell, pp. 25–26, 33.

25. Bancroft, *Works*, Vol. 31, pp. 677–87. A variety of Montanans sought to obtain territorial or county subsidies for railroad construction between 1873 and 1881. This included attempts by both Helena and the UP management to make Helena the Montana terminus of the U&N. Bancroft gives a brief synopsis of these events. However, the reference to the U&N reaching Helena on page 687 is certainly a typographical error; the U&N never built beyond Garrison.

26. Beal, p. 21, Ferrell, p. 64.

27. Beal, pp. 59–61, 134–40; Ferrell, pp. 33, 36.

28. The OSL connected with the Oregon Railway & Navigation Co. (OR&N) at Huntington, Oregon. After Henry Villard lost control of the OR&N in 1883, the UP eventually acquired control of it by means of long-term lease, gaining access to Portland, Oregon. Athearn, pp. 324–29.

29. Anaconda *Standard*, October 23, 1891, p. 5; Ibid., December 22, 1893, p. 7.

30. Wood, pp. 56, 204. David Wood was a freighter in Colorado, but his business left records which were used by the authors to document the operation of freighting in the Rocky Mountain region during the period of railroad construction. Wagon freighters tended to state weight in pounds, which have been converted to tonnage figures here for simplicity of comparison to freight car capacities, given in tons.

31. Ferrell, p. 71; *Official Railway Equipment Register,* November, 1928, p. 613. The capacities are confirmed from *Equipment Register* listings for equipment owned by the Sumpter Valley Ry. (SV), an Oregon short line equipped with former U&N equipment following its conversion to standard gauge. Some ex-U&N cars remained in service on the SV until 1947.

32. Interstate Commerce Commission (ICC), Records. ICC Bureau of Valuation, Union Pacific Railroad, Valuation Summary, Account 53, Freight Cars, approved June 30, 1919.

33. Freight train crews at this time consisted of a conductor, responsible for all aspects of operating the train; two brakemen who coupled and uncoupled the cars, set brakes, and repaired minor mechanical problems on the cars between stations; an engineer who operated the locomotive; and a fireman responsible for maintaining steam pressure in the locomotive and assisting the engineer in its safe operation.

34. Railroad practice is to refer to the capacity, rather than the light weight of freight cars. A ten-ton car is one with a ten ton capacity, not a car weighing ten tons.

35. Hofman, pp. 265–67; Goodale, pp. 608–09; *Mining and Scientific Press,* Vol. 48 (March 22, 1884), p. 206.

36. Butte *Daily Miner*, July 15, 1884.

37. Interstate Commerce Commission. "Valuation Docket No. 959, Northern Pacific Railway, et al.," 25 Val. Rep. 700–701. The Montana Railway was incorporated December 17, 1881, and was controlled by the NP through stock ownership at the time of its sale to the NP on October 7, 1898. The Montana Ry. was also the legal entity responsible for building nearly six miles of mine spurs on the Butte Hill. Between August 1, 1896, and May 17, 1898, the Montana Ry. trackage was operated by the Montana Union Railway.

38. Ibid. Also see Patrick F. Morris, *Anaconda Montana: Copper Smelting Boom Town on the Western Frontier* (Bethesda, Maryland: Swann Publishing, 1997), p. 37. Morris is in error in his reference to "Stanley Dillon"; the Union Pacific executive he is referring to was Sidney Dillon.

39. U.S. Geological Survey, *Minerals Resources,* 1885 (Washington, D.C.: GPO, 1886), p. 216; *Engineering and Mining Journal,* Vol. 34 (October 18, 1884), p. 272.

40. Car trucks, often simply called trucks, contain the wheels of a railroad car. The following definition of car trucks is from Matthias N. Forney, *The Railroad Car Builder's Pictorial Dictionary* (New York: Railroad Gazette, 1879; repr., New York: Dover Publications, 1974), pp. 35–36. "Car truck. A group of two or more pairs of wheels and axles attached to a frame with suitable journal boxes, springs, jaws, etc. to form a complete carriage, and intended to carry one end of a car-body."

41. Indicative of the importance of the Wyoming coal traffic, the U&N from Pocatello to all Montana points was standard-gauged in 1887, but the line from Ogden to Pocatello remained narrow gauge for another three years. Ferrell, pp. 55–56.

42. Smalley, pp. 408–09. Smalley was writing as the railroad neared completion, but as of the publication date in August, 1883, it was not quite finished. The NP did not enter Butte on its own until 1890.

43. Schwantes, *Railroad Signatures*, pp. 57–60 describes the events at Gold Creek; as does Winks, pp. 259–60.

44. Bill and Jan Taylor, *The Butte Short Line* (Missoula, Montana: Pictorial Histories Publishing Co.1998), p. 28; Louis T. Renz, *Northern Pacific Data Tables* (Walla Walla, Washington: Louis

T. Renz, 1974), p. 21. Renz gives May, 1890, as the opening date; the Taylors cite the June 15, 1890, Helena *Daily Independent* reporting the opening of the line on that day.

45. Interstate Commerce Commission, "Valuation Docket No. 959," *ICC Valuation Reports*, Vol. 25, pp. 427–28, 700–705. The Montana Railway was incorporated in 1881, and built the line from Stuart to Anaconda, and over five miles of mine spurs on the Butte Hill. This trackage was operated by the U&N until 1886, when it was leased to the Montana Union Railway. The Montana Union Railway was incorporated in Montana on June 28, 1886, and controlled by the NP through stock ownership. The MU owned no trackage, but leased the U&N between Butte and Garrison, and the entire Montana Ry. The U&N trackage was leased for a period of 999 years, commencing in 1886. The practice of transcontinental railroads locally incorporating branch lines, which were later consolidated into the parent company though outright purchase, or long-term lease, was quite common. Readers can observe this in detail in the case of the NP, from a close reading of ICC Valuation Docket No. 959. A layman's treatment of this method of organizing NP branch line construction in eastern Washington is contained in Peter B. Lewty's *Across the Columbia Plain*, Pullman, Washington: WSU Press, 1995.

46. NP practice came to refer to the Helena line as the "freight line," and the Butte line as the "passenger line." The NP had a yard in Butte, but did not directly serve either the mines or the smelter. Instead it relied on the MU, and later the BA&P to move cars to mines on the Butte Hill or to the Anaconda smelter.

47. Morris, pp. 31.

48. Malone, *The Battle for Butte*, p. 41.

49. Malone, *The Battle for Butte*, pp. 42–45. Conservation of natural resources became a national issue during this period. Samuel P. Hays, *Conservation and the Gospel of Efficiency: the Progressive Conservation Movement, 1890–1920*, is an overview of federal conservation policy and practice. Chapters Three and Five pertain to forests and public lands. Bringing the study of this subject closer to the present, Elmo Richardson examines federal conservation policy in the post-WW II period in *Dams, Parks and Politics* (Lexington, Kentucky: University Press of Kentucky, 1973). Both show how federal policy has often worked to support short-term use of resources rather than long-term conservation policies.

50. Martin, *Opening*, p. 348.

51. Ralph W. Hidy, Muriel E. Hidy, Roy V. Scott, and Don L. Hofsommer, *The Great Northern Railway: A History* (Boston, Massachusetts: Harvard Business School Press, 1988), pp. 72–73. Hill's first section of the GN was the St. Paul & Pacific, which Hill reorganized as the St. Paul, Minneapolis & Manitoba. The Manitoba, along with several other Hill railroad properties, was merged into the Great Northern Railway on January 31, 1890. The Montana Central is discussed in Hidy et al., pp. 57–60. Hill has been the subject of numerous biographies. One of the most readable, as well as the shortest and most objective, is Michael P. Malone, *James J. Hill:*

Empire Builder of the Northwest (Norman, Oklahoma: University of Oklahoma Press, 1996).

52. Martin, *Opening*, p. 348.

53. Malone, *Hill*, pp. 115–27.

54. Malone, *Hill*, pp. 114, 119–23. Commissioner of Indian Affairs. *Annual Report, 1887* (Washington, D.C.: US GPO, 1887) p. 38. St. Paul, Minneapolis & Manitoba Railway Co. "Annual Report for the Year Ended June 30, 1888," p. 19.

55. Ferrell, p. 55. Interstate Commerce Commission, "Valuation Docket No. 959, Northern Pacific Railway Co., et al.", 25 Val. Rep. 703–706. The MU leased the U&N between Meaderville (Butte) and Garrison.

56. Switching charges are fees charged to the shipper for spotting cars at his facility for loading or unloading. Switching charges are charged in addition to the freight charges, which only cover the cost of transportation from the point of origin to their destination. Many railroads would agree to spot cars for loading and unloading for free within certain limitations.

57. Anaconda *Standard*, March 20, 1891, p. 5.

58. Ibid., p. 4.

59. Ibid., p. 4; Ibid., March 21, 1891, pp. 2, 5.

60. Ibid., October 22, 1891, pp. 1–2; Ibid., October 23, 1891, pp. 2–3, 5.

61. Ibid., October 26, 1891, p. 3.

62. Interstate Commerce Commission, *ICC Valuation Reports*, Vol. 25, pp. 427–28.

63. Trackage rights agreements are typically found where two railroads desire to serve the same community or industry, but want to avoid the expense of duplicating facilities. One railroad owns the track, and acts as landlord, while the other, as tenant, pays for the privilege of operating trains over the track. In this case, the UP paid the NP for the use of the track between Silver Bow and Butte.

64. Derleth, pp. 265–87. The initials CM&StP are correct for the period when the company built through Butte. After its reorganization as the Chicago, Milwaukee, St. Paul & Pacific, the CMStP&P initials are correct. Part of the Pacific extension was operated as the Chicago, Milwaukee & Puget Sound (CM&PS) prior to 1913.

65. Derleth, pp. 188–90 discusses the connections between the ACM, Montana Power, and the CM&StP briefly, with little analysis of the situation.

66. Max Lowenthal, *The Investor Pays* (New York: Alfred A. Knopf, 1933). Lowenthal argued the Pacific extension of the Milwaukee was indeed one transcontinental railroad too many in his study of its financial collapse. Thomas H. Ploss, *The Nation Pays Again* (Chicago: Thomas H. Ploss, 1984). As former CMStP&P legal counsel, Ploss offers an insider's view. He argued the railroad was wrecked by outside financial interests which had been looting it over the long haul. Ploss concluded that the final economic failure was due to mismanagement.

Chapter Three

THE COPPER SHORT LINE

Butte people manifested a great deal of interest in the formal opening of the B.A.&P. for passenger business today, [December 27, 1893] and there was quite a crowd at the Great Northern depot at 8:55 this morning to see the first train come in from Anaconda. It was the Great Northern through express and bore a number of Anaconda people, who came up to Butte for the express purpose of taking a ride on the first passenger train on the new road out of the future capital.[1]

AS A RESULT OF FRUSTRATION, Daly and ACM entered the transportation business in 1891, to assure cost effective and timely movement of ore to the Anaconda smelter at fees lower than the Montana Union had demanded. With the construction of the Butte, Anaconda & Pacific, the ACM became an increasingly vertically integrated enterprise, controlling the copper from its mining through its transportation and smelting to its use in finished products. The railroad, though only one link in the corporate chain, was nonetheless a crucial link. Over the next ninety years, the BA&P hauled the vast majority of the output of the Butte mines to the Anaconda smelter.

Much of Daly's reasoning behind his decision to build the BA&P must be left to conjecture, since his personal papers were destroyed by his wife and attorney after his death, as Daly had willed. Thus all information contained therein was consigned to the flames, and not to posterity.[2] Evidence suggests that Daly may have considered building a railroad as early as 1888. In the January 23, 1889, Missoula *Gazette*, were reports that the ACM had ordered a survey for a railroad from the company's mines in Butte to the smelter. An interview with Daly, in which he discussed the possibility of building his own railroad, was published in a Helena paper three days later. Another report of ACM interest in building an independent railroad to haul its ore was published in early November 1889.[3] The first solid indication of ACM interest in railroading appeared in the newspaper early in 1891. Readers of the Anaconda *Standard* learned some of the details about the incorporation of the Anaconda Mining Company, which had been filed with the Silver Bow County Clerk on January 19, 1891, following two months of preparation. Among the objects the com-

pany was permitted to engage in was transportation.[4] While the second article of the new corporate charter did not specifically call for ACM to engage in the railroad business, it left the possibility open under the rubric of "constructing, owning, or operating…roads, tramways, and other means of conveyance and transportation." Another clue is contained in the organizational notice of the BA&P: "This new road has been discussed for nearly two years…", which would have indicated about November or December 1890, twenty-two months before the BA&P charter was filed. That places the idea of the railroad within the time frame of the incorporation process of the Anaconda Copper Mining Company.[5]

Another curious obervation, judging from the noticeable absence of his name in newspapers and other public records, was Daly's secrecy during incorporation of ACM. His name does not appear in public records from the days of the early corporate existence of either ACM or the BA&P. His name is not even listed among the incorporators![6]

Despite lacking Daly's personal records, we understand the reason that Daly and his partners ordered the closure of the ACM mines and smelter in mid-March 1891. It was a last-ditch effort to shock MU management into making concessions to the copper company.

For ACM, the timing of the closure was advantageous, as world copper prices had been depressed for several years, and a shutdown might actually bolster copper prices by reducing the volume of copper in the market. Montana copper production had figured into the efforts of the French-based Secrétan Syndicate to manage world copper prices in the 1880s, but the plan failed in 1889.[7] On March 19, 1891, ACM mines in

Butte stopped loading ore for shipment to Anaconda. The smelter operated until it was finished with the ore on hand, and then it closed.

Both the railroad and ACM attempted to use the power of monopoly to force the other to concede to their desires. Though the railroad had no competitors, the mining company provided virtually all the business on this lucrative section of the Montana Union Railway. The ACM closure lasted a little over six months, until October 22, 1891.[8] During that time, Daly and his partners were busy with arrangements to build their own railroad.

In April 1891, during the mine closure, Daly met with railroad baron James J. Hill. Hill visited Daly in Anaconda, causing the town's residents to speculate about a possible Great Northern extension from Butte to Anaconda.[9] Such a move would have been perfectly feasible, and would have given the GN direct access to the smelter traffic without the need for sharing the revenue with the Montana Union for the Anaconda to Butte mileage. Because of the impasse between ACM and the MU, Daly was receptive to a visit from Hill, who in turn was seeking additional traffic for the GN.

Although Daly and Hill apparently got along better than Daly did with either the UP or NP and their MU subsidiary, Daly would have been aware of the self-interest operating behind the magnate's visit. Hill was astute enough to recognize that he could capture a significant share of the business by being cooperative with large shippers. Anaconda's partners would provide a large volume of business. If the GN extended the Montana Central from Butte to Anaconda, it would certainly be profitable. An extension to the west could be important if more mineral wealth were encountered in the mountains of western Montana. The possibility of a secondary line across the state to compete with the Northern Pacific for business in Missoula and other towns on the NP route was also a consideration. However, from Hill's perspective, if Daly built a railroad to Anaconda, the GN could get the profitable freight business without having to invest in a western extension of its Helena to Butte branch. As it turned out, the BA&P was incorporated as an Anaconda subsidiary, and not as a part of the GN.

While miners and smeltermen were idle, lawyers and surveyors were busy. On May 11, 1891, the Butte, Anaconda & Pacific Railway was incorporated by five Montanans: Stephen A. Estes, William L. Hodge, Judson B. Losee, William M. Thornton, and Shelley Tuttle. Capitalization was set at $5,000,000. The new

railroad was to be built from Butte to Anaconda, then west to Missoula by way of Warm Springs Creek and the Bitterroot Valley.[10] Daly appeared uninvolved in the early phases of the project. When asked if the new railroad was actually being built by the ACM, William Hodge was evasive, stating that, "Nobody connected with the Anaconda company figures among the incorporators."[11] True enough, but who was going to buy $5,000,000 worth of stock? Local investors outside of the Anaconda company seemed unlikely. Proof of the ACM's interest became evident in October 1892, when the *Railroad Gazette* reported that a charter for the BA&P was filed by Daly.[12] One obvious reason Daly kept himself out of the picture, at least in the beginning, was to prevent land owners from boosting prices for land the BA&P needed for its right-of-way. As one of the largest businesses in the region, the ACM probably expected the worst from its neighbors, who would ask more for the property if they knew that ACM money was behind the railroad than if they thought it was a group of relatively small-time local businessmen. Daly's shrewdness was likely justified; the U&N entry into Butte from Silver Bow had been delayed by high prices demanded by several placer claim owners who thought a big railroad like the UP, which was financing the U&N, could afford to pay big prices for the land.[13]

Organization of the BA&P was largely accomplished by means of a very quiet series of gentlemen's agreements and verbal contracts, unlike the highly publicized marketing of stocks and securities associated with most common-carrier railroads. Many important details were worked out by Daly and his partners in private. Daly then handled arrangements with Hill verbally, again leaving virtually no paper trail. The verbal contract with the GN effectively made Hill's railroad responsible for financing the building and equipping the new railroad. In return, the GN would receive shares of Butte, Anaconda & Pacific stock and first mortgage bonds. As the Anaconda Mining Company paid for the construction of the BA&P, the GN would turn the BA&P securities over to the mining company.[14] From 1895 on, the ACM held the majority of the BA&P stock.

Rumors that the BA&P would become a subsidiary of the GN, like the Montana Central, persisted. The *Railroad Gazette*, a prominent industry trade journal, reported that the BA&P would be operated by the Great Northern after it was completed.[15] There was good reason to assume this. Incorporation of locally chartered railroad companies, headed by local businessmen, was a standard tactic of large railroad companies at the time. Hill was a master of the technique. In addition, a local precedent existed: Charles Broadwater, the publicly recognized man building the Montana Central, was merely a figurehead; everyone knew that the MC was financed by the Great Northern and was every bit Hill's railroad.

Because Daly played his cards close to the vest, speculation about the real power behind the BA&P continued until well after the line opened for business. It was wondered if Daly actively sought a GN takeover of the BA&P. It was common knowledge that Daly wanted to see his smelter town become the state capital. But in 1892 Anaconda was too remote, served only by a branch of the Montana Union, while Helena was on the main line of the NP as well as on the Montana Central branch of the new Great Northern. However, if the GN took over the BA&P along with the Montana Central, it would put Anaconda on an important branch line, allowing the operation of through long-distance passenger trains between Anaconda and Saint Paul or Chicago. A truly transcontinental connection was possible if the BA&P were extended west to the Bitterroot Valley, then north to Missoula, and ultimately connecting with the Great Northern main line at Kalispell.[16] Anaconda would then be on a secondary GN main line, similar to the NP line that served Butte. Anaconda's boosters believed such a route would accord Anaconda passenger service comparable to that received by Helena.[17]

Survey crews headed into the field immediately. Work began at Butte on May 16, 1891, locating spurs from mines on the Butte Hill to a point where trains could be composed for the trip to the smelter at Anaconda.[18] The point chosen as the Butte district's main yard for the BA&P was Rocker .[19] Here the Missoula Gulch line branched off of the main line to begin its climb up the flanks of the Butte Hill to the mines. The main line was surveyed east to join the GN's Montana Central subsidiary at the west end of its Butte yard.[20] Survey work continued through the summer. One crew worked in the Silver Bow canyon, between Butte and Anaconda, which was the most critical area along the surveyed route. The BA&P had to locate its line to avoid interfering with the already existing Montana Union track through the narrow canyon. In July, BA&P officials ordered another survey party to locate a route from Anaconda west to Phillipsburg.[21]

Little more was done that year. Anaconda and Butte celebrated the resumption of work in the mines and smelter in late October, 1891. Daly reported that

James Ben Ali Haggin had finally concluded a satisfactory contract with executives of the two parent companies of the Montana Union Railway in New York.[22] Having determined to build its own railroad, ACM went back to work producing copper, along with silver and gold as valuable by-products. The days of dealing with the MU were numbered.

Construction got off to a slow start in 1892. In February the Missoula *Gazette* reported a proposal to build a railroad from Anaconda to Missoula by way of the Bitterroot Valley "as soon as practicable," though little happened. Newspaper enthusiasm not withstanding, the BA&P line down the Bitterroot valley was to remain a paper railroad.[23] Most of the construction season went by, and with no work occurring except surveying. Finally in the autumn of 1892, stirrings of activity again were evident. A new charter was filed for the BA&P, which listed Daly as an investor.[24] Less than two weeks later, construction began along the surveyed route between Anaconda and Butte. Ninety teams were put to work, with another sixty expected to be on the job soon. Graders were expected to complete a half-mile a day.[25] At that rate, the grade between Butte and Anaconda was estimated to take about 50 working days to complete. The primary concentration was on the roadbed between Butte and Anaconda, but some grading was done near Silver Lake, sixteen miles west of Anaconda. Construction of the proposed western extension was terminated by the onset of winter.[26]

Regional lore has it that the BA&P was built by Daly's miners who were unemployed as a result of the dispute between Daly and the Montana Union Railroad. Reality appears to differ from the popular account.[27] The mines and smelter were shut down in 1891, and serious construction work on the BA&P did not start until the fall of 1892, by which time both the mines and smelter were back in operation. Doubtless some unemployed miners were hired by the railroad subcontractors to help grade the BA&P, but the work was not overseen by Daly or the ACM.

The Great Northern Railway acted as a resource for Daly, who initially acted as the general contractor building the BA&P. Daly oversaw the construction work and generally managed the project, but subcontracted the actual grading work to the firm of Toole & Twohy.[28] On July 5, 1893, Daly assigned his contract to the Great Northern, which then officially became the general contractor—although correspondence suggests that actual responsibility for construction remained in the hands of Daly or his subordinates in Montana. Although the GN recommended civil engineers and other technical advisors to the BA&P, the mining company appears to have exercised control over its construction and operation; the GN's interest was essentially financial, rather than operational.[29]

Grading, except where rock was encountered, was done using the standard technology of the times. Horse- or mule-drawn fresno scrapers gouged up the earth and moved it to form the grade. The largest fills were built up with earth or rock removed from the deepest cuts nearby, moved by animal power.

Between Butte and Anaconda, grading continued through the winter, and neared completion by the end of 1892. Once the grading was finished, the roadbed was allowed to settle until April, 1893, when the management planned to lay track.[30]

Allowing the raw grade to settle was wise, because the line expected to begin hauling heavy ore as soon as it opened for traffic. After the roadbed had gone through a spring thaw-and-dry cycle the construction crews could find low spots, add fill to bring them up to grade, and stabilize soft sections before laying track and ballasting it.[31]

There were other good reasons not to hasten track laying. In fact, a considerable amount of work remained to be done. Blasting cuts through rock had not been completed at several locations in Silver Bow canyon. Most of the bridges and culverts also needed to be constructed, including two large bridges in the canyon. One bridge carried the BA&P from the north side of the canyon to the south side, across both the creek and the Montana Union track. Sub-contractors could not drive piles for the bridge crossing the Montana Union until the frozen ground had thawed. Elsewhere, especially on the portion east from Anaconda, the grade was not only ready, but ties had been distributed along it, in preparation for laying rail.[32] In Anaconda itself, terminal facilities needed to be constructed. Shops, a roundhouse and engine terminal, company offices, and freight and passenger stations needed to be completed—hints to the observant that the new railroad would operate independently of the Montana Central.[33] Track connections to the smelter also had to be built. The Montana Union was not going to permit its competitor to use its own tracks to enter the smelter, nor was it willing to allow the BA&P to cross its Anaconda branch without a legal challenge. By December 1892, there was still a year's worth of work—legal and physical—to be done before the BA&P was operational.

The BA&P was built for heavy traffic, using new, seventy-five pound steel rail. Common to large construction jobs, unforeseen delays were encountered. For example, rail laying was supposed to begin in early summer 1893,[34] but the steel mill only began shipping rail in late July 1893.[35] Track laying began at Butte in August, working toward Anaconda.[36] Reports in mid-October that "…train service will probably begin in a few weeks," proved overly optimistic.[37] It wasn't until December that the BA&P started carrying a small volume of freight, with the expectation of soon offering passenger service.[38] The BA&P was far from completed, however, with an engine terminal, yards, and freight and passenger stations remaining to be built in Butte. During the first few months of operation, the BA&P used the GN's Montana Central station, roundhouse, and yard in Butte. Passenger service began on December 27, 1893, though the first passenger train actually arrived in Anaconda on the night of December 26, when the GN began running its Montana Central passenger trains through Butte to Anaconda.[39] Twelve years after the city's first train arrived on the U&N, Butte again received a shiny new railroad for Christmas.

Concurrently, Daly and Anaconda's business and civic leaders busied themselves with seeking to make their town the state capital. Montana, admitted to statehood in 1889, had not yet selected a state capital. While Daly had no interest in holding office himself, it was clear that he wanted his town to become the political capital of the state, matching the economic dominance of his mining company.[40] For Anaconda to become Montana's capital, however, direct train service to important eastern political and commercial centers was vital. Therefore Daly negotiated with Hill to provide Anaconda with through passenger service via the GN.[41]

Passenger service between Helena and Anaconda was instituted in December 1893. GN Montana Central passenger trains Nos. 1, 2, 23, and 24 were scheduled to run through Butte and terminate or originate in Anaconda.[42] But disagreement over the division of revenue and operating expenses ensued, and the agreement was terminated on February 23, 1894, after only two months. The issue was revisited the following year, when the GN offered to reinstate the Anaconda service of Montana Central trains Nos. 1 and 2.[43] Helena had by then secured the state capital, consigning Anaconda and Butte to become economic, but not legislative, centers in the Treasure State. Doubtless, past experience with outside carriers discouraged the ACM from contracting again with the Montana Central for this service. Passenger trains on the BA&P ceased to be advertised as linked with long distance carriers serving between Anaconda and the Midwest. The BA&P passenger service contented itself with primarily local travelers, mail, and express operating between Butte and Anaconda.

It is apparent why rumors that BA&P was actually a GN subsidiary would have been common between 1891 and 1894, since the railroad had obvious ties to the GN. For example, construction of BA&P began in 1892, when the expansion of the Great Northern main line was also under way.[44] The larger railroad acted as the general contractor for the construction of the new railroad after Daly assigned his contract to the GN in July 1893.[45] The first rolling stock used by BA&P was supplied by GN, or obtained as part of larger orders placed by GN. When the original wooden bridge at milepost 11.02 was replaced, GN assisted with the engineering for a steel structure, including the bid process.[46] However, the relationship appears to have been strictly an investment on Hill's part, with little desire to actually acquire the BA&P and merge it into his railroad.

⚒

The first locomotives acquired by BA&P were purchased from GN. Engines 1 through 5 of the BA&P Railway were 0-6-0 switch engines, with 19 x 26-inch cylinders, 49-inch diameter driving wheels,[47] and Belpaire fireboxes built by the Brooks Locomotive Works in 1892 for GN. For freight service, four Brooks 2-6-0's (Mogul) locomotives were delivered in 1893. Numbered 30 through 33, they were identical to GN No. 362. Three of these locomotives were built together by Brooks as part of their order number 501, which had been placed by GN.[48] The fourth, No. 33, although ordered in 1893, was delivered in 1894, making it the first new locomotive built expressly for the BA&P. All four Moguls had 19 x 24-inch cylinders and 55-inch driving wheels.[49]

For passenger service, the BA&P acquired a pair of 4-4-0 (American) type locomotives from GN, which became BA&P Nos. 50 and 51. These were both the oldest and the smallest motive power on the roster. Numbers 50 and 51 were part of a six-locomotive order for the St. Paul, Minneapolis & Manitoba (later Great Northern) delivered in 1882 by the Rhode Island Locomotive Works.[50] The 4-4-0 was the all-purpose locomotive of the 1850s through the 1870s, but by 1890 greater motive power was needed for many

The crew of 0-6-0 switch engine No. 5 posed with the engineer's daughter in front of the Anaconda coal chutes, ca. 1905. *World Museum of Mining, #1316*

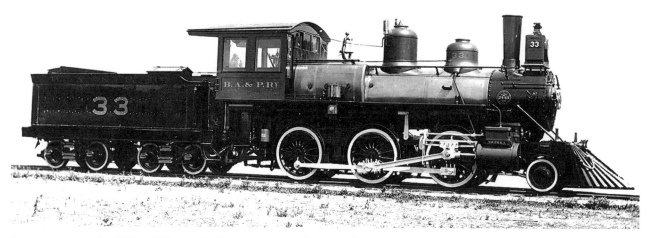

Brooks constructed 2-6-0 No. 33 for the BA&P in 1894. It was identical to locomotives Brooks built for the GN at the same time. Although equipped with air brakes, the locomotive had link-and-pin couplers when new. *Brooks Locomotive Works Photo; ALCO Historic Photos, #B-1170*

passenger trains. Although many western railroads continued to rely heavily on Americans as passenger power in the 1880s, by 1890 the heaviest main-line passenger trains were becoming too heavy for a single 4-4-0. Like its competitors, the NP and UP, the GN's predecessor had bought numerous 4-4-0's in the 1880s, and now needed to replace them with larger motive power. As 4-6-0's (Ten-Wheelers) assumed main-line passenger train duties, smaller locomotives were downgraded to hauling local trains on the main lines, and

to branch line service, or were sold. The GN had plenty of 4-4-0's that were too small for use on transcontinental passenger trains, but which were more than adequate for the relatively short passenger trains of secondary lines such as the Montana Central or the BA&P. As inexpensive, readily available locomotives, they met the BA&P's immediate needs. However, both had relatively short careers on the BA&P, and were replaced by larger, newer locomotives before 1906.[51]

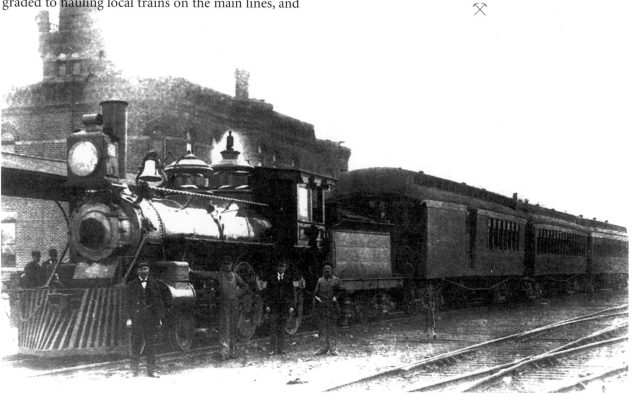

Marcus Daly's funeral train, behind one of the 4-4-0's, in 1900. The crew wrapped black crepe around the handrails, domes and over the number plate—official observance of mourning for the railroad's founder. *World Museum of Mining, #127*

When it opened for service in December 1893, the BA&P owned ten locomotives and a small number of passenger cars. The BA&P differed from the large railroads with which it connected in that passenger service was not a primary concern. Three secondhand coaches were purchased, adequate for local service on a short line like the BA&P.[52] More passenger cars were added later, but only as they were needed to meet local traffic.

The freight car roster reflected the priorities of the Anaconda Mining Company. Although some of the equipment was secondhand, the majority of it was new and the best available. Freight business aside from ore was mostly inbound merchandise and mining supplies originating off-line, so there BA&P had no need for the large number of boxcars, solid-bottom gondolas, or other freight cars usually required on larger roads. Flats and ore cars predominated, with a handful of box cars for general freight business, and nine stock cars.

The stock cars were acquired primarily to move horses for AMC's owners.[53] Daly and Haggin fancied themselves horsemen, and both owned estates for raising horses.[54] Three of the cars were designed for use on passenger trains, rather than freight trains—a practice associated with expensive racehorses or carriage horses for the wealthy. These express horse cars rode on passenger trucks, constructed for smooth riding at high speeds.[55]

In 1893 the freight car generally requested by most shippers was the box car. Almost everything that was theft-prone or subject to weather damage was shipped in box cars. Lumber, grain (both sacked or in bulk), canned goods, small machinery, petroleum in barrels, ore concentrates, hides, wool, buggies, blasting powder, rye whiskey, cigars, and all manner of general merchandise required by the residents of Anaconda and Butte was shipped in box cars.[56] Even coal could be shipped in box cars during times of car shortages. Consequently, most railroads had large numbers of them.

But the BA&P ordered just enough to supply the general needs of the two company towns.

Coal was the lifeblood of North America before 1920, and an important commodity for rail traffic. Railroads commonly hauled coal in hopper-bottom cars, or in flat-bottom cars with or without doors in the floors. Though the hopper cars were becoming common in the eastern states in the 1890s, the solid, flat-bottomed gondola still predominated in the Rocky Mountain West. The solid-floored gondola was basically a flat car with sides and ends, and could be used to haul anything from lumber and pipe to coal, ore, and gravel. In coal service, the cars were easily loaded by gravity at a mine tipple, but a crew of men was required to shovel the contents out of the car at its destination. Such cars were typically thirty or thirty-six feet long, eight feet wide, with a capacity of twenty to thirty-five tons.[57] Because the BA&P did not have a coal source on its line, it relied on the railroad where the coal was loaded to supply the cars for shipping the load to Butte or Anaconda. Therefore, there was no reason for the BA&P to purchase many gondola cars for coal and general rock service.

The St. Lawrence Mine, circa 1895. At the lower left snakes a train of Rogers Convertible Ballast cars, ready for loading. *World Museum of Mining, #3965*

Flat cars, however, were a necessary component of the new railroad's inventory, primarily used to transport forest products. Timbering for the mines and wood used in the smelting process were largely obtained from ACM's Bonner, Montana, forestry division. By supplying its own cars or those of its railroad subsidiary, ACM held down its costs of moving wood products to its operations. Initially, the BA&P bought thirty-ton capacity all-wood flats.[58]

Not surprisingly, ore cars comprised the majority of BA&P's rolling stock. Five hundred Rogers Convertible Ballast cars were purchased. As its name implies, the Rogers car was designed for multipurpose use. It could be used for ballasting track as well as for carrying coal or ore. The car was equipped with almost body-length horizontal doors, which could be opened easily by a single man operating the door-release mechanisms. Built to handle loads of thirty tons, it was anticipated that the cars would be used for ore service between Butte and Anaconda, and for coal service between Sand Coulee and Anaconda.[59] But in actual practice, they were kept solely in use on the BA&P, hauling ore between Butte and Anaconda.[60]

Operational relations between BA&P and GN were strained as the new company began operations in 1894. Billing for freight and passenger interchange traffic, and the use of GN's Butte yard by BA&P remained a source of friction until the latter built its own engine facilities and spurs to most of ACM's mines in Butte. As it built, and during the first years of operation, the BA&P had no Butte terminal, and paid the GN for the privilege of using the Montana Central yards and engine facilities. Physically, the BA&P main line began where the GN's Montana Central main track ended, an invisible line on a map of Butte, where the tracks crossed Wyoming Street. Because the BA&P track began at the west end of the GN's Butte yard, and the roundhouse and wye[61] were located at the east end of the yard, the new railroad had to pay for the use of GN tracks to turn locomotives and passenger trains after their arrival in Butte.[62]

In February 1894 the through GN passenger trains to Anaconda ceased operating. The two railroads spent the next two years sorting out the details of paying the GN for the construction of the BA&P, and wrangling over expenses incurred from the use of GN equipment and facilities. To avoid paying for the use of the GN's roundhouse and wye for turning its locomotives and passenger trains, the BA&P subsequently built a wye of its own in Butte.[63] Engines were sent to Rocker for servicing. Accounting matters were resolved largely at the mid-management level, though occasionally Daly and Hill were involved.[64] Business was good for the new railroad, which scheduled ten trains a day over the line—two passenger and three freight trains in each direction.[65] These scheduled trains, plus any

Interior of the BA&P machine shop at the Anaconda yard. The machine shops were built originally to service steam locomotives, but adapted along with the railroad to maintain the fleet of electrics and diesel electrics. *BA&P Records, Butte-Silver Bow Public Archives*

unscheduled or "extra" ones, kept the Anaconda dispatcher busy directing the movement of trains on the single track main line.

BA&P's first year proved to be an eventful one for the railroad industry. Labor unrest disrupted many railroad operations throughout the western United States in 1894, although not the BA&P's. Working conditions and wages were the underlying issues behind the strikes that paralyzed much of the nation's railroad system. Leading labor organizer Eugene V. Debs led the newly formed American Railway Union (ARU), which challenged both railroad management and the older railroad labor brotherhoods. A strike by the ARU against the Great Northern in April shut off interchange between the BA&P and the GN at Butte, halting the shipment of coal from Sand Coulee, which was served by the GN.[66] Although the GN was struck, the BA&P was not, continuing to move ore to the smelter. Coal for the smelters and mines was obtained from mines served by the UP and NP. Inbound coal was interchanged with the BA&P at Silver Bow on the UP or at Butte or Stuart on the NP.

When GN settled on terms favorable to the ARU, it emboldened the union's leaders. A few months later, Debs brought the ARU into a sympathy strike in support of the workers of the Pullman Palace Car Company on June 21, 1894. The so-called Pullman Strike had catastrophic results for the union.[67] A nation-wide railroad strike developed, as ARU members refused to handle trains with Pullmans. Federal troops soon broke the strike, and the ARU in the bargain.[68]

The BA&P seems to have been little affected by the labor unrest, probably due to the nature of the railroad and its operations. Train crews on the 25-mile railroad were able to work fairly regular hours and live at home. These were not common conditions for train and engine crews on the transcontinental railroads in 1894. Railroad work was hazardous; brakemen, switchmen, and to a lesser extent, conductors, faced the constant threat of injury or death on the job due to being struck by moving equipment, crushed between it, or falling from it. Engine crews had their own hazards to contend with, such as being crushed or scalded to death in a derailment if the locomotive turned on its side. Railroaders had to be alert on the job to work safely. On the transcontinental roads the work day was especially long, and most crews had to eat and sleep away from home half the time. The length of a typical run over an operating division of a transcontinental road was between 80 and 120 miles. Freight crews' work days

often exceeded sixteen or eighteen hours, and then they faced the prospect of a night in a hotel or boarding house.[69]

Another event of national prominence rode the rails through Butte, but did not involve the BA&P. Economic depression gripped the United States following the collapse of the silver market in 1893. An "army" of unemployed citizens marched on Washington, D.C. in 1894, demanding employment and economic reforms. The movement took its name from one of its leaders, a Massillon, Ohio, stone quarry owner, Jacob S. Coxey. A unit of Coxey's Army made headlines when they commandeered an NP freight train in Butte on their way east.[70] Again, the BA&P remained figuratively on the side-track of national events and watched them pass by. While the nation's railroad industry as a whole endured a turbulent year, 1894 was a year of growth and labor peace on the BA&P.

When ore trains began running over the BA&P in January, 1894, the company did not have spurs to the mines it intended to serve. Because the existing spurs and sidings serving Butte's mines were those of the Montana Union (NP) or the Montana Central (GN), the BA&P was at a disadvantage until it could build its own track to the mines. Consequently, the ore traffic involved interchange with GN until BA&P built its own trackage to serve the mines on the Butte Hill. Cars were loaded on GN tracks and brought to GN's Butte yard, where they were picked up by BA&P for the trip to Anaconda.[71] At Butte, empties from the smelter would travel the final few miles to the mines on GN tracks.

Completing BA&P spurs required crossing Montana Union tracks at various locations on the Butte Hill, and at the smelter at Anaconda. MU management sought injunctions from the Deer Lodge County Superior Court to prevent installation of the crossings, but achieved only a delay. None of the disputes was particularly violent, and no pitched battles ensued between rival construction crews that occasionally occurred in similar circumstances. Orderly process through the courts postponed the completion of the BA&P, but only briefly. By late 1894 most of the important ACM mines were served by the BA&P.[72]

To reach the mines, BA&P built its Missoula Gulch branch north and east from the BA&P main line at Rocker, 3.9 miles west of Butte. Rocker, to a large extent, served as the eastern end of the BA&P main line after 1895. Although the actual main line ended where it met the Montana Central in Butte, the heaviest traffic did not arrive on the BA&P main line at milepost 0.00.

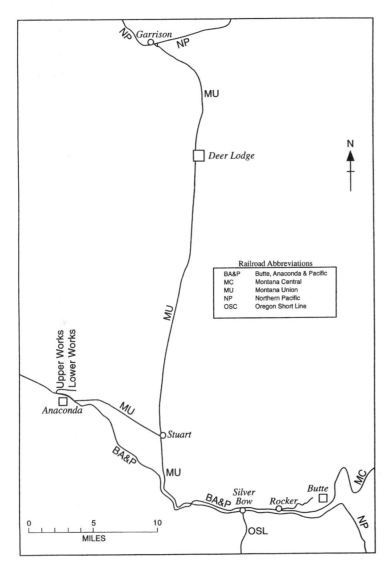

Railroad Abbreviations

BA&P	Butte, Anaconda & Pacific
MC	Montana Central
MU	Montana Union
NP	Northern Pacific
OSC	Oregon Short Line

Butte, Anaconda & Pacific Railway, 1895.

Gulch line to the Butte Hill yard, where they would be dispatched to the waiting mines. Empties for ore loading were not the only traffic bound for the mines. Flat cars of mine timbers, an occasional flat with a large item of machinery, and box cars of mining supplies were regularly delivered to the mines, and returned to Rocker empty. Before electricity replaced steam for pumping and hoisting, there were cars of coal for powerhouses at many of the mines as well.

After completion of the Missoula Gulch line and the multitude of spurs on the Butte Hill, most of the ore bound for the smelter originated on the line, and did not require interchange with GN or NP. The main line to downtown Butte proper was primarily used to interchange freight with GN and NP, and by the passenger trains, which used it to reach the BA&P depot.

There is some evidence to indicate that Daly may have initially been considering selling BA&P to GN, then decided not to do so. The Interstate Commerce Commission suggests that GN actually operated BA&P for the first few months; but by the end of February, 1894, BA&P had assumed full responsibility for its operations.[76] However, this evidence is contradicted by the commission's valuation report for BA&P, and by correspondence in BA&P records and the James J. Hill papers, which strongly indicate that BA&P was always operated as an independent carrier.[77] The prospect that BA&P would become part of GN faded fast after 1894. Although newspapers had promoted the idea of putting Anaconda on a GN transcontinental line, none of these grandiose plans ever came to pass. Two additional preliminary surveys were done in 1894. One proceeded west from Anaconda, went over two mountain passes, into the Bitterroot Valley, and then north to Missoula. From there it climbed another mountain pass on its way to Flathead Lake, where the line would join the GN line to Kalispell. The other survey turned north at Rock Creek, proceeded to Bonner where it crossed the NP, then up the Blackfoot River, through a pass in the Mission Mountains to the Swan River, then to Kalispell, a distance of 230 miles, including a 12,900 foot tunnel at the Mission Mountain divide.[78] After the reports were filed, no more work was done on the Kalispell extension.

Instead, it rolled through back yards and alleys of Butte before winding down Missoula Gulch to Rocker, milepost 3.9.[73] Here the BA&P built a large yard and a wye for turning locomotives,[74] plus a three-stall engine house, coal chutes, and a water tank.[75] Rocker served as both a busy junction and as the eastern engine terminal for the BA&P main line. Given that most of the heavy ore traffic came off the Missoula Gulch line, it was logical to make Rocker the operational center instead of downtown Butte.

From the completion of the Missoula Gulch line in 1895, Rocker became the focal point of Butte operations, and remained so for more than half a century. Cars of ore gathered from mine spurs on the Butte Hill were brought down to Rocker where they were made up into trains bound for the smelter. Trains of empty ore cars were received from the smelter, and broken into shorter ones for the trip up the Missoula

viaduct over the creek itself, was built during 1897 with engineering assistance from the Great Northern.[86] During the winter of 1897–98 a three-stall, rectangular, frame engine house was built at the Butte Hill yard for the switch engines that worked the mine spurs.[87] This eliminated the need for either running the switchers to Rocker for routine work during the winter, or attempting to perform the work out-of-doors in the cold. These improvements helped make the railway more efficient, but the company was still having a hard time keeping up with the ACM's transportation needs.

✕

In 1896 BA&P's equipment was representative of most of the industry. Small locomotives and a fleet of wooden cars, some equipped with link and pin couplers, comprised its rolling stock.[88] All of the engines were simple locomotives, meaning that the steam was used once in the cylinders, then exhausted out the smokestack. Although GN and NP both had numerous 4-4-0's and 2-6-0's, these were no longer commonly used on mountain grades or for heavy trains. Both the NP and GN had been buying eight-coupled freight power since the 1880s, as had many other western railroads. In 1897 the BA&P began adding new equipment to its roster, starting a program of modernizing which would continue over the next fifteen years.

When BA&P realized that its Moguls were no longer adequate for the size of trains demanded by the smelter, the management sought the latest in locomotive technology. Three compound 4-8-0, or "Mastodon" type locomotives arrived from the Schenectady, New York, works of the American Locomotive Company in 1897. Mechanically, the 4-8-0's were identical to similar locomotives built earlier that year for the neighboring Northern Pacific. These were two-cylinder, cross-compound locomotives. Compounds, which used the steam twice, theoretically got more work out of each pound of coal and gallon of water than simple (single-expansion) locomotives. Steam from the boiler went into a 23 by 30-inch high pressure cylinder, where it was used once to push a piston connected to the driving wheels on one side of the locomotive. From the high pressure cylinder, the steam was exhausted into a 34 x 30-inch low pressure cylinder on the opposite side of the locomotive, where it again was used to push a piston before being exhausted through the smoke stack. A theoretical tractive effort of 35,000 to 40,000 pounds of pulling power at the tender coupler (drawbar pull), was achieved in tests of NP's identical compound 4-8-0's.[89]

When the BA&P took delivery of these new compound locomotives, they were numbered 36 through 38, following the group of 2-6-0's.[90] Retirement of the

Cross-compound 4-8-0 ("Mastodon") No. 19 near the Old Works on the north side of Warm Springs Creek at Anaconda, probably soon after delivery in 1901. *Marcus Daly Historical Society of Anaconda*

oldest and smallest locomotives became possible as the new locomotives assumed the heavy work of hauling ore trains from Rocker to Anaconda. Based on age and tractive effort, the pair of former GN 4-4-0's were the most logical candidates for retirement, since they were too light to haul ore trains unassisted. Passenger trains were generally short and relatively light, and the 2-6-0's, which had been replaced by the Mastodons in ore service, replaced the 4-4-0's.[91]

Larger locomotives allowed the movement of longer, heavier ore trains, but they were only part of the modernization program. Two substantive changes in railroad car design and construction came to fruition nation-wide at the close of the nineteenth century. One was the universal application of automatic couplers and air brakes on equipment that was interchanged with other railroads; the other was a revolution in freight car design. Air brakes and automatic couplers finally became standard equipment on the nation's railroads in 1903. The hand brakes and link-and-pin couplers, which had been the accepted standards since the 1840s, were extremely dangerous. Cars were coupled together with large wrought-iron links, which fit into cast iron pockets on the ends of the cars, and were secured in place by an iron pin. A man had to stand between cars to make the coupling, guiding the link into the pocket with one hand and securing it in place with the pin using his other hand. Coupling and uncoupling cars equipped with link-and-pin couplers was terribly hazardous, and many brakemen were lucky if they lost only a few fingers, and not their lives. It was a horrible technology, with nothing to recommend it except that it was ridiculously simple and cheap. Various self-activating couplers were designed and patented by 1873, but it took the industry thirty years to adopt one, and to require its use on all locomotives and cars engaged in interstate service.

The story behind brakes was similar. Hand brakes were individually set on each car, so brakemen had to run from car to car on moving trains to set or release brakes as needed. Falls from car roofs were common and often fatal. Power brakes had been successfully developed and patented by 1869, but railroads were slow to adopt them.

In both cases, the federal government finally forced action. Through a series of acts, Congress required common carrier railroads in the United States to use air brakes and automatic couplers. The Safety Appliance

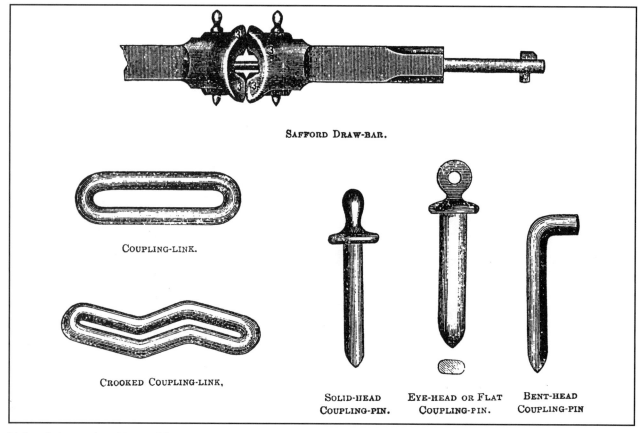

Link and pin couplers. (*Car Builders Dictionary.* Used with permission of Simmons-Boardman Publishing Company.)

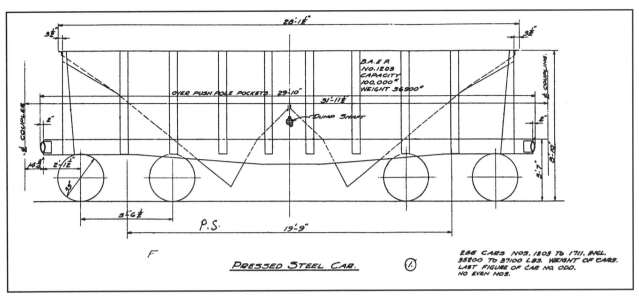

Pressed Steel Car Co. 50-ton steel hopper car. (Side elevation only, not reproduced to original scale.) (BA&P Records, "Cars and Shop Equipment," 3-4-13. *Used with permission of the Butte-Silver Bow Public Archives.*)

Act of 1893 required safe couplers and brakes on railroad equipment in interstate service by 1898, but later extensions set back the date for compliance to 1903. Ironically, the real pay-off for most railroads was the ability to haul heavier trains than had been possible before the safety appliance acts went into effect. Link-and-pin couplers were literally the weak link in the chain, where the load the coupling would hold, rather than locomotive pulling power, limited train size. Lack of braking power also worked to limit train size. Most BA&P cars were equipped with safe couplers and brakes from the beginning, which helped make the movement of increasingly heavy ore trains possible. Unfortunately, much of the rolling stock in service throughout North America in 1893 still had the murderous link-and-pin couplers, and some cars were devoid of air brakes. The BA&P routinely handled these cars in interchange service until 1903.[92]

Freight car design had been advancing rapidly during the 1890s. Wooden cars were still the rule, and a thirty-ton capacity was considered to be basically standard for an all-wood car.[93] Efforts to design and build all-steel cars dated back to the 1860s, with the iron "pot" hoppers built by the Baltimore & Ohio. Throughout the 1880s and 1890s, the railroad industry had been attempting to standardize freight car construction. As part of this move toward standardized car trucks, framing, brakes, and couplers, there was also an increased interest in the structural use of steel for car construction. Most railroads continued to buy wood cars until after the turn of the century because they were sub-

stantially less expensive than steel. Pound for pound, though, steel cars offered the ability to carry more weight than their all-wood counterparts—with the exception, perhaps, of all-wood box cars. Because box cars relied on the framing of the car sides to help carry the load, they could be engineered to carry 40, even 50 tons, as demonstrated by Ferdinand Canda in 1899.[94]

Shortly after Charles Schoen began marketing his steel hopper car in 1897, the BA&P started examining how to increase the tonnage it could move over its road. Adding more 30-ton capacity wooden cars was one possibility. Besides costing less, wooden cars offered the relative simplicity of local maintenance. BA&P car shop employees were familiar with the work involved in maintaining wooden cars. However, one of the disadvantages of an all-wood ore car consisted of the truss rods in the underframe that interfered with the placement of hoppers or drop doors in the floor of the car.

Schoen's steel cars offered potential advantages. With their 50-ton capacities, they could haul 20 more tons of ore per car than wood ones. They were arguably less maintenance intensive; there were no truss rods to tighten or loosen periodically, as were required on most wooden underframed cars.

An order for a trial group of four of Schoen's 50-ton steel hoppers for ore service was placed with the Pressed Steel Car Company (PSC) in 1899. When they were tested in service, the BA&P was delighted, and promptly ordered another 140 from PSC in 1900.[95] As copper production by the ACM soared between 1900 and 1910, general modernization of the freight car fleet occurred, and most of the all-wood Rogers cars were retired. Three hundred steel hopper cars of 50-ton

The "Butte Hill" circa 1910. In the right distance, the Neversweat Mine's seven stacks add to the haze of coal smoke which typified Butte's mining area before electric power replaced steam. In the foreground, a cut of Pressed Steel Car Co. 50-ton hopper cars waits to be loaded. *Montana Historical Society, Helena, #PAc 98-57.19*

capacity had replaced the 500 wooden Rogers cars by 1903. Though these new steel cars were hauling the same amount of ore as the older, larger fleet, it was still not sufficient to meet the ACM's expanding needs.

When the ACM's new smelting plant east of Anaconda, named the Washoe Works, came on line in 1903, more ore cars were required to keep it supplied to its calculated 5,000 ton-per-day milling and smelting capacity. In fact, the Washoe plant soon proved to be able to mill and smelt over three times that amount of ore, processing as much as 17,000 tons per day during World War I.[96] To keep up with the smelter's increasing capacity, 300 additional 50-ton steel hoppers were purchased between 1903 and 1910.[97]

Young men on a Pressed Steel Car Co. steel-underframe box car built for the BA&P in 1906. *World Museum of Mining, #1289*

Though ore cars were the most important, BA&P's modernization program extended to other rolling stock as well. Two orders of fifteen all-steel gondolas came from Pressed Steel Car, first in 1904 and again in 1907. The first order included only thirty-ton cars, but the second involved 50-ton cars, comparable to the ore cars. In 1906 PSC built 46 steel underframed, 30-ton box cars for the BA&P. These were a transitional design, with a steel underframe beneath a more traditional, framed wooden body. Standard Steel Car

Opposite: The new Washoe works nearing completion, ca. 1902–1903. Across the valley, the old works are visible. *Montana Historical Society, Helena, #PAc 82-62.95*

Co. built 75 steel-framed flat cars for the line in 1907, rated to carry 40 tons. The only all-wood cars to remain in any number were 30-ton capacity flat cars, primarily used for the transport of mine timbers.[98] Some cars were simply retired or sold without being replaced. Three refrigerator cars had been on hand in 1900, used for perishable foodstuffs. Two were retired by 1915, and not replaced. Also retired, between 1900 and 1905—after Daly's death—were the nine stock cars bought to transport Daly's and Haggin's racehorses.[99]

Passenger business remained an afterthought. The total number of passenger cars remained constant at 13, though as some of the oldest coaches were retired, they were replaced with new ones. American Car and Foundry delivered five coaches and a baggage-mail car in 1904.[100] Another addition was a car purchased by ACM for the use of its business executives. Although actually owned by the mining company, it was added to the BA&P equipment roster.[101]

The business car *Anaconda*. Although lettered for the BA&P, the business car was actually owned by the ACM. *Photo #92-2145, Philip C. Johnson Collection, K. Ross Toole Archives, University of Montana, Missoula*

Exemplifying a typical passenger train before the BA&P electrified, Baldwin-built No. 20 is hauling a baggage-mail car and two coaches in Silver Bow Canyon, ca. 1902. *Marcus Daly Historical Society of Anaconda, #18503*

When the ACM began planning for the new Washoe smelter in 1900, the BA&P owned 18 locomotives, only three of which were suited for pulling heavy freight trains. A decade later, 16 new, larger locomotives had been purchased, and six of the oldest and smallest freight and passenger locomotives had been sold. Both of the 4-4-0's were gone, replaced by larger 4-6-0 (Ten-wheeler) types for passenger service. One of the 4-4-0's had been disposed of before 1898, but the other remained on the BA&P until 1906, when it was sold to the Yellowstone Park Railway. The oldest four of the 2-6-0's were sold in 1905. Four new compound 4-8-0's built by the American Locomotive Company's Schenectady works between 1901 and 1905 had rendered the Moguls surplus. Even with larger locomotives, the BA&P could not keep pace with the increasing traffic, and additions to the locomotive roster continued. Two more 4-8-0's and the first two consolidations, or 2-8-0's, were purchased in 1906. While the Mastodons were compounds, and identical to the

others of that type on the BA&P, the 2-8-0s were simple locomotives, only using the steam once. Four more identical 2-8-0s were added in 1907. The last new steam locomotives were delivered in 1910, one a simple 2-8-0, and the other a compound 4-8-0.[102]

During the first decade of the twentieth century, the BA&P experienced several significant changes that related to its future operations. Of minimal importance, but immeasurable local pride, was the planned presidential visit of 1901. A special train carrying President of the United States William McKinley and guests was scheduled to operate over the BA&P on June 1, 1901, bringing the party to Anaconda at 4:30 A.M., then departing for Butte at 10:30 A.M.[103] Mrs. McKinley became ill, however, and much of the trip, including the Montana stops, was canceled.[104]

Of greater importance to the BA&P was the arrival in Butte of the Chicago, Milwaukee & St. Paul

(CM&StP), on its way from the Midwest to Puget Sound. Construction crews reached Butte in 1907, and the BA&P leased some of its remaining Rogers ballast cars to the CM&StP.[105] Effective August 1, 1908, a trackage rights agreement was concluded to allow the transcontinental road to use 14 miles of the BA&P between Colorado Junction, in Butte, and Cliff Junction in Silver Bow canyon. While this saved the CM&StP time and the initial expense of laying its own track, it also added to the traffic congestion on the BA&P, since Rocker was situated between the two junctions.[106] Although the arrangement proved less than ideal to both companies, corporate cooperation was encouraged by the interlocking directorship positions represented by John D. Ryan. Ryan, who was the president of the ACM, was also president of the BA&P, as well as actively interested in the Montana Power Company and the CM&StP. Six years later, when the CM&StP completed its own line paralleling the BA&P between Butte and Finlen, the transcontinental road stopped operating

its trains over the BA&P, and abandoned the connection at Cliff Junction.[107]

Although BA&P managers were not especially happy about delays caused by CM&StP trains on their rails, they had at least eliminated a bottleneck of a different sort by 1908. Emptying each ore car at the Washoe smelter had previously required five minutes of labor: a car's hopper doors had to be opened manually, and then closed and latched by a worker after the contents were emptied into a receiving bin at the concentrator. In 1908, the railroad began using a technological solution that had been developed for unloading carloads of coal. It was called a rotary car dumper. A barrel-like steel framework held the car in place on a short section of track within the frame, and then was rotated 180 degrees to dispense the contents from the top of the car in a matter of seconds. Called "the tipple" by ACM and BA&P personnel, the car dumper accelerated the process of moving ore from the mines to the smelter.[108]

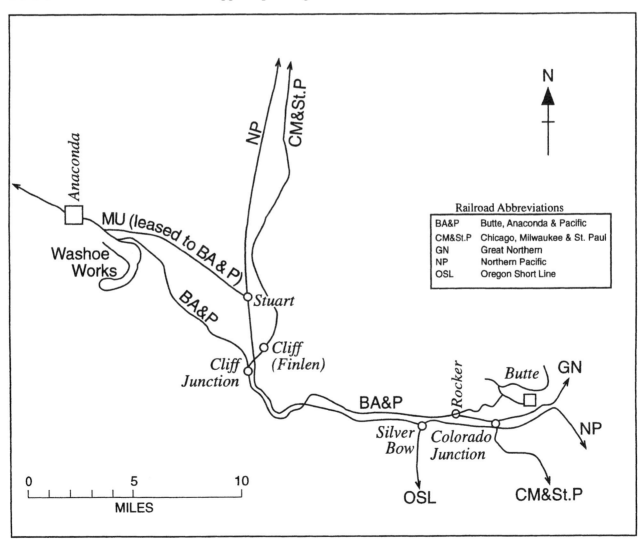

Butte, Anaconda & Pacific Railway, 1910.

The first ore delivered to the concentrator at the Washoe Works, 1903. *World Museum of Mining, #5965*

Locomotive and car purchases had been steady for ten years, keeping pace with the needs of the mining company. In June 1910, the BA&P was hauling an average of over 9,100 tons of ore to the Washoe smelter every day. The railroad also moved a daily average of 1,700 tons of limestone and silica flux, 1,100 tons of coal, and 450 tons of coke to the smelter to process the ore. A remotely secondary consideration in the company's business was the average of 412 passengers carried daily in June, 1910.[109] It was a far cry from the daily average of 3,000 tons of ore the BA&P had delivered to Anaconda in 1894. Freight business was booming, but the railroad was nearing its capacity. The ACM, however, continued to expand the Washoe works, putting more pressure on the railroad to meet its needs. A single track railroad with passing sidings can only move a limited number of trains at a time. Double-tracking the BA&P would have increased the railroad's carrying capacity, but no records indicate that this was considered. The expense would have been significant, and there was another option, which the BA&P began to consider with increasing interest: namely, to become a test track for General Electric, to prove the efficacy of the company's electric locomotives in heavy freight service.

NOTES

1. Anaconda *Standard*, December 28, 1893, p. 1.

2. Toole, "Marcus Daly," p. i. Toole indicates that Daly's penchant for secrecy was honored after his death by many of his close associates, who destroyed their copies of correspondence with Daly, or records in which he was the subject.

3. Missoula *Gazette*, January 23, 1889, p. 1; Helena *Independent Record*, January 26, 1889, p. 3; Butte Semi-Weekly *Miner*, November 6, 1889, p. 4.

4. Anaconda *Standard*, January 20, 1891, p. 5.

5. *Railroad Gazette*, October 14, 1892, p. 777.

6. Anaconda *Standard*, January 20, 1891, p. 5; *Railroad Gazette*, October 14, 1892, p. 777.

7. The efforts to manage world copper prices between 1880 and 1910 are effectively summarized in Hyde, pp. 60–61 and 204–207; Navin, pp. 113–116; and Malone, Battle, pp. 34–40. Copper, which had been selling for $0.22 per pound in 1897

dropped to $0.11 per pound in 1885, partially due to increased production from the western United States.

8. Anaconda *Standard*, March 20, 1891, p. 5, Anaconda *Standard*, October 23, 1891, p. 5.

9. Ibid., April 13, 1891, p. 2.

10. Ibid., May 16, 1891, p. 3.

11. Ibid., May 16, 1891, p. 3.

12. *Railroad Gazette*, October 14, 1892, p. 777.

13. Ferrell, pp. 45, 47.

14. ICC, *Statistics of Railways in the United States*, 1894, (Washington, GPO, 1895), pp. 226–227, 316–317; ICC, *Statistics*, 1895, (Washington: GPO, 1896) pp. 246–247, 336–337; ICC, "Valuation Docket No. 1018, Butte, Anaconda & Pacific Railway," *ICC Reports*, Vol. 141, pp. 748–751. The idea of making contracts involving millions of dollars on a handshake clearly was acceptable to Daly, Haggin and Hill, and thoroughly frustrating to the federal regulators.

15. *Railroad Gazette*, October 13, 1893, p. 757.

16. Anaconda *Standard*, October 23, 1892, p. 5; Ibid., November 5, 1892, p. 2, p. 6.

17. BA&P Records, "Letterbook," August 16, 1894–December 31, 1894, pp. 345–356; *Railroad Gazette*, July 6, 1894, p. 485.

18. Anaconda *Standard*, May 17, 1891, p. 4.

19. Rocker is named for the placer mining tool used to wash gold from gravel. Cheney, p. 191.

20. BA&P Records, "GN Station Map of Butte Montana," [n.d.] BA&P Records, Butte Silver Bow Public Archives. See also Emmons and Tower, which includes a topographic map of the Butte Hill showing mines and railroads.

21. Anaconda *Standard*, July 3, 1891, p. 2. Phillipsburg was never reached by the BA&P. A Northern Pacific branch served the mining camp. Renz, p. 30.

22. Anaconda *Standard*, October 22, 1892, pp. 1–2; Anaconda *Standard*, October 26, 1891, p. 3.

23. Anaconda *Standard*, February 15, 1892, p. 6; Ibid., October 23, 1892, p. 9; BA&P Records, Letter Book, August 16, 189–December 31, 1894, pp. 345-356. The only railroad to be built along a portion of this route was the Northern Pacific's Bitter Root branch line, from Missoula south to Darby. The BA&P never got west of Georgetown Lake. Renz, p. 31.

24. *Railroad Gazette*, October 14, 1892, p. 777.

25. Ibid., October 28, 1892, p. 815.

26. Anaconda *Standard*, October 23, 1892, p. 5.

27. Gordon Rogers, "Butte, Anaconda & Pacific," *Trains* Magazine, July 1963, pp. 16–28, p. 19; Marcosson, p. 53.

28. BA&P Records, "Administrative Correspondence," GN to BA&P, June 1, 1896, XVI 1:2; Brian Shovers, Mark Fiege, Dale Martin and Fred Quivik, *Butte and Anaconda Revisited: An Overview of Early-Day Mining and Smelting in Montana*, Special Publication No. 99, (Butte, Montana: Montana College of Mineral Science and Technology, 1991), p. 51.

29. Hill to Daly, March 6, 1893. James J. Hill Papers, James J. Library. ICC "Valuation Dockct No. 1018, Butte, Anaconda & Pacific Railway Company," *ICC Reports*, Vol. 141, p. 759.

30. *Railroad Gazette*, January 6, 1893, p. 17.

31. Fahey, *Inland Empire*, pp. 42–43. The problems encountered by Daniel C. Corbin's Coeur d'Alene Railway & Navigation Co. represent the perils of attempting to operate over raw roadbed that had not been adequately tamped down or allowed to settle naturally. Trains derailed frequently, and service was finally suspended until the ground dried out enough to allow the sunken spots in the roadbed to be located and filled, and adequate ballast added to the track to support the weight of trains.

32. *Railroad Gazette*, April 7, 1893, p. 271.

33. BA&P, Records, "Maps," "BA&P Anaconda Shops and Yard," n.d. (ca. 1894?); BA&P Records, "Building Elevations and Floor Plans, Roundhouse, Machine Shop" 1893, BA&P Records, Map Cabinet. The original yard map shows the BA&P approximately a city block south of the Montana Union trackage at Anaconda.

34. Anaconda *Standard*, June 22, 1893, p. 3; Railroad *Gazette*, June 30, 1893. Rail size is measured by weight in pounds per yard (ppy); seventy-five pound rail weighs 75 ppy, or 975 pounds per 39-foot length. Rail length has normally been dictated largely by the length of most commonly used flat cars or gondolas which could be used for hauling it. Thus the 39-foot rail length became standard after 1900 because it would fit the typical 40-foot car in use at the time.

35. *Railroad Gazette*, July 21, 1893, p. 557. Interstate Commerce Commission, Bureau of Valuation Records, Summary, p. 3 indicates that the entire BA&P was built with new rail, a combination of 75-pound rail and 80-pound rail, on fir ties.

36. *Railroad Gazette*, August 11, 1893, p. 613.

37. Ibid., October 13, 1893, p. 757.

38. Ibid., December 15, 1893, p. 916.

39. Anaconda *Standard*, December 25, 1893, p. 3; Anaconda *Standard*, December 27, 1893, pp. 2–3; Anaconda *Standard*, December 28, 1893, p. 1.

40. Malone, *The Battle for Butte*, pp. 93–105, especially pp. 94, 99, and 104.

41. BA&P Records, "Letters," Daly to Hill, December 30, 1893, XVI:1. Letter is a file copy contained in the general correspondence of the BA&P. Hill's replies to Daly doubtless were destroyed along with the bulk of Daly's personal papers after his death.

42. BA&P Records, "Correspondence," GN, GN Traffic Department, Memorandum to Passenger Agents, December 22, 1893, XVI:1.

43. Ibid., GN to BA&P, July 16, 1894, XVI:1; GN to BA&P, February 9, 1895, XVI:1.

44. Hidy et al., pp. 72–85; and Malone, *Hill*, offer good overviews of the construction of the GN, and of Hill's role in developing Montana.

45. BA&P Records, "Letters," GN to BA&P, July 21, 1896, XVI, 1:2. ICC, "Valuation Docket No. 1018, Butte Anaconda & Pacific Railway," *ICC Reports*, Vol. 141, p. 748.

46. Great Northern Railway Co. Records. Montana Historical Society. "Drawing No. 3198. GNRy Bridge No. 13 Silver Bow Creek Special 96 Foot Truss Span. Trusses and Laterals. Lassig Bridgc & Iron Works, Chicago. Order 1709A., November 5, 1897." The original drawing has been annotated, with "No. 13" marked through, and "11.02" penciled in. Milepost 11.02

on the BA&P is the location of this bridge. The 1897 date indicates that GN support of an informal nature continued for several years after construction.

47. Brooks Locomotive Works Order Book, from Steven A. Delibert. Steam locomotive cylinder size is given showing the diameter of the bore (19 inches in this case) by the length of the stroke of the piston (26 inches), rather than cubic displacement of the cylinders, as is common for internal combustion engines. North American practice has been to identify steam locomotives by wheel arrangement, using the Whyte system of notation which lists the leading or pilot truck, driving wheels, and trailing truck, each group of wheels separated by a hyphen. The six-wheeled switch engines described thus are 0-6-0 wheel arrangement. Steam locomotives are normally assumed to be equipped with a tender, a separate vehicle semi-permanently coupled to the engine to carry fuel and water. Tank locomotives, carrying fuel in a bunker behind the cab, and water in a tank or tanks over or alongside the boiler, are given the suffix "T" in the Whyte system, i.e. 0-4-0T. The Belpaire firebox was not commonly used on the majority of North American steam locomotives. The Great Northern and the Pennsylvania were the two railroads in North America to make extensive use of the Belpaire firebox. Most locomotive builders did not normally produce locomotives with the Belpaire design of firebox. Technical information on firebox and boiler design can be found in editions of Roy V. Wright, *Locomotive Cyclopedia of American Practice.*

48. Brooks Locomotive Works Order Book, Order No. 501; Norman C. Keyes and Kenneth R. Middleton, "The Great Northern Railway, All-Time Locomotive Roster, 1861–1970," *Railway & Locomotive Historical Society Bulletin No. 143,* pp. 60–61.

49. Brooks Locomotive Works Order Book, Order No. 464.

50. Keyes and Middleton, p. 49.

51. BA&P Records, "Locomotives, Steam," I, 4:3:A. Dispositions are not certain, as the earliest BA&P locomotive roster held by the Butte Silver Bow Public Archives was prepared sometime around 1915, and there had been at least two renumberings of locomotives prior to that date, in 1898 and 1905. Probably one was disposed of by sale or scrapping in 1898, and the BA&P steam roster indicates that one 4-4-0, number 15, was sold in 1906. Much of the federally mandated bureaucracy which enabled the precise tracking of locomotive ownership through inspection records did not exist before 1900.

52. ICC, Records, Valuation Bureau, "Valuation of Butte, Anaconda & Pacific Railway," 1915.

53. BA&P Records, "Correspondence," J.B. Haggin to P.M. Halloran, BA&P Auditor, October 3, 1898; BA&P to J. B. Haggin, September 28, 1898; XVI, 1:5A.

54. Malone, *The Battle for Butte,* p. 81; Morris, pp. 84–88.

55. *Official Railway Equipment Register,* May 1898, p. 218.

56. John H. White. *The American Railroad Freight Car: From the Wooden Car Era to the Coming of Steel,* (Baltimore, Maryland: Johns Hopkins University Press, 1993), pp. 192–236.

57. Ibid., pp. 312–348.

58. ICC, Records, Valuation Bureau, "Valuation of Butte, Anaconda & Pacific Railway," 1915.

59. Anaconda *Standard,* December 10, 1893, p. 3; Anaconda *Standard,* January 3, 1894, p. 5.

60. BA&P Records, "Correspondence," M. Donahoe, Vice President, BA&P to William Scallon, August 16, 1895, XVI 1:7A. The BA&P apparently relied on the ACM legal counsel when it needed representation. Scallon was the ACM's lawyer in Butte. Marcosson discusses Scallon's role in ACM affairs in *Anaconda,* his official history of the ACM.

61. A wye is a track arrangement used for turning locomotives. It looks like a letter "Y" extending from the main track, which runs across the top of the letter. To turn the locomotive, it is backed from the main line onto one leg of the wye, and down to the stem. The switches are thrown to run forward out the other leg of the wye, and onto the main track, now pointed in the opposite direction.

62. BA&P Records, "Correspondence," A. H. Melin, Auditor, BA&P to R. I. Farrington, Comptroller, GN, September 8, 1894, XVI, 1:1.

63. Ibid., R. I. Farrington, Comptroller, GN to A. H. Melin, Auditor, BA&P, June 6, 1896, XVI 1:2.

64. Ibid., R. I. Farrington, Comptroller, GN to A. H. Melin, Auditor, BA&P, July 21, 1896, XVI, 1:2.

65. Anaconda *Standard,* December 28, 1893, p. 1.

66. The GN strike began on April 13, 1894, and continued until May 1, 1894. Hidy et al., pp. 137–143 provide a good overview of the strike from a management perspective.

67. Colston E. Warne, *The Pullman Boycott of 1894: The Problem of Federal Intervention,* Boston, D. C. Heath, 1955, pp. v–vi, although dated, provides a good synopsis of the ARU Pullman boycott and strikes.

68. Malone, *Hill,* pp. 155–156. The Anaconda *Standard* and the BA&P correspondence files held by the Butte Silver Bow Public Archives do not mention strike activity on the BA&P.

69. White, *Freight Car,* pp. 70–80.

70. Carlos Schwantes, *Coxey's Army: An American Odyssey,* (Lincoln: Nebraska, 1985), pp. 149–165.

71. The term used by railroaders for adding cars to a train is "pick up"; cars removed from a train are "set out." A local freight train on the Butte Hill might pick up loads of ore at the Anaconda Mine, and set out empty ore cars for loading before moving on to the next mine.

72. Anaconda *Standard,* August 22, 1893, p. 5; Anaconda *Standard,* August 27, 1893, p. 5; Anaconda *Standard,* August 30, 1893, p. 5; Anaconda *Standard,* September 4, 1893, pp. 6, 8; Anaconda *Standard,* September 13, 1893, p. 4, Anaconda *Standard,* September 19, 1893, p. 5; Anaconda *Standard,* September 22, 1893, p. 3; Anaconda *Standard,* December 2, 1893, p. 4.

73. BA&P, "Timetable 16," p. 3. Unless otherwise indicated, all timetables cited will be employee timetables, which are intended for the information and guidance of employees. Public timetables contain information about services and connections offered to passengers, but do not contain information required for the safe operation of trains. Employee timetables contain information required for the operation of trains, including such information as siding length, locomotive tonnage ratings, speed restrictions, weight restrictions, impaired clearance, and other special instructions.

74. Steam locomotives, except switch engines, are normally turned so that they are run forward whenever possible. Visibility out of the cab when running tender first is very poor, because the tender blocks the engineer's field of vision. Additionally, because steam locomotives, especially those without trailing trucks, track better running forward than backing up, the speed is generally restricted for road locomotives running tender first. Because none of the BA&P steam locomotives had trailing trucks that would guide them through curves and switches while running backwards, backing up at normal road speeds would be much more hazardous than operating pilot first.

75. BA&P Records, "Map of Rocker Yard," [n.d.]

76. ICC, *Statistics of Railways in the United States for the Year Ending June 30, 1894,* (Washington, GPO, 1895), pp. 226–227; ICC, *Statistics of Railways in the United States for the Year Ending June 30, 1895,* (Washington: GPO, 1896), pp. 246–247; BA&P, "Correspondence, GN, 1894" BA&P Records, XVI, 1:1.

77. ICC, "Valuation Docket No. 1018," ICC Reports, vol. 141, p. 759. Correspondence in the James J. Hill Papers, James J. Hill Library, include the following that indicate Hill's financial interest in the BA&P was as an investment to aid Daly more than a strategic railroad property: Hill to Daly, March 6, 1893; Daly to Hill, March 1, 1893, February 23, 1893; and Daly to J. B. Haggin (copy to Hill), March 3, 1893.

78. BA&P Records, "Letter book, August 16, 1894–December 31, 1894," pp. 159–163, 345–356. BA&P Records, Montana Historical Society. Maps. "Location of the BA&P Railway. Clearwater Surveys, December 1894, E. L. Wooley, Locating Engineer." The map shows the location for a line passing Summit Lake, Lake Dell, Lake Inaz and along the Clearwater River. Kalispell's days on the GN main line were relatively brief, as winter conditions on Haskell Pass, between Kalispell and Libby, soon proved difficult for the railroad, and the GN main line was re-routed to the north, along the Kootenay River.

79. Hill's belief in maximizing operating efficiency is well covered in standard biographies and Hidy et al., p. 75. Improvements were made to the GN to lower operating costs where possible by reducing mountain grades and curves. Two examples include the 1911 line change to eliminate the crossing of Haskell Pass, west of Kalispell, and the 1928 Cascade Tunnel, in Washington State. Both were designed to reduce mountain grades and curves, and to avoid areas with severe winter snow problems.

80. Malone, *The Battle for Butte*, 31, 41.

81. Anaconda *Standard*, January 3, 1894, p. 5.

82. BA&P Records, "Locomotives, Steam," I, 4:3:A.

83. BA&P Records, "Locomotives, Steam," I, 4:3:A.

84. BA&P Records, "Plan and Elevations, BA&P Passenger Station and Freight House, Butte, Montana"; Butte *Daily Miner*, January 15, 1896, p. 6. Railroads generally did not hire architects to design buildings. An architect often was hired by a large railroad to design a large passenger station in an important city. The Chicago, Milwaukee & St. Paul (Milwaukee Road) passenger depot in Butte fits this category. Ordinarily, the company used a standard design created by its own engineers, who stressed functionality more than architectural charm. The BA&P depot was attractive, but functional. The BA&P depot and freight house in Butte were razed in the late 1990s.

85. BA&P Records, "Letter Book, October 1, 1897–November 10, 1900," p 14.

86. BA&P Records, "Engineering Dept," J. F. Stevens, Chief Engineer, GN, to M. Donahoe, Vice President, BA&P, August 10, 1897, and M. Donahoe, Vice President, BA&P, to F. A. Jones, Chief Engineer, BA&P, August 14, 1897, XVI, 8:3. John F. Stevens is known for his stint of work on the Panama Canal after leaving the GN.

87. BA&P Records, "Letter Book, October 1, 1897–November 10, 1900," pp. 16, 61, 62.

88. BA&P Records, "Letters," Vice President M. Donahoe to Legal Counsel William Scallon, August 16, 1895; Anaconda *Standard*, January 3, 1894, p. 5.

89. *Railroad Gazette*, February 26, 1897, p. 125.

90. BA&P Records, "Locomotives, Steam," I, 4:3:A; ALCO photo of BA&P No. 37. Locomotive builders generally took a photograph of a representative of each group of locomotives they built as a record of their work, not one of each locomotive. The builder's photo for the group of BA&P 4-8-0's was of number 37.

91. Ibid., [n.d], I, 4:3:A.

92. White, *Freight Car*, pp. 490–546. The BA&P's ore cars were equipped with automatic couplers at the factory, as noted earlier.

93. Ibid., pp. 197–201; *Railroad Gazette,* 1890–1900.

94. White, *Freight Car*, p. 600; *Railroad Gazette*, July 14, 1899, p. 501. Ferdinand Canda, an executive for two freight car manufacturers, designed and built 50-ton all-wood cars in 1899. Canda argued the superiority of all-wood car construction with Charles Schoen in a series of letters to the editor of the *Railroad Gazette*, a leading trade publication.

95. ICC, Records, Valuation Bureau, "Valuation of Butte, Anaconda & Pacific Railway," 1915.

96. BA&P Records, "Tonnage and Revenue Reports, 1909–1952," XX, 1:1; Morris, p. 103.

97. BA&P Records, "ICC Valuation," XX, 1:4; ICC, Records, Valuation Bureau, "Valuation of Butte, Anaconda & Pacific Railway," 1915.

98. ICC, Records, Valuation Bureau, "Valuation of Butte, Anaconda & Pacific Railway," 1915; BA&P Records, "ICC Valuation, 1915," XX, 1:4; *Official Railway Equipment Register*, June, 1905.

99. ICC, Records, Valuation Bureau, "Valuation of Butte, Anaconda & Pacific Railway," 1915; BA&P Records, "ICC Valuation," XX, 1:4 ; *Official Railway Equipment Register*, June 1900, p. 247; *Official Railway Equipment Register*, June, 1905. [n.p.]

100. ICC, Records, Valuation Bureau, "Valuation of Butte, Anaconda & Pacific Railway," 1915; BA&P Records, "ICC Valuation," XX, 1:4; *Official Railway Equipment Register*, June, 1905, *Official Railway Equipment Register*, June, 1908.

101. BA&P Records, "Washoe Business Car," I, 3:4:B, *Official Railway Equipment Register*, June, 1908.

102. BA&P Records, "Roster, Locomotives, Steam," [n.d. ca 1953], I, 4:3:A.

103. BA&P Records, "Miscellaneous Correspondence," VII, 1.

104. Anaconda *Standard*, May 16, 1901, p. 1.

105. Ibid., F. A. Jones, Superintendent, BA&P, to P. M. Halloran, Auditor, BA&P, October 31, 1907, VII, 1.

106. Ibid., F. A. Jones, Superintendent, BA&P to P. M. Halloran, Auditor, BA&P, June 16, 1909.

107. Chicago, Milwaukee & Puget Sound Railway Co. "Third Annual Report (June 30, 1912)," p. 3. reports a contract was let for construction of its own track between Butte and Cliff Junction, to be completed in early 1913. Chicago Milwaukee & St. Paul Railroad Co. "Station Plat, Finlen, Montana, ICC Valuation Section V.M. 4-A / S4. Corrected to January 1, 1921."

Reference to AFE No. 12390, covering the retirement and dismantling of BA&P connection between Cliff Junction and Finlen, December 8, 1914. This was a year before the first CM&StP electric operations west of Butte, which occurred in December 1915.

108. Morris, p. 185.

109. BA&P Records, "Tonnage and Revenue, Six Months Ending June 30, 1910," "Tonnage and Revenue Reports, 1909–1952," BA&P Records, XX, 1:1.

Chapter Four

White Coal vs. King Coal

The railway, electrical, and mining worlds and the country in general are indebted to the BA&P railway for the pioneer work it is now doing, as it undoubtedly marks the beginning of the electrification, within the comparatively near future, of all transcontinental roads between the Missouri River and the Pacific coast.[1]

AMERICAN INDUSTRY in the Gilded Age was powered by steam. There were exceptions to the rule, but the state-of-the-art power-generating technology in the heaviest industrial applications was steam. From ocean vessels to hoisting engines, sawmills to locomotives, steam powered the republic. For railroads, especially, steam equaled progress and success. Dirty, noisy, and ubiquitous, the steam locomotive was perhaps the most visible symbol of American technological prowess during the half-century following the Civil War. However, by the 1890s, the noise and smoke accompanying busy steam railroads were becoming problems in some urban areas. It was time to find a cleaner alternative. Fortunately one was on hand: electricity—the power source already changing domestic life.

The combination of rails and electricity was already in place in many large cities in the 1890s, through their urban transit systems. Railroad technology had been applied to urban transit needs as early as 1832, when the first horse car line opened in New York City. Over the next half-century, horses, small steam locomotives, and underground cables were all used to power street railways throughout the world's growing urban centers.[2] Each of these technologies had its disadvantages, and inventors sought cleaner, less expensive means to power street railways. In Scotland, Robert Davidson built an experimental electric locomotive in 1842, when electrical engineering was in its infancy, but his battery-powered electric locomotive failed to perform reliably.[3] By 1872 engineers had mastered the fundamentals of electricity and started to demonstrate commercially viable motors and generators. Werner von Siemens demonstrated an electric locomotive at Berlin in 1879. The following year, Thomas A. Edison built an experimental electric locomotive (but oddly, did nothing to promote its use). Though operators of steam railroads took no interest in electric gimmickry, urban street railways needed an alternative to horses,

and their interest promoted the early designs for railroad electrification.[4]

Some technological problems required solving before electricity could be harnessed to power street cars and later, locomotives. For example, a method had to be developed for mounting motors so that they would not suffer excessive breakdowns or damage under normal service. Also, of more broad consequence, was figuring out how to deal with electricity's particular properties in order to transmit electrical power effectively over substantial distances from the source.

It was known that line loss, due to the internal resistance of wires conducting electrical current, was greater at lower voltages and less at higher voltages. The quantity of power transferred through a power line or trolley wire is proportional to the voltage at its input, and the amount of current passing through it. The voltage drop, or degree of power loss, of a power line is proportional to the resistivity of the wire, the length of the wire, and the amount of current passing through it. Any motor requiring substantial power will not operate properly if the voltage drop of the line is too great. The longer the distance between the power input at the substation and the motor, the greater the voltage drop. This phenomenon limited the maximum distance between substations.

Because alternating current could be economically generated and transmitted at high voltages, transmission lines carrying 100,000 to 220,000 volts alternating current (AC) became common. Moreover, AC transformers could convert a lower voltage to a higher one, which was not feasible for direct current (DC). On the other hand, the DC motors of the time were better suited for use in street cars and electric locomotives than AC motors. Problems associated with safely insulating wire used in motors, and concern about safety for persons working around high voltages, indicated that street car voltages had to be kept

A pair of Mastodons (4-8-0's) climb upgrade on the Missoula Gulch line with a train of empty ore cars near the western edge of Butte, ca. 1910. *Marcus Daly Historical Society of Anaconda*

as low as possible. Six-hundred-volt DC became the nominal industry standard for street railways.[5] This was not ideal for transmission of current from a power-house to the cars, as transmission was effective only to a distance of eight to twelve miles from the power supply before the line loss caused a noticeable decline of power to the trolley cars.[6] This meant that substations, which would boost the voltage in the trolley wire back up to the 600-volt maximum, were required approximately every sixteen to twenty-five miles along the line.

Generation and transmission of electric current for commercial and residential purposes was relatively easy, but transmission for street railway use required a technology that was both dependable and safe. The simplest system, a current-bearing third rail laid parallel to the railway tracks, posed the greatest risk to public safety. Concern about the danger of electrocution posed to pedestrians and draft animals made third-rail systems undesirable for use on city streets. Experiments with power distribution through a wire strung over the center line of the track resulted in a system which gave the public the popular name for the electric street car in the United States: the trolley. The trolley took its name from the current collector,

initially called a "troller," which was mounted on the car roof. The first experiments used a wheeled collector riding on top of a pair of wires over the track. Later experimentation proved that it was less expensive and more reliable to position the wheeled collector on the underside of a single wire.[7]

Frank J. Sprague pulled it all together in one package, adopting 500-volt DC, and mounting a trolley on the car roof for current collection. He also devised a method of mounting motors on car trucks which would allow the motor to flex up and down on uneven track without stripping gear teeth or damaging the motor itself. Sprague's so-called "wheelbarrow mounting" allowed the electric street car, and later the electric locomotive, to become practical realities instead of experimental novelties. Opened in 1888, Sprague's pioneer installation in Richmond, Virginia, was the start of successful electric railroading. Trolley cars were more efficient than horse cars, quieter and cleaner than steam-powered street railways, and much less expensive to construct than cable railways. Within a decade urban transit had been revolutionized, and electric transit accounted for over ninety percent of the nation's street railway systems.[8]

Initially, electrification of main line railroads was given little thought. Even though the electric street car was preferable to steam-powered street railways, economics were seldom the primary consideration for early proposals to electrify steam railroads. As busy railroads through large cities caused noise and smoke pollution, city governments began agitating to abate the nuisance caused by having too many steam locomotives downtown. The first heavy railroad electrification was undertaken by the Baltimore & Ohio Railroad (B&O) to alleviate smoke problems in the company's tunnel under downtown Baltimore, Maryland. Electric operation was not intended to replace steam in this application, but to supplement it, by hauling entire trains, steam locomotive and all, through the tunnel. A total of 3.3 route miles of line was electrified in 1895, using 600-volt DC.[9]

After the successful operation of the B&O electrics, other localities with smoke problems also turned to electricity. One of the busiest railroad terminals in the world was Grand Central Terminal, used by the New York Central Railroad (NYC), and smoke created problems for city residents living near the tracks. More importantly, smoke was a threat to safe operation of the railroad. A two-mile-long tunnel under Park Avenue was used to reach the terminal. Smoke and steam exhausted by the numerous locomotives using the tunnel caused poor visibility, which was the direct cause of a collision on January 8, 1902, resulting in fifteen deaths.[10] Minor accidents and near misses had also become increasingly common by that time. Although demand for train service to New York City was increasing, the limiting factor for the NYC was the Park Avenue tunnel. As part of its plan to build a larger terminal, the NYC decided to electrify thirty-four miles of line from the passenger terminal to Harmon, where the change from electric to steam motive power took place.[11] General Electric received the contract to elec-

trify Grand Central Terminal, which included not only installation of the current generating equipment and the distribution system, but also the electric locomotives required. Power distribution was provided by a third rail, located outside the running rails of the track. Energized at 600-volts DC, the third rail was mounted in brackets upon long ties placed in the track at regular intervals. Electric operation began in 1906, ending the smoke problems under Park Avenue for good.[12]

General Electric had been very successful in promoting the use of 600-volt DC for street cars. Applying the standard trolley voltage to the B&O and NYC was another feather in the company's cap. However, its competitor, Westinghouse, advocated using high voltage AC for railroad operations because of its greater transmission efficiency, and designed an AC electric locomotive.[13] The company's first test engine was produced in 1905. The 135-ton machine drew 6,000-volt AC from an overhead contact wire. Tests at the Westinghouse plant were satisfactory, and the concept of single-phase AC electrification was deemed ready to market to the railroad industry.[14]

In 1906 Westinghouse teamed up with the Baldwin Locomotive works to build single-phase AC electric locomotives for both the Spokane & Inland, and the New York New Haven & Hartford. The two railroads were significantly different. The Spokane & Inland, soon reorganized as the Spokane & Inland Empire (S&IE), was an interurban based in Spokane, Washington. One portion of its system was constructed to standard interurban specifications, using 600-volt DC drawn from a single overhead trolley wire. However, the line from Spokane to Colfax, Washington, and Moscow, Idaho, was operated under a catenary system (addressed at length below), energized with 6,600-volt single-phase AC.[15] In all other respects, the S&IE was a typical interurban, with sharp curves and steep grades that made heavy freight business expensive. Six 50-ton electric locomotives were built for the S&IE, designed to haul 400-ton freight trains at speeds of 30–35 miles

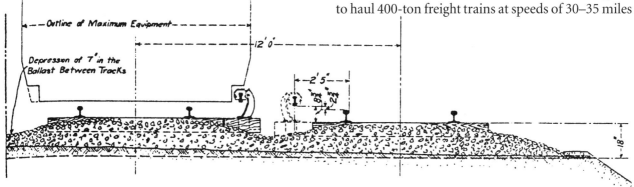

New York Central. Half cross-section of standard four-track roadbed showing location of third rail for 600-volt DC. *Railroad Gazette,* September 1, 1905, p. 199. *Used with permission of Simmons-Boardman Publishing Company.*

per hour (mph).[16] A 400-ton freight train represented about seven loaded freight cars—a light load by the standard of most steam railroads in 1906.

A completely different application was the 11,000-volt single-phase electrification of the New York, New Haven & Hartford (New Haven), which also began running under electric motive power in 1906. A high-speed, busy main line with heavy freight and passenger trains, the New Haven electrification was well suited to test the possibilities of main-line electric operation. Westinghouse delivered the first New Haven electrics in 1906. Given the high voltage involved, catenary distribution was used instead of third-rail current distribution. Catenary line construction was developed to permit higher voltages and operating speeds than were possible with the single-wire construction used on most city trolley lines. In catenary construction, the contact wire carrying the current was suspended from large ceramic insulators, and supported by other wires to give more rigidity than single-wire street car lines. Catenary wire did not tend to push aside or up away from the current collector at high speed, reducing the risk of lost contact or wire damage.[17] Instead of a trolley pole with a wheel, normally used on city street cars, a pantograph with a wide frame and contact area was used for current collection from catenary overhead.[18] The pantographs on New Haven locomotives had flat, sliding shoes which made contact with the energized wire overhead. Unlike the comparatively small S&IE electrics, the New Havens were geared to run at 60 mph with a 250-ton passenger train.[19]

Long tunnels and their accompanying smoke problems were not limited to cities. Colorado and Washington State had long tunnels under mountain passes at the summit of steep grades, where trains normally used multiple locomotives. Engine crews on the Great Northern line over Stevens Pass in Washington state found the trip through the two-mile long Cascade Tunnel simply hellish.[20] The bore was used too frequently for the wind to naturally ventilate the smoke from the tunnel between trains. In order to allow safer operation through the tunnel, the GN, following the examples of the B&O and the NYC, opted to electrify its track through the Cascade Tunnel in 1909. This section involved a scant four miles, extending only between the two stations at each end of the tunnel.[21] Operations at the Cascade Tunnel were similar to that of the B&O at Baltimore: a steam-powered train would stop at the yard on its approach to the tunnel and be coupled to an electric locomotive to pull the entire train, steam engine and all, through the tunnel. Since the steam locomotive would drift[22] through

the tunnel using a minimum of energy,[23] its exhaust would be negligible. After stopping at the station outside the far end of the tunnel, the electric would be uncoupled and the steam locomotive would continue the haul.

Great Northern's first electric railroad was different from the NYC in two important respects. The GN used 6,600 volt, three-phase AC, which was distributed to the locomotives through overhead wires above the center line of the track. Though high-voltage AC was more efficient than low-voltage DC for railroad purposes, three-phase systems required *two* overhead contact wires instead of one, which added to the expense of construction and maintenance. Three-phase electrification failed to attract many railroads in the United States.[24]

In each of these cases, electric traction was adopted to eliminate the use of steam locomotives in tunnels. None of these railroads viewed electric operation as preferable to steam for purely economic reasons, but proponents of railroad electrification were already starting to argue that "white coal," as electricity was called in the popular press, could do the job more efficiently than steam.

The first decade of the twentieth century was a time of significant advance in the engineering of electric power and its applications. However, one of the problems of electrifying, as encountered by the railroad industry, was one which had haunted it for the past quarter century: standardization. It had taken over thirty years, and the increasingly strenuous efforts of Congress to standardize couplings, brakes, and other safety appliances on railroad equipment.[25] Now again the railroad industry was encountering hindrances associated with the lack of standardization, stemming primarily from the competition between electrical motor manufacturers. General Electric, based in Schenectady, New York, promoted direct-current electrification based on the research and development of its engineers. Westinghouse, a leading producer of air brake equipment for railroads,[26] advocated high-voltage alternating current for railroad electrification based on its company's developments.

Because GE had become the leading supplier of street railway motors by 1893, the firm was in a good position to expand into steam-railroad electrification. Hence, when GE received the contracts for two of the first instances of steam railroad electrification—the B&O and the NYC—the company implemented its 600-volt DC system. Rather than choosing the streetcar wire option, however, the railroads opted

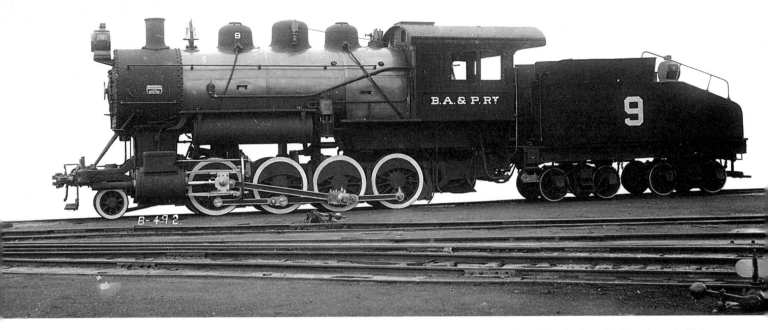

Consolidation type No. 9 was designed for heavy switching work as well as freight service, as indicated by the slope-back tender tank. This design provided a better field of vision for engine crews when backing, but reduced the tender water capacity. Photographed in 1906, No. 9 was one of the last BA&P steam locomotives in service, retired and scrapped in 1953. *ALCO Brooks Works Photo; ALCO Historic Photos, #B-1093*

for third-rail current distribution, believing the third rail would require less maintenance than trolley wire.[27]

Underlying the competition between GE and Westinghouse was the belief that railroads were the next logical market for electric motors. Trolley cars and the B&O's Baltimore tunnel electrification had proved the technological feasibility of electric traction by 1900, just as steam locomotive size appeared to be reaching its maximum limits. Steam generation was limited by the size of boiler that one man could fuel single-handedly. Heavy trains required two or three locomotives, each with its crew of engineer and fireman. Over the next decade, GE and Westinghouse heavily promoted electrification as a money-saving alternative to the steam locomotive, which appeared to have reached its practical limits in size and tractive effort. Innately conservative, the railroad industry, however, showed no enthusiasm to electrify. Two new technological improvements for the steam locomotive were also under development at the turn of the century: oil firing and a mechanical stoker. Both technologies would enable larger steam locomotives to be built and operated than was possible with hand-fired coal burners.[28] Nonetheless, the burgeoning electric manufacturing industry continued to promote electric traction as more cost-efficient than larger steam locomotives. Between 1900 and 1910, while the nation's steam railroads and locomotive builders struggled to develop larger steam locomotives to move heavier trains, the

BA&P looked with increasing interest at the claims of electric motive power.

Vastly more efficient than the horses it replaced, the steam locomotive was undeniably still a labor-intensive machine in 1910. Requiring a high level of maintenance, it was not unusual for a locomotive to spend at least six hours a day being serviced.

Preparation for a day's work started at least two hours before the engine was needed. A locomotive which had been kept under steam overnight in the roundhouse usually had had the fire banked to save coal. In the morning a hostler[29] checked the water level in the boiler, then broke up the banked fire and prepared it for optimal steam generation. While the steam pressure was rising, the hostler started the air pump, drained the air reservoirs, and filled the lubricators. These tasks were essential, for it was dangerous to move a locomotive without being certain that it could be stopped. The steam-powered air pump (compressor) provided the compressed air for braking the locomotive and train, and for any air-operated appliances, such as fire doors and power reverse. The air reservoirs were drained of water to prevent damage to brakes and other appliances, and corrosion of the air reservoir itself. Along with these duties, a careful and on-going inspection of the locomotive was required. After completely checking for mechanical defects, the hostler backed the locomotive out of the roundhouse and moved it to the ash pit, where the fire was cleaned and the ash pan dumped. After the fire cleaning was completed, the locomotive was moved to the coal chute to fuel its tender and to a water tank or water column (standpipe) to have its cistern filled. Sand, necessary for traction when starting or stopping, was added to the sand box, a dome located on top of the boiler. Lubrication of the crank pins, and all the pins and bushings in the rods and valve gear followed. The hostler then moved the locomotive onto the ready track to wait for its crew. The servicing process often took up to two hours.

In addition, the engine crew might take as much as an hour at the terminal to conduct their own mechanical inspection of the locomotive, checking the lubricators, fuel, water, sand supplies, and the tool box before putting the locomotive to work.[30] At the end of their shift, typically eight to twelve hours, the crew returned the locomotive to the hostler at the roundhouse.

The very best that management could hope for was another two-hour servicing period before the locomotive was returned to the business of hauling trains and earning revenue for the BA&P. If the locomotive was finished for the day, the hostler would put it into a roundhouse stall, bank the fire, and perform light maintance work. In any case, the fire would not be dropped, and the boiler allowed to cool, for several reasons. Firing up a locomotive from stone cold to working steam pressure took several hours. Thermal stress to the boiler from rapid heating and cooling could result in leaky boiler tubes and flues, and was to be avoided if at all possible. Once under steam, it was best to keep a locomotive steamed up for a full thirty days. At the end of this period, it would be removed from service to have the boiler washed out and inspected.[31]

In short, reliance on steam locomotion required roundhouse personnel to be available around the clock to service the locomotive fleet. The optimum level of work any locomotive could perform was about 75 percent of its capacity. Therefore, to efficiency-minded corporate executives, electric motors were appealing. It was not insignificant that electric street cars were available for service virtually around the clock, and could be shut down and left unattended when not in use. Nearly every city of any size had a street railway system, and it looked promising that electric technology could replace steam power on the railroads.

Ultimately, it was probably a web of corporate relationships that influenced the decision to electrify the BA&P. Mining had been one of the first heavy industries to change from steam to electric power on a large scale, starting in the 1890s. When the Anaconda Copper Mining Company began using electricity to power hoists, air compressors, and other equipment at the mines in Butte, it was greatly pleased with the savings compared to the cost of coal-fired steam engines to do the work. Not surprisingly, the ACM believed that it could effect similar savings in fuel costs by electrifi-

At the BA&P passenger station in Anaconda, the public has turned out to see the railway's first electric passenger train. *Marcus Daly Historical Society of Anaconda*

cation of its railroad subsidiary. Such savings would enhance the profits already made from the sale of the copper needed for contact wire and motors. Profitability to the ACM was doubtless considered as much as increased operating efficiency for the BA&P. If the BA&P proved the efficiency of electric operation, ACM could expect to sell a lot of copper when the nation's main line railroads electrified.

In 1909 control of the Anaconda operations passed to John D. Ryan, an energetic man with close personal ties to Marcus Daly, who had assisted his rise to prominence in Montana financial circles. Under Ryan's management, ACM consolidated its holdings and attained a state of vertical integration from mine to finished copper product that was unmatched by most of the other major copper producers until years later.[32] Furthermore, the relationship between Ryan and the ACM directorate with other influential corporations was interconnected. The Anaconda Copper Mining Company was controlled by men who were second tier executives of the Standard Oil Company. Ryan was one of the most successful of this group, but as a whole, they linked the boards of ACM, the Montana Power Company, and the CM&StP railroad. As a subsidiary of the mining company, the BA&P was a small player in the larger financial dealings of these corporations. Although the BA&P operated as an independent entity, the ACM owned 51 percent of the capital stock, and the CM&StP held most of the remaining 49 percent, save for a few shares held individually by the corporate officers.[33] Clearly, the electrification of substantial portions of the nation's railroad network would create a large domestic market for copper, which would in turn benefit the ACM. Sales of power from utilities controlled by the group would increase if railroads electrified. Ryan and his business associates could theoretically profit at each stage of the process.

From the outset, it was clear that the BA&P would not need to generate its own electricity, but could purchase it from the Great Falls Power Company, an affiliate of the Montana Power Company.[34] High voltage transmission lines of the Great Falls Power Company already served Butte and Anaconda.

Development of hydroelectric power in Montana had been rapid, and had kept pace with the growing demand for energy created by the expansion of the Anaconda Copper Mining Company. Small units were tied together into a larger electrical system, both electrically and administratively.[35]

The Canyon Ferry plant, located on the Missouri River seventeen miles east of Helena, was completed in 1898, and served as that city's main generating station. Consisting of a thirty-nine-foot high timber crib-and-rock-fill dam, the plant had a generating capacity of 7,500 kilowatts. As more efficient transmission over long distances became possible, the Canyon Ferry plant was tied into the transmission system to Butte, primarily to serve the power demand of the mining industry.[36] A sixty-five-foot high rock-filled crib dam and 3,000 kilowatt (kw) generating plant were completed on the Big Hole River, twenty-two miles south of Butte, in 1899. Connected to the city by a 15,000-volt transmission line, most of the Big Hole plant's power served Butte's domestic and business customers and the street railway system.[37]

At Great Falls, a 25,000 kilowatt hydro-generating plant went into service in 1910. Electrical energy for the Great Falls smelter was transmitted at 6,000 volts, and a 100,000-volt transmission line was constructed to Butte and Anaconda.[38] By the time BA&P electrified, the Montana Power Company system included eleven plants, with a total generating capacity of 72,100 kilowatts.[39] Butte and Anaconda were supplied by several power plants, so it was unlikely that the failure of any one would cause a complete loss of power to either the mines or to the railroad. Purchasing electricity from the Montana Power Company allowed the BA&P to avoid duplication of existing generation and transmission facilities, and gave some assurance that a source of energy could be guaranteed.

By 1910, when BA&P management began to study the operational economies of electrifying, there were several precedents established to recommend railroad electrification for environmental benefits. But railways had not given serious consideration to electrifying their roads for the purpose of operating economy. It was with the economy argument that GE, desiring to showcase its direct-current technology in hopes of advancing sales, convinced BA&P management that the railroad would save money and move more tonnage with electricity. A contract to electrify most of the BA&P road was awarded to the persuasive manufacturer in late 1911. All of the main line, the trackage at the Washoe Smelter, and the branch from Rocker to the main yard on the Butte Hill were to be wired for electric operation. Only a few spurs and branch lines were to remain steam worked.

Construction began in the winter of 1912, and proceeded slowly. Over a year passed before the first electrically powered train operated. Regular electric freight and passenger services were not fully implemented

No. 20 at the Anaconda shops, ca. 1910. A 4-6-0 built by Baldwin for passenger service, No. 20 was rendered surplus by the electrics, and sold to a Cuban sugar plantation in 1917. Spare locomotive tires are piled on the ground in front of the locomotive. *Marcus Daly Historical Society of Anaconda*

until October 1913. By 1915, GE and BA&P were broadly proclaiming the success of the project in terms that any railroad accountant could appreciate: more tonnage moved at a lower cost under wires than behind steam.

Acting as the general contractor, GE built the locomotives (often called "motors"), designed the electrical distribution system, and supervised all construction.[40] The construction work was performed by railroad employees who would later take responsibility for the maintenance of the electrical distribution system and the new motive power when it arrived. Employee training was important, because the slated BA&P electrical current was 2,400 volts, four times more powerful than the standard 600 volts of a trolley line. GE engineers believed that this voltage would permit the use of existing GE traction motors, while reducing line voltage loss. Because of the high voltage involved, along with the heavy nature of its train loads, the catenary suspension system was chosen for this railroad.[41]

As engineered by GE, the BA&P catenary consisted of a single No. 0000 copper contact wire, hung

A "wire train," consisting of Motor 52 and a box car equipped with a work platform, is adjusting the new catenary in the Anaconda yard, May 6, 1913. *Montana Historical Society, Helena, #PAc 82-62.2116*

from a 1/2-inch galvanized steel cable, called the messenger. Hangers for the contact wire were placed at eleven points within each 150-foot distance between poles on tangent (straight) track. The hangers consisted of a pair of malleable iron jaws riveted to a strap which was hung over the messenger. The jaws were clamped over the upper half of the contact wire and bolts secured the entire assembly in place, giving the contact wire a greater degree of rigidity than was possible with single-wire suspension. The messenger cable was hung from 3 1/2-inch high by 4 1/2-inch diameter ceramic insulators on bracket arms bolted to cedar poles. The messenger and contact wire were both energized, allowing the messenger to serve as an auxiliary conductor for the electric current.[42]

During 1912 line crews installed poles, starting as soon as the ground had thawed sufficiently to allow excavation. Work continued into 1913. Setting poles was followed by the task of constructing the catenary and suspending the contact wire from it. Stringing wire was complicated by the need to work around the regular freight and passenger trains on the railroad. On straight, single track, the catenary was hung

Under a copper and steel web of catenary, Hopper No. 2513 rests at the Butte Hill yard, ca. 1950. In the foreground, an electrical "bond," the stout copper jumper between lengths of rail, is visible. *World Museum of Mining, #4819*

from steel brackets bolted to cedar poles. Brackets and single poles could be used on some curves, but often two poles were placed opposite each other, with the catenary suspended from a span wire between them. Span wire suspension was also used at sidings and yards where two or more tracks needed to be electrified.[43]

All rail joints along trackage being converted to electric operation had to be bonded for electrical conductivity. Good conductivity was necessary because the rails served as the return route for the current. The angle bars which held the lengths of rail together made a good mechanical connection, but the pounding of trains moving over them tended to loosen joints, and weather caused them to rust, resulting in high electrical resistance. Good electrical conductivity between rail joints was achieved by running a copper bond—a short, stout jumper wire—from a clean, newly drilled hole in the end of one rail to a clean, newly drilled hole in the next.[44]

At the GE plant in Schenectady, fifteen freight motors and two passenger motors were constructed for the BA&P. The seventeen motors were externally indistinguishable, but the passenger units had gear-

ing for higher speed than their freight counterparts. All were 37 feet, 4 inches over the pulling faces of the coupler knuckles, 10 feet wide, and 15 feet, 6 inches high excluding pantographs. Each unit rode on two four-wheeled trucks, with 46-inch diameter wheels. Each of the four axles was powered with a 300 horsepower (hp) motor, for a total of 1,200 hp per unit. For the freight units, the rated tractive effort was 25,000 pounds for normal service; but a short-time rating of 48,000 pounds was possible without damaging the motors.[45] One radical departure from steam technology was a feature called multiple unit control. Whereas every steam locomotive required an engine crew to operate it, multiple unit control allowed two or more electric units coupled together to be run by an engineer from one cab. This was not a particularly new technology, having been applied to passenger use in the East, but the BA&P application was the first time multiple unit control was used for hauling heavy freight.

Electric operation began at the Anaconda end of the line in the spring of 1913. Portions of the railroad were converted to electric operation gradually, as the work was completed, rather than waiting until all of

Motor 54 with a cut of ore cars at the concentrator yard, Washoe smelter. The roller-shoe pantograph, with which these units were initially equipped, is clearly visible. *Marcus Daly Historical Society of Anaconda, #13017*

the catenary construction had been completed. First electric freight operations took place at the Washoe Works, starting May 28, 1913.[46] Full electric operation of the main line began in October 1913. Both freight and passenger traffic were handled by the new motors, and most of the company's steam locomotives were stored out of service by the end of the year. Only switching on part of the Butte Hill, the leased trackage from Anaconda to Stuart, and the lines west of Anaconda remained steam operated. This

included the 15 1/4-mile extension from Browns to the mines above Georgetown Lake, completed in the spring of 1913.[47]

Once the wire was up, a test of the new motive power was conducted using the Smelter Hill lines. These tracks ran from the East Anaconda yard to serve various locations within the Washoe Works, including the concentrator, where ore began the process of becoming copper ingots. From the yard at East Anaconda the track climbed 7 1/4 miles on a 1.1 percent

Cross-compound 4-8-0 No. 37 was delivered in 1897. Renumbered No. 17, it was one of the largest steam locomotives on the BA&P. Slow and labor intensive, compared to both the new electrics and simple steam locomotives, most of the compound Mastodons, including No. 17, were sold during World War I. *ALCO Schenectady Locomotive Works Photo; ALCO Historical Photos, #S-160*

grade to reach the concentrator yard.[48] Standard operating practice in 1910 was to assign one of the big 4-8-0's to work between East Anaconda and the concentrator yard, bringing sixteen loads upgrade on each trip, and a like number of empties down on the return trip. Normal running time for the trip upgrade was forty-five minutes for the Mastodon. Downgrade trains were restricted to 25 mph, so the trip with the empties took only approximately 18 minutes. However, the steam locomotive had to take water at regular intervals, and was only making six round trips during a shift, for a total of 96 loads of ore delivered.[49]

The 4-8-0 working the Smelter Hill run pulled cuts of cars only from East Anaconda to the concentrator yard. At the concentrator yard, a 2-8-0 worked as the switch engine. This job was called "the spotter locomotive," or just "the spotter" by railroaders, because the locomotive spotted cars for weighing and unloading. Finally, the spotter crew shunted empties onto outbound tracks in the concentrator yard, ready to be picked up and returned to East Anaconda by the Smelter Hill crew.[50] Coal, coke, limestone and other supplies were delivered to the smelter stock bins by

another switching crew and a 2-8-0 type locomotive working out of the East Anaconda yard.[51]

Change from steam to electricity was implemented gradually. Instead of having the GE staff train all the enginemen, the BA&P chose to have GE explain the operation of the electrics to one of the BA&P's steam locomotive engineers, who in turn taught the rest of the railroad's enginemen how to run electrics. Most of the men at the Anaconda end of the line were able to learn during the gradual change on the Smelter Hill lines, starting in May. As more trained men became available, steam power was replaced with the new electrics. On May 27, 1913, the first electrics were tested in freight service running to the concentrator yard. Starting May 28th, the day shift ceased using a 4-8-0 steam locomotive, and began using a pair of electrics for this run. With multiple-unit control, a single engine crew operated the pair of electrics as a single unit. The steam switcher doing the day shift spotting at the concentrator yard was replaced by a single-unit electric on June 20th. Finally, sure that all the "bugs" had been worked out of electric operation, night-time operations of both the Smelter Hill and concentrate yard spotter were electrified on July 2, 1913.[52]

The advantages of the new electrics became obvious almost immediately. Unlike the steam locomotives, they allowed virtually around-the-clock availability. Equally impressive was the greater work they could

Opposite: A typical mixed train on the Georgetown branch probably required only a single coach, but otherwise was much like this consist. *Marcus Daly Historical Society of Anaconda*

Electrics took over operation first on the Smelter Hill line. In 1913 a pair of new motors bring loaded ore cars upgrade to the concentrator.
Montana Historical Society, Helena, #PAc 82-62.2170

accomplish. When the electrics began working the Smelter Hill trains, a pair of motors pulled sixteen loaded cars at a time to the concentrator yard. With an identical load as in the past, the electrics proved able to pull the train upgrade much faster, enabling the crew to make eight round trips during their shift. The electric motors delivered 128 cars to the concentrator per shift, vs. 96 loads under steam power—a 25 percent increase. Incrementally, the number of loaded cars was increased until the standard train on the Smelter Hill was twenty-five cars long. Operating the electric units in groups of two or three using the multiple unit control feature allowed one electric engine crew to perform the work of two or more steam locomotives and their crews. In addition to hauling more tonnage, the electrics could make the trip in twenty-six minutes—nearly half the time it had taken a 4-8-0 to drag sixteen loads upgrade. They were so much more efficient than steam engines that railroad management decided to eliminate the night shift spotting crew, leaving the Smelter Hill night shift crew to do its own spotting.

Electric operations on the Smelter Hill provided a good opportunity for the engine crews to familiarize themselves with the operation of electrics. Electrified operations on the main line and from Rocker to the Butte Hill yard did not begin until October, four months after the Smelter Hill trackage. The results on the main line were equally pleasing. Steam-hauled ore trains had typically consisted of 50 cars, with a maximum of 55 loaded cars between Rocker and East Anaconda. Gross tonnage for such a train was approximately 3,500 to 4,000 tons.[53] A single 4-8-0 pulling a 4,000-ton train averaged a little over 13 mph, making the 20-mile run from Rocker to East Anaconda in 90 minutes. A pair of electrics replaced a 4-8-0 on the main line starting October 10, 1913. As at the Smelter Hill, the train size initially was kept the same as it had been with steam operation, then was gradually increased—from 55 loaded cars to 65 cars, approximately 4,620 tons gross weight.[54]

On this route too, the pair of box cabs proved that they could not only move more tonnage, but move it faster than steam power. It was nothing short of impressive how a pair of electrics could haul 65 loaded cars and a caboose up the 0.3 percent grade from Gregson to East Anaconda at 16 mph, doubling the 7 mph speed that the 4-8-0's had struggled to maintain with less tonnage. Elimination of routine water stops also helped increase the trains' running time. For example, running time between Rocker and East Anaconda dropped from 90 minutes to an hour.[55]

The electrics also brought welcome changes for their passengers. The accompaniments of steam travel had been smoke, soot, and road grime. In winter, steam heat, though common on most main-line trains by 1910, was not the norm on most short lines, which generally heated with coal stoves at each end of the car.[56] Summer compounded passenger discomfort, since windows opened for ventilation also let in dust from the roadbed, and soot and cinders from the engine. When the BA&P electrified, passengers found the new amenities pleasing. The annoyance of smoke and cinders had vanished, and electric resistance heating and electric lighting were provided in each coach.[57]

At the end of the year, BA&P management could reflect with pride on its achievements in 1913. The railroad now had reached what would become its maximum length, with the completion of the Georgetown Lake extension, 22 miles west of Anaconda. Although BA&P had surveyed from Anaconda to Missoula and even Kalispell, the track would never get west of the Atlantic Cable mine, located in the mountains on the eastern shore of Georgetown Lake. Electrification had replaced steam locomotives on the busiest portions of the railroad. The ACM was pleased with the increased carrying capacity of the railroad brought about by the introduction of electric traction.

General Electric found the BA&P to be an excellent proving ground, as the railroad substantiated GE's claim that direct current could be applied to heavy freight hauling for greater cost efficiency. Almost immediately after the BA&P was wired for electricity, GE received a contract for the electrification of 440 miles of the connecting CM&StP between Harlowton, Montana and Avery, Idaho. Interestingly, the CM&StP was controlled by the same group that controlled the ACM and the Montana Power Company. Even as Ryan, William Rockefeller, and other major investors in ACM and Montana Power anticipated additional sales of copper to the CM&StP, advocates of railroad electrification anticipated wholesale conversion from steam to electric operation of western main lines in mountainous territory.[58] Trade journals discussed plans to

An eastbound passenger train at Durant, ca. 1915. The electric conduit for the lights is visible on the car roofs. *Marcus Daly Historical Society of Anaconda, #18513*

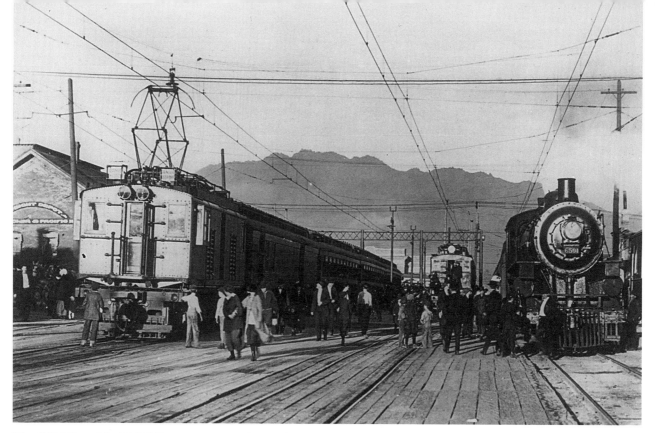

The CM&StP used the BA&P's Butte passenger station until its own was built in 1917. The BA&P passenger train with Motor 66 is on the left; a new CM&StP electric, No. 10200, is in the center; and CM&StP steam engine No. 6501 is on the BA&P-GN connection, ca. 1915. *Butte-Silver Bow Public Archives, #347*

electrify portions of the Chicago, Milwaukee & St. Paul, Denver & Rio Grande, Great Northern, Norfolk & Western, and Southern Pacific.[59]

General Electric immediately moved to begin electrification of CM&StP's main line between Harlowton, Montana, and Avery, Idaho.[60] Electrification of the mountain grades of the CM&StP gave GE an opportunity to make improvements on its basic DC system, utilizing knowledge it had gained from its BA&P experience. The first change made was to increase the voltage on the line from 2,400 volts to 3,000. Secondly, GE dropped the roller-contact idea for the CM&StP motors, finding through experience with the BA&P that using roller pantographs for current collection was not satisfactory. The rolling trolley wheel that worked well for current collection on street cars at 600 volts DC did not work on the BA&P electrics. Roller replacement was much more frequent than anticipated, because the BA&P rollers revolved fast enough to throw out the oil lubricating the bearings. The loss of lubrication caused bearing failure, resulting in seized-up rollers that would soon wear through where the wire contacted them. GE resorted to using a sliding contact shoe, fitted to the top of each pantograph. This was the same technology first used in the East in 1906 on AC equipment running at 6,600 or 11,000 volts.[61]

Lastly, regenerative braking, the use of the electric motors for braking purposes, was introduced on the new CM&StP electrics. When an electric motor's armature is mechanically turned, the motor acts as a generator, producing electric current rather than consuming it. Using the motors as generators, an electrically hauled train going downgrade actually produced current, rather than drawing it, and could feed this back into the power distribution system. The force required to turn the motor armatures as generators acted as a brake, slowing the train, and making it possible to keep heavy trains under control with greatly reduced use of the air brakes, consequently reducing the wear and tear on wheels and brake shoes. Regenerative braking was not designed into the BA&P units, and GE touted the CM&StP's electrics as the first to incorporate this feature.[62]

Although GE had successfully used the BA&P to prove the viability of direct current for heavy-duty freight hauling, the results were less positive on the main-line CM&StP railroad. Operationally, the electrics performed as GE had promised, but financially the results were disappointing. Much of this doubtlessly was attributable to the lack of freight traffic, but the decision to electrify contributed to the expense side of the ledger.[63] The bonded indebtedness of the CM&StP had tripled by the time the Pacific extension had been completed and 658 miles of it electrified. Bad as this was, the contracts for electricity the CM&StP signed were extremely one-sided, in favor of the utility company. The Interstate Commerce Commission noted that Ryan had simultaneously served on the governing boards of ACM, BA&P, CM&StP, and Montana Power Company. Obviously, Ryan successfully promoted his agenda to favor the interests of the power company (to sell power) and ACM (to sell copper) at the expense of the CM&StP.[64]

An additional expense associated with the electrification of the CM&StP was the construction of its own track between Colorado Junction, in Butte, and Cliff (Finlen) in 1913. Operation of CM&StP trains over the BA&P began when both railroads were steam operated. However, the decision to electrify the CM&StP at 3,000 volts, instead of the 2,400 volts used by the BA&P, made it necessary for each railroad to have its own track and electrical system. The CM&StP connection between Cliff Junction, on the BA&P, and

Finlen was removed from service on December 8, 1914, and dismantled.[65]

Another major expense cropped up for the CM&StP. It has been noted that line loss due to the resistance of the wire was greater for the GE's DC system than it was for the AC system designed by Westinghouse. Even raising the DC voltage to 3,000 volts did not change the fact that the voltage in the contact wire dropped below the desired level about fifteen miles away from a power supply station. This electrical loss required that substations be built approximately thirty miles apart to maintain the catenary voltage at or near the maximum 3,000 volts on which the locomotives were designed to operate. Each substation required an electrical operator around the clock, equaling three men, each of whom worked an eight-hour shift. Labor costs, in addition to those of capital and maintenance for the substations, added to the expense of electric operations. On the electrified lines of the CM&StP, the

A BA&P ore train and a CM&StP freight at BA&P bridge 11.02, ca. 1915. Both railroads used GE electrics, but because of the difference in operating voltages, each needed its own track and electrical system. *Butte-Silver Bow Public Archives, #345*

railroad built twenty-two substations which existed for the sole purpose of maintaining the 3,000-volt current in the catenary. On the Butte, Anaconda & Pacific, the substation expenses were less of an issue, because the portion of the main line which had been electrified was less than thirty miles long. Power could be fed from each end of the railroad, for a total of two substations. While the BA&P had to assume a share of the cost of operating the substations which served it, both had been built to serve other operations of the ACM, so the railroad application was an added function to an already extant facility.

The decade between 1906 and 1916 was a brief period when railroad electrification appeared to have great promise. General Electric and Westinghouse both sought to showcase their competing systems, and by 1914 extensive main line mileage had been electrified with each system, allowing a fair comparison of the two. The BA&P, with over 100 miles of main line, branch, and siding under wire, operated at 2,400 volts DC. While not complete, the CM&StP was in the process of having 658 miles electrified with 3,000-volt DC in the contact wire of the catenary. These two railroads were GE's showcases for the feasibility of direct current railroad electrification. Westinghouse countered with its 11,000-volt system applied to seventy-four miles of the New Haven, and thirty miles of the Norfolk & Western.[66]

The period of railroad expansion in the United States ended with World War I. Electrification and other large capital investments in the industry became less common after the war. Railroading had dominated transportation since the 1860s, but after the federal government assumed rate-making authority in the early 1900s, many railroads found themselves in an economically weakened condition. They complained that federally set freight rates failed to keep up with inflation, especially during the war. In addition, railroads began facing increasingly stiff competition from automobiles and trucks after 1916.[67] Lack of capital for railroad improvements was one reason for the lack of enthusiasm for electrification; improvements to steam locomotive design was another. Between 1900 and 1920 significant advances in steam locomotive design allowed the production of larger steam locomotives than would have been thought practicable in 1897, when the BA&P compound 4-8-0's appeared to be some of the largest steam locomotives possible. Both mechanical stokers and successful oil firing technologies were

perfected between 1900 and 1915, causing most railroads which had been considering major electrification to abandon the idea in favor of larger, more powerful steam locomotives. Under federal control during World War I, the nation's railroads firmly committed themselves to modern steam power, much of which was designed by the United States Railroad Administration (USRA). While the federal agency designed a dozen standard steam locomotives and a variety of freight cars, no electric motive power or catenary designs came off its drawing boards, indicating that the mechanical engineers and planners responsible for shaping railroad policy during the war had concluded the future still belonged to the steam locomotive.[68]

Hence, rather than replace existing technology, the Great Northern and Northern Pacific bought larger steam locomotives instead of electrics. Stoker-fired coal burners predominated on the NP, while the GN gradually moved to a preponderance of oil-fired steam locomotives. When the GN did electrify part of its main line, it was for only seventy miles, through the new, eight-mile Cascade Tunnel in Washington, opened in 1929. From Skykomish to Wenatchee, Washington, an 11,000-volt, single-phase alternating current powered trains through the tunnel, where the decision to use electricity had once again been made for smoke abatement reasons.[69]

In the middle of the depressed 1930s, the Pennsylvania Railroad undertook to operate its main line from Harrisburg, Pennsylvania, to New York and Washington, D.C., with 11,000-volt AC electrification. This was the last major railroad electrification project in the United States engaged by a private company. The only large post-World War I electrification project in North America to use GE's direct current system was Mexico's thirty-mile section of the Ferrocarril Mexicano between Orizaba and Esperanza, completed in 1924.[70] This was also a 3,000-volt system. Although the electrics provided better service on this steeply graded portion of the Mexicano than steam power, steam remained the motive power of choice in Mexico as well as the United States. Mexico, which was still suffering from the economic dislocation of its revolution, was an even less likely market for extensive electrification than was the United States.

Electrification occurred at a very fortunate time for the ACM. Less than a year after GE completed electrifying the BA&P, World War I began, causing an increased demand for copper. For the railroad, the increased carrying capacity due to electrification was a blessing.

In 1894 Daly had ordered construction of the BA&P with modern equipment to maximize its operating efficiency. Two decades later, the copper-carrying short line was still one of the most modern railroads in the United States, largely dependent on clean, hydroelectric power to move its trains. However, the majority of the nation's railroads found no economic justification for electrification, and the steam locomotive remained the industry standard for another thirty-five years, until after World War II. By that time, the BA&P electrics were older than many of the steam locomotives in use, and direct current electrification was relegated mostly to remaining street railways and mass transit systems, and a handful of railroads electrified before 1930. General Electric's DC systems continued to operate on the Canadian National, the Chicago, Milwaukee & St. Paul, the Ferrocarril Mexicano, and the Paulista Railway in Brazil.

Most of the main-line electrification in North America installed after 1925 used the AC system. These included the GN's eight-mile Cascade Tunnel, and the extension of the Pennsylvania Railroad's electrification of its Washington, D.C.-to-New York City main line. Both were 11,000-volt, 25-cycle, single-phase AC systems. Westinghouse's hypothesis that alternating current was preferable for main line railroad electrification had been proven true.

General Electric successfully used the Butte, Anaconda & Pacific to demonstrate the viability of electric traction for heavy freight hauling. Economically, the 2,400-volt DC system had proved satisfactory for the BA&P—successful more in spite of the system than because of it. On the twenty-six mile line from Butte to Anaconda, line loss on the catenary's direct current was not a significant problem. As a pioneering application, the electrification of the BA&P gave engineers and economists additional data for use in planning additional railroad electrification. GE made three changes in its heavy electrification design which were incorporated on the CM&StP electrification after observing the early operation of the BA&P electrics: 1) the catenary voltage was increased from 2,400 to 3,000 volts, 2) the locomotive pantographs were equipped with sliding contact shoes instead of rollers, and 3) regenerative braking was introduced.

Ultimately, however, railroad electrification—AC or DC—failed to reach the enthusiastic goals of its proponents. The BA&P electrics, heralded as the harbingers of change in 1915, were regarded as something of a curiosity thirty years later when steam locomotives finally began to lose their primacy to diesel-electrics.

NOTES

1. R. E. Wade, "The Electrification of the Butte, Anaconda & Pacific Railway," *Transactions of the American Institute of Mining Engineers*, Volume 46, p. 820.

2. George W. Hilton and John F. Due, *The Electric Interurban Railways in America* (Stanford, California: Stanford University Press, 1964), pp. 4–7. Interurban railways were generally more lightly built than steam railroads, though not always. Electrically operated, interurban lines ran both in city streets (like city street cars), and on private right-of-way between cities. For this reason the cars were larger, heavier, and geared for faster speeds than city street cars. The Hilton and Due volume is the standard overview of the history of interurban railways.

3. Hilton and Due, p. 4; William D. Middleton, *The Time of the Trolley* (Milwaukee, Wisconsin: Kalmbach Publishing Co., 1967), p. 54.

4. The term "steam railroads" came into common use after electric traction became common on street railways. It was generally assumed that all railroads were operated with steam unless otherwise specified. Most steam railroads were built with heavier rail, and designed to carry heavier loads than city street car lines. Electrified steam railroads were generally referred to in the trade as "heavy electrification." After the use of electric traction on street railways and interurbans became common, the engineering phrase "electric traction" was shortened to "traction" in trade and engineering circles. The term was soon adopted by the general public in reference to electric street and interurban railway operations. Modern readers of *Babbitt* may find the term curious, but in Sinclair Lewis's day, readers knew exactly what he was talking about. Sinclair Lewis, *Babbitt* (New York: Grosset & Dunlap, 1922), pp. 30, 45, 375–76, 397–98. The term "light rail" is the present term for what would have been called a trolley line in 1915.

5. Alexander Gray, *Principles and Practice of Electrical Engineering* (New York: McGraw-Hill, 1947), pp. 253–254.

6. International Textbook Company, *Electric Railway Systems* (Scranton, Pennsylvania: International Textbook Company, 1908), pp. 15–16.

7. Hilton and Due, pp. 5–7.

8. Ibid., p. 7. Cable cars remained in cities with steep hills, like San Francisco, and Seattle, Washington. The definitive history of cable car operations is George W. Hilton, *The Cable Car in America* (Berkeley, California: Howell-North, 1971), an overview of the technology and economics of cable railways in the United States.

9. *Railroad Gazette*, July 14, 1893, p. 527. "Electric Motors for Steam Roads—A Step in Progress." Design work and construction began two years before the B&O electric operation

commenced, indicating that there were technological difficulties which took time to correct. *Railroad Gazette*, January 2, 1893, p. 3; July 19, 1895, pp. 480–82; November 8, 1895, pp. 735–36.

10. New York *Times*, January 9, 1902, p. 1; January 25, 1902, pp. 1–2.

11. *Railroad Gazette*, October 20, 1905, pp. 366–69.

12. Ibid., September 1, 1905, pp. 198–200; June 15, 1906, pp. 648–52.

13. The amount of power required by an electric locomotive is proportional to the weight of the train and other factors, including gradient and curvature. For a fixed electrical power requirement, such as a fixed train tonnage, and grade, the voltage drop can be reduced by increasing the voltage in the trolley wire and hence reducing the amount of current passing through it. Alternatively, for a fixed voltage drop, a heavier train can be pulled using a higher voltage since the current is the same. These factors indicated clear advantages of using higher line voltage for railroad electrification.

14. *Railroad Gazette*, June 2, 1905, pp. 609–10.

15. Ibid., August 24, 1906. A condensed history of the S&IE is included in John R. Fahey, *Shaping Spokane: Jay P. Graves and His Times* (Seattle, Washington: University of Washington Press, 1994).

16. *Railroad Gazette*, August 24, 1906.

17. International Textbook Company, *Single Phase Railway System* (International Textbook Company: Scranton, Pennsylvania, 1908), pp. 78–83.

18. Ibid., pp. 72–76.

19. *Railroad Gazette*, April 13, 1906, pp. 379–82.

20. Hidy, et al., pp. 84–85, 115, 166. The original GN line crossed Stevens Pass by a series of temporary switchbacks, completed in 1892–93. The first Cascade Tunnel was completed in 1900, and was used until the present Cascade Tunnel was completed in 1929.

21. John A. Dewhurst, "A Review of American Steam Road Electrifications," *General Electric Review*, 17:11 [November, 1914], pp. 1144–45. Hidy, et al., pp. 115, 166.

22. Steam locomotives are external, rather than internal combustion engines. To lubricate the cylinder walls and piston rings, lubricating oil is injected into the cylinders along with steam. To prevent damage to the cylinders and pistons, the engine must always work enough steam to provide oil to lubricate the cylinders. When moving downgrade, or being towed by another locomotive, a steam locomotive should have the throttle cracked to admit just enough steam to lubricate the cylinders, but not enough to perform any work pulling the train. This is known as "drifting." A dead locomotive (one not under steam) is normally towed only after disconnecting the main rods so that the pistons will not move, thus preventing scoring of cylinder walls. D. C. Buell, *Basic Steam Locomotive Maintenance* (Omaha, Nebraska: Rail Heritage Publications, 1980), p. 178.

23. Dewhurst, "Review," p. 1144.

24. Ibid.

25. Interstate Commerce Commission. *Interstate Commerce Commission Activities, 1887–1937* (Washington, D.C.: GPO, 1937), pp. 117–21.

26. George Westinghouse held patents for the air brake system which eventually became the industry standard in North America. Once skeptical railroad managers realized the advantages of air brakes, Westinghouse's fortune was made. After 1885 the Westinghouse Company expanded into all aspects of electrical manufacturing, from industrial motors to consumer electronics. "George Westinghouse," *Dictionary of American Biography*, Vol. 20, pp. 16–18.

27. While the third rail was easily accessed by railroad maintenance crews, it was not an ideal system in terms of public safety. At highway crossings it was necessary to have "breaks" where the electrified third rail did not cross the roadway. Even so, the possibility of accidental contact with the energized rail was a hazard at public grade crossings. Careless trespassers risked electrocution if they touched the third rail while walking on the tracks.

28. Roy V. Wright, Editor, *Locomotive Cyclopedia of American Practice*, Seventh Edition (New York: Simmons-Boardman Publishing Co., 1925), p. 327. Wood firing, although still common on logging railroads and in parts of Africa and South America, had been discontinued in favor of coal firing by most main-line railroads in the United States after 1880.

29. The term was carried over from the age of horse power. A hostler was the stable hand responsible for the care and feeding of horses. A railroad hostler was responsible for the routine servicing of locomotives (iron horses) under steam in the roundhouse.

30. Observation and timing of the process was conducted by the author at the Chama, NM, engine terminal of the Cumbres & Toltec Scenic RR in 1983. The C&TS operates locomotives of approximately the same size as the largest BA&P steam locomotives. The facility and practices are largely unchanged from the early 1920s, when the present coal tipple replaced an earlier one with a higher coal delivery track on a long trestle. The BA&P coal chutes at Anaconda were similar to the original coal chutes at Chama.

31. The ICC held responsibility for regular locomotive boiler inspection under the terms of the *Locomotive Boiler Inspection Act of 1911*, *Statutes at Large*, 36, sec. 103, 913 (1911).

32. Navin, pp. 203, 211.

33. Montana State Railroad Commission Records, "BA&P Annual Report, Year Ending June 30, 1914," p. 5.

34. J. B. Cox, "The Electrical Operation of the Butte, Anaconda & Pacific Railway," *General Electric Review*, Vol. 17:11 [November, 1914], pp. 1049–50; Max Hebgen, "Hydro-electric Development in Montana," *Transactions of the American Institute of Mining Engineers*, Vol. 36 (1913), pp. 789–815.

35. Hebgen, pp. 789–815.

36. Ibid., p. 793.

37. Ibid., p. 792.

38. Ibid., p. 797.

39. Ibid., pp. 802–04.

40. Electric railroaders generally referred to electric motive power as "motors" rather than "locomotives." The technical distinction is that a locomotive is self-propelling, i.e., has a self-contained power source. A steam locomotive produces its own steam in its boiler and uses it in the engine, which has two or more cylinders, to pull the train. An electric motor does not have its own power source, but draws current from an

overhead wire or a third rail. A diesel-electric locomotive (which many North Americans simply call a "diesel") contains its own power plant. The diesel engine drives an electric generator, which produces the electricity that drives the electric traction motors powering the wheels.

41. International Textbook Company, *Single Phase*, pp. 78–83.

42. *Electric Railway Journal*, August 31, 1912, p. 340.

43. *Electric Railway Journal*, August 31, 1912, p. 340; General Electric Co. "Railway Line Material for Catenary Construction," Schenectady, New York: [n.d.], pp. 4–5.

44. International Textbook Company, *Line and Track* (Scranton, Pennsylvania: International Textbook Company, 1908), pp. 14–27.

45. BA&P Records, "Electrics," Specification Sheet [n.d.]; Wright, *Locomotive Cyclopedia*, Seventh Edition, 1925, p. 894.

46. Cox, p. 1052.

47. ICC, "Valuation Docket No. 1018, Butte, Anaconda & Pacific Railway Company," *ICC Reports*, Vol. 141, p. 759; BA&P Records, "Annual Report to the Montana Railroad Commission," 1914, p. 13.

48. Cox, pp. 1047–48, 1051.

49. Ibid., p. 1052.

50. Ibid., p. 1053.

51. Ibid.

52. Ibid.

53. A 4,000-ton train indicates that the nominal 50-ton capacity of the ore cars was routinely exceeded, and the typical load in each car averaged slightly more than 54 tons. (55 empty cars @ 18 tons each = 990 tons, plus one caboose @ 20 tons gives a subtotal of 1,010 tons, leaving 2,990 net tons of ore.)

54. Cox. p. 1055.

55. Ibid.

56. John H. White, *The American Railroad Passenger Car* (Baltimore: Johns Hopkins University Press, 1971), p. 394.

57. *Electric Railway Journal*, March 14, 1914, Volume 48:11, p. 579. BA&P Records. A circa 1914 photograph of a BA&P passenger train at the Durant, Montana depot shows the electrical conduits on the coach roofs for electric lighting. Passenger cars before 1900 were often heated by coal stoves. Steam heat, supplied by the locomotive, became the common source of heating after 1900. See White, *Passenger Car*, pp. 391–400.

58. Wade, "Electrification," p. 820.

59. *Railroad Gazette*, September 6, 1907, pp. 249–50; *Electric Railway Journal*, June 7, 1913, pp. 1006–10; *Railway Age*, November 2, 1912, p. 1001.

60. *Railway Age*, January 2, 1914, pp. 11–12; *General Electric Review*, vol. 18:1 [January, 1915], pp. 5–9.

61. *Railroad Gazette*, June 2, 1905, pp. 609–10; April 3, 1906, pp. 379–82.

62. A. H. Armstrong, "The Electrification of the Puget Sound Lines of the Chicago Milwaukee & St. Paul Railway," *General Electric Review*, Vol. 18, No. 1 (January, 1915), pp. 8–9.

63. Lowenthal, pp. 13–14; pp. 21–24.

64. ICC, "Docket No. 17021," *ICC Reports*, Vol. 131, pp. 634, 637–38, 642.

65. Chicago Milwaukee & St. Paul Railroad. "Station Plat, Finlen, Montana," January 1, 1921. Map shows track removed, cites Authorization For Expenditure number 12390, dated December 8, 1914. The station plat indicates that sometime prior to 1921, the station originally called Cliff on the CM&StP had been renamed Finlen.

66. Dewhurst, p. 1144.

67. Gabriel Kolko, in *Railroads and Regulation, 1877–1916* (Princeton, New Jersey: Princeton University Press, 1965) argues that during the Progressive period, the railroad industry systematically subverted federal regulation attempts, and used the ICC as a shield to protect itself from citizen reform movements. Kolko views the ICC as ineffectual, arguing that it served the needs of the railroads more than the public. The USRA, Kolko concludes, saved the railroads from the effects of poor private management at taxpayer expense. John F. Stover, *The Life and Decline of the American Railroad* (New York: Oxford University Press, 1971). Stover concludes that the industry reached its maximum size and importance to the United States economy in 1916. Competition since 1916, in conjunction with increased regulation, has reduced the profitability of railroads since World War I. Albro Martin, *Enterprise Denied: Origins of the Decline of American Railroads, 1897–1917* (New York: Columbia University Press, 1971). Martin argues that the regulatory climate had become so restrictive after 1900 that railroads could not charge rates that were profitable. Martin's thesis is that the railroads needed to earn enough to provide adequate capital for reinvestment in improvements, in addition to an attractive return on investment; but that this was impossible under the rate structure created by Progressive legislators.

68. Wright, *Locomotive Cyclopedia*, Seventh Edition.

69. An alternative to electrification had already been demonstrated in 1928, when the six-mile Moffat tunnel opened for service in Colorado. Forced-air ventilation cleared out smoke and exhaust steam. Steam locomotives used the tunnel regularly from its opening until 1956. Diesel-electrics still use the tunnel, depending on the fans to remove the diesel exhaust from the bore. Charles Albi and Kenton Forrest, *The Moffat Tunnel: A Brief History*, (Golden, Colorado: Colorado Railroad Museum, 1986), p. 14. Forced air ventilation of the Cascade Tunnel allowed the GN to discontinue electric operations in 1956. Hidy et al., pp. 267–68.

70. Glen H. Walker, "Electric Locomotives for Mexican Railway," *Railway Age*, vol. 75:22 [December 1, 1923], pp. 1021–23; W.D. Bearce, "Mexican Railway Begins Electrical Operation," *Railway Age*, vol. 78:27 [June 6, 1925], pp. 1385–86. Electrification of the Mexican Railway was to reduce operating costs on this steeply graded section of the railroad.

Chapter Five

THE BUSIEST LITTLE RAILROAD IN THE WORLD

The Butte, Anaconda & Pacific handles trains of the heaviest freight class and its success in regard to both reliability of service and economies effected contributed in no small measure to the decision to electrify a considerable part of the main line of the Chicago, Milwaukee & St. Paul Railway lying in the same territory.[1]

FOR THE NEXT THIRTY YEARS, the BA&P was one of the few electrified railroads in North America operating heavy freight trains. From 1915 through 1945, while the GE-built box cabs rolled up an impressive performance record, the railroad industry changed considerably. What was a state-of-the-art railroad in 1915 became an example of economic conservatism by 1945—far from a role-model for progressive voices in the industry. During those three decades, American society and the business world endured the traumatic changes of two world wars and a crushing economic depression. After 1915, railroads moved from directing economic and political currents—as they had for the latter half of the nineteenth century—to reacting to them. Steam locomotives grew larger and more powerful during these years. A serious challenger to steam appeared just as the United States entered World War II, combining internal combustion and electric traction motors: the diesel-electric locomotive.

The BA&P managed to change very little during this era. In 1945 it was still operating older, smaller locomotives and freight cars than were the transcontinental railroads. Ore remained the primary traffic between Butte and Anaconda, along with coal, coke, and supplies for the ACM's mines and smelter. As from the railroad's day of origin, all other freight and passenger business was incidental.

Although chartered and operated as a common carrier, the BA&P was unlike its transcontinental railroad neighbors in one fundamental respect. The NP and GN were owned and operated to provide transportation as common carriers; they made a profit for their stock holders by carrying freight and passengers. The BA&P was a mining company railroad, which had been built to provide economical transportation of ore from the ACM's mines to its smelter. As such, the railroad's role as a common carrier was secondary to its function within ACM's Montana copper production system. Because the BA&P moved ore and sup-

plies at lower cost than the transcontinental railroads, it was a success—as long as the total cost of producing copper was profitable to the ACM. For these reasons, the BA&P was not particularly driven to make technological changes in keeping with national, common-carrier railroads.

Electrification of the Butte, Anaconda & Pacific was completed just as the demand for copper was increased by the outbreak of World War I. Butte's mines shipped 3,772,294 tons of ore to the Washoe Works over the BA&P in 1914, the first full year of main-line electric operation.[2] Output of the mines rose over the next two years. In 1916 the BA&P carried 5,850,480 tons of ore from Butte to the Washoe Works for concentrating and smelting.[3] The volume of ore carried by the railroad dropped slightly in 1917, and rebounded to over 5,500,000 tons in 1918, before the end of the war softened the demand for copper.[4] Average daily ore traffic in 1916 was just over 16,000 tons per day, or 320 50-ton car-loads per day.[5] A record for productivity was set in January 1917, when over 18,000 tons of ore, or 360 cars per day, were handled.[6]

Upon conversion to electric traction, it became immediately obvious that the electrics' capability of multiple-unit control greatly facilitated productivity and economy of labor. Steam-powered ore trains pulled by one 4-8-0 had been limited to 4,000 tons gross, or about 50 to 55 loaded cars and a caboose, between Rocker and East Anaconda.[7] Experience highlighted the superiority of the electrics. Initially a pair of box cabs was rated at 4,680 tons, or 65 loaded cars and a caboose. This was eventually increased to 5,600 tons for two units and 8,400 tons for three units, equalling 75 loads or 116 loads, respectively.[8]

Because increased ore production soon overwhelmed the BA&P shortly after electrification of the main-line freight operations in 1913, steam locomotives were retained to help with the increased traffic.[9] Meanwhile, another four freight motors and three booster units were ordered from GE.[10] A booster, called a tractor truck by the BA&P, involved a single, four-wheeled truck with two traction motors (one per axle) which could be semi-permanently coupled to a box cab to increase its tractive effort.[11] A booster was energized by the electrical power of the locomotive, since it had no pantograph or electrical control gear of its own. The tractor trucks were among the first units designed to provide added tractive effort in the form of powered axles without requiring a complete second unit of motive power containing a power source.[12] Ideally, a single unit and booster (called a "cow and calf" by BA&P crews) was intended to be used for switching service, and would be able to replace some of the steam switchers still in use. General Electric completed two locomotives and two boosters in December of 1914, and two locomotives and the last tractor truck in Janu-

Motor No. 48 and Tractor Truck No. T3 were photographed by the American Locomotive Company in 1914. GE supplied the electrical gear and traction motors, but ALCO built the trucks and cab. *ALCO Schenectady Works Photo; ALCO Historic Photos, #S-1062*

ary of 1915.[13] Despite the arrival of all these units by early 1915, the railroad was still short of motive power. Steam locomotive usage actually increased in 1915 and 1916.[14]

Control of the Butte, Anaconda & Pacific remained firmly in the hands of the Anaconda Copper Mining Company, but reflected the financial course undertaken by the Standard Oil Gang. The Great Northern Railway, which had overseen the original construction of the BA&P, was paid in BA&P securities. These securities were then redeemed by the ACM, which held the majority of stock of the railroad. By 1915 the BA&P stock was held in nearly equal parts by the ACM, in the person of William G. Rockefeller, and by the Chicago, Milwaukee & St. Paul Railroad. Rockefeller held 51 percent of BA&P common stock, the CM&StP held about 49 percent of the

The changing of the guard in Butte, as 2-8-0 No. 10 backs out of the way of brand new electric No. 57. Many Butte residents lived with the noise of trains in their back yards. *World Museum of Mining, #1068*

stock, and the officers each held shares to entitle them to vote.[15]

As a subsidiary of the mining company, the railroad was expected to meet the transportation needs of the parent company more than to generate a profit from conducting general transportation. As ACM's operations expanded and changed, the mining company adjusted the operations of its railroad subsidiary accordingly. When a new ACM subsidiary, the International Smelting and Refining Company, was created, a rail connection to the new smelter near Tooele, Utah, was needed. The Tooele Valley Railway (TV) was incorporated in 1910 to meet that need, and was partially equipped with second-hand rolling stock from the BA&P.[16] Judging from the locomotive sale to the TV in 1915, one can infer that the larger needs of the ACM took precedence over the immediate needs of the BA&P. One of BA&P's newest 2-8-0's was sold to the TV that year, despite the need to press steam engines as well as electrics into service to handle the overwhelming load on the BA&P.[17]

Records indicate that much of the actual decision-making for the railroad was undertaken by the ACM, not by the BA&P. For example, the contract for a group of 100 steel ore cars purchased from Pressed Steel Car Company in 1916 was made between the Anaconda Copper Mining Company and the car builder; the BA&P appeared only as a penned annotation to the contract.[18]

✂

Equipment acquisitions in 1915 and 1916 included 400 additional 50-ton capacity steel hoppers, and a unique new three-ton vehicle called a Federal truck. The truck was a labor-saving device intended to eliminate the use of work trains for wire maintenance. In the past, for construction and maintenance of the catenary, work platforms for electrical crews were built on top of a pair of box cars.[19] This work train required the services of a two-man engine crew and a train crew, in addition to the electricians. The Federal truck facilitated catenary maintenance. Fitted with flanged railroad wheels, a telescoping tower to reach the overhead wire, and room for a small stock of parts and tools, a small electrical crew could drive itself to specific locations. When the crew reached the job site, the power was shut off, the wire grounded, and the truck's tower was raised to provide a small platform for the electricians working on the catenary. By using the converted truck for most electrical work, and using a work train only when a larger crew was required, the BA&P reduced the cost of maintaining the catenary substantially.

As the demand for copper increased during World War I and the BA&P found itself short of motive power, it placed two more orders with GE for more electrics. The first group of three was delivered in 1916, and the last set in 1917.[20] All of them were mechanically identical to the first 15 box cabs delivered in 1913, giving the BA&P a total of 28 electric locomotives, and three booster units. Only two of the 28 box cabs were geared for passenger service; the other 26 and all three of the tractors were geared for hauling freight.

Increased ore movement also required an expansion of the freight car fleet. As expected, the rate of production at the mines and smelter was in direct proportion to the railroad's ability to move ore. In a two-year period, 545 new, 50-ton capacity ore cars were added to the roster, nearly doubling the number of ore cars. Pressed Steel Car Company delivered 145 cars in 1914. An order for another 100 went to Western Steel Car & Foundry for 1915 delivery. Two more batches of ore cars arrived in 1916: Pressed Steel Car delivered 100, and Western Steel Car & Foundry delivered 200 cars.[21] All of these were virtually identical to those built in 1900, riding on arch bar trucks. Arch bar trucks were still in wide use at the time, but no longer state-of-the-art technology. Single-piece cast truck sideframes produced by the Bettendorf Axle company were already beginning to dominate new freight car construction because of their superior construction.

Twelve all-wood flat cars were built in the Anaconda car shops using second-hand trucks during

Line Car M-1 was a converted Federal truck, equipped with a telescoping tower. *Marcus Daly Historical Society of Anaconda*

A pair of box cabs could handle 25 cars of ore on the Smelter Hill branch in less time than steam locomotives. May 14, 1914. *Marcus Daly Historical Society of Anaconda, #18568*

the four years of the World War I traffic boom.[22] Although the superiority of steel construction had been effectively demonstrated on the BA&P as early as 1899, steel was in great demand for military purposes and railroads were encouraged to save steel where possible. Wooden cars really were obsolete by 1918 because of the heightened efficiency of steel, but wood materials were relatively easy to obtain, and most car shops had men who were experienced in the craft of maintaining wooden equipment. The war gave the wooden car a lease on life on the BA&P just as it did on other railroads across North America. Many of the standard freight car designs developed by the United States Railroad Administration (USRA) during this era were of composite construction, having steel underframes and wooden car bodies.[23]

Upon receipt of the final two batches of electrics in 1916 and 1917, the BA&P finally had sufficient electric motive power to meet its needs. Then the railroad began wholesale retirement of the steam fleet. In 1915 the steam roster totaled 24 steam locomotives of varying ages between 12 and 22 years. Initial sales were made to other ACM subsidiaries, such as the six-mile-long Tooele Valley Railway in Utah, which connected the ACM subsidiary International Smelting Company plant with the Union Pacific system and with the Western Pacific at Warner, Utah, southwest of Salt Lake

City.[24] When an eight-year-old 2-8-0 was sold to the Tooele Valley Railway in January 1915, it joined two other ex-BA&P locomotives there.[25] The Black Eagle smelter in Great Falls, Montana, was sold one of the 0-6-0's for use as a switcher in June, 1916.[26]

World conditions contributed to the increased demand for used locomotives just at the time the BA&P found itself with a roundhouse full of surplus steam locomotives. New locomotives could not be obtained on short notice. Not only did U.S. railroads need additional motive power for the increased business, but foreign governments had ordered large numbers of locomotives from U.S. builders because military production was overtaxing factories in Europe. Industries and common carrier railroads were often faced with long delays for new locomotives, making used locomotives more attractive under the circumstances. The BA&P was thus fortuitously able to sell its surplus steam locomotives for more than their scrap value. Fourteen steam locomotives were sold in 1917, and one in January, 1918. A steel company in Minneapolis bought one of the 0-6-0's on January 1, 1917. Six weeks later, the Great Northern purchased a pair of ten-year-old 2-8-0's. The lone Baldwin 4-6-0 was sold to a Cuban sugar mill in August, and in January, 1918, a steel mill in Harrisburg, Pennsylvania, purchased an 0-6-0.[27] Three of the oldest 4-8-0's were sold to the Nashville, Chattanooga & St. Louis in October, 1917.[28]

The largest single purchaser was a New York City equipment dealer working on behalf of the Penoles Mining Company in Mexico. Mexico's railroads had suffered losses due to the ongoing military campaigns of the Mexican Revolution. Some private enterprises, such as mining companies, had found it necessary to obtain their own equipment in order to attempt to achieve rail service in parts of Mexico. During the summer of 1917, two 0-6-0's and five 4-8-0's were sold to General Equipment Company, which in turn sold them to Penoles.[29]

All of these surplused locomotives were smaller than the new ones manufactured for main-line service in 1915, and, given that they were at least ten years old, they would have been unlikely candidates for prompt sale under peace-time conditions.

Added complication for BA&P's equipment disposition was created about the time the United States entered World War I, as the railroad came under the auspices of the United States Railroad Administration. Federal operation of most of the railroads in the United States by the USRA was mandated in December 1917 as a war-time measure to facilitate the movement of troops and war materiel.

The USRA was given management responsibilities over U.S. railroads because of a crisis that had developed as the European war progressed. All across the United States, train traffic had increased dramatically from 1914 through 1916, as manufacturers and agricultural dealers sold war materiel and foodstuffs to European customers. When the United States entered the war in 1917, the railroad system was nearing a standstill, choked by an overabundance of business and a shortage of freight cars. By Thanksgiving 1917, freight cars clogged yards for miles around Atlantic ports, waiting to be unloaded onto ships bound for Europe. These standing cars exacerbated the car shortage in the nation and blocked movement of other trains.

Soon, the shortage of railway cars began to affect the movement of coal, the nation's primary heating and industrial fuel. This shortage threatened war production and heating just as winter grew severe in the northeastern states. Railroad industry efforts to meet this challenge through voluntary pooling arrangements were ruled illegal, and the problem grew more desperate. Driven to exasperation by the situation, President Woodrow Wilson gave the USRA control over most of the nation's railroads for the duration of the war.[30]

Consequently, in December 1917, the BA&P came under the management of the USRA. Regular daily operations continued to be conducted by BA&P management, but overall policy decisions were made by the USRA. Reduction of the equipment shortage was addressed in the short-term by reassigning equipment to locations where the USRA determined it was most needed for the war effort. During BA&P's period under federal management, the railroad's wreck train[31] was moved from Anaconda, and stationed at Lima, Montana.[32]

As a more permanent solution for the nation's freight-hauling problem, the USRA undertook development of standard designs for locomotives and freight cars which could be efficiently produced and distributed to the railroads as directed by the federal managers. The BA&P, because it was already adequately equipped with motive power and hopper cars for the ore business, received no USRA-designed rolling stock.

After a few months of USRA operation, the Anaconda Copper Mining Company began complaining that the government was not operating the BA&P as efficiently as the company could under its own management. In a series of protests to the USRA, the railroad argued that it served no useful purpose to force the BA&P to remain under federal control: 1) because it was not a common carrier, but a railroad primarily dedicated to hauling ore for the ACM; 2) because most of its equipment was used for hauling ore on its own track; and 3) because it did not

Wrecker No. D-2 re-railing a car loaded with 50 tons of ore, winter of 1953. *BA&P Records, Butte-Silver Bow Public Archives*

Motor 66 and a typical four-car passenger train posed in Silver Bow Canyon, near Durant. *Marcus Daly Historical Society of Anaconda, #18565*

serve any Atlantic ports. Recognizing the validity of ACM's arguments, the USRA relinquished control of the BA&P to its owners in the autumn of 1918.[33] Most other railroads in the United States remained under federal control until returned to their private owners under the terms of the Transportation Act of 1920.[34]

In 1918 the 51 percent of the BA&P stock held by William G. Rockefeller was transferred to the Anaconda Copper Mining Company. Forty-nine percent of the BA&P common stock continued to be held by the CM&StP.[35] But that stock was soon to end up in ACM's hands. The war had not created windfall profits for the CM&StP. After being returned to its owners following the period of federal control, the CM&StP defaulted on its bonds, and went into financial collapse in 1923. As a result, the transcontinental railroad sold its share of BA&P stock to the mining company, an act which consolidated the ownership of the BA&P as a wholly owned subsidiary of Anaconda Mining by 1924.[36]

In spring 1921, while CM&StP still was a major corporate owner of the BA&P, the two companies formed an agreement to jointly use the Milwaukee's Butte passenger terminal. This was a favorable agreement for the BA&P, since it allowed the short line to eliminate the expenses of staffing and maintaining its own station in Butte. The Milwaukee agreed to employ the station staff and take care of building maintenance. The BA&P was only held responsible for maintaining the catenary over its two tracks. For the next 34 years, BA&P passenger trains used the Milwaukee passenger station.[37]

The imposing, brick passenger station fronted on Montana Street in the south part of Butte. It was served by six tracks, which far exceeded the operational needs of either railroad by itself. Because the two railroads used different voltages for their electric locomotives, compatibility became an issue. The BA&P used only the two northern tracks under catenary energized at 2,400 volts, fearing that the 3,000-volt direct current used by the CM&StP would damage the BA&P's units. The four southernmost tracks were used by Milwaukee trains, under 3,000-volt catenary.[38]

All thought of through passenger service east from Anaconda was long forgotten. Local passenger business, typified by railroads like the BA&P, was dwindling. The all-time yearly high for passengers carried was achieved in 1916, when over 408,000 rode the BA&P.[39] Five years later, when the BA&P and Milwaukee agreed to share the latter's passenger station, the BA&P was carrying only a third of the number it had in 1916. Passenger business began an even more precipitous decline in 1921, when only 152,592 passengers rode its line.[40] In three years the number of fare-paying passengers dropped to a mere 32,026.[41] These declines, though steeper than transcontinental service declines, reflected a national trend in railroad passenger service as improved roads, new highways, and increasing automobile ownership began to reduce American's dependence on trains.

A reduction of passenger equipment followed, as the BA&P sold or rebuilt what was now surplus rolling stock. In January 1924, passenger Motor No. 65 was regeared for use in freight service.[42] Only Motor No. 66 retained passenger gearing and continued to provide passenger service, making two round trips per day. One 4-6-0 remained in the Anaconda roundhouse as a stand-by passenger locomotive. Some of the oldest cars and locomotives were sold to the Tooele Valley in 1924 and 1925. Three passenger cars went to the TV in 1924, followed by another coach and a caboose

in January 1925.[43] The TV bought a locomotive and twenty-two steel hopper cars that fall.[44] With reduced ore loading from Butte after the war's end, the BA&P was able to spare some of its surplus cars for the Utah short line.

Eight steam locomotives remained on the BA&P roster after mid-January 1918, and were used for minor portions of track in the early 1920s. One six-coupled switcher, one 4-6-0 passenger locomotive, two Mastodons and four 2-8-0's were still stabled in the Anaconda roundhouse. Keeping one of the 4-6-0's gave the company a spare passenger locomotive. The 4-8-0's and 2-8-0's were well suited for use hauling mixed trains or freight. These remaining steam locomotives were used on branches and industrial trackage that couldn't justify the expense of electrification.

One such branch line was the extension constructed to the mine at Southern Cross, above Georgetown Lake. Originally, the BA&P had surveyed west of Anaconda for the publicly stated purpose of building to Missoula or to Kalispell. A five-mile extension from Anaconda to Browns had been completed in 1898, to reach a source of limestone, which was quarried for use as a flux in the smelting process. A 15¼-mile extension from Browns to Southern Cross was completed in spring 1913, with operation beginning April 1, 1913.[45]

No. 30 and the mixed train prepare to leave Southern Cross for Anaconda in the early 1920s. The small depot had none of the grandeur of those built at Butte or Anaconda. *Montana Historical Society, Helena, #PAc 88-67*

During the nine operational months of 1913, only 31,381 tons of ore were shipped from the mine at Southern Cross to the Washoe Works. This averages out to 115.37 tons, slightly over two 50-ton carloads per day.[46] In 1914 the Southern Cross mine shipped 69,104 tons of ore, a daily average of 189 tons, or a scant four carloads.[47] Maximum production occurred in 1916, when 80,520 tons were shipped, averaging about 4 1/2 50-ton carloads per day.[48] Subsequently, ore loadings at Southern Cross dropped rapidly: 63,754 tons in 1917, dropping nearly 20,000 tons per year for the next three years before reaching a low of 102 tons in 1921.[49] That coincided with greatly reduced production in Butte, as well—but while Butte production returned to 1912 levels and maintained them over the next three years, such was not the case at Southern Cross. Operating revenues on the Georgetown extension in 1922, for both freight and passengers, were $10,000 less than operating expenses. When taxes were added to the loss, it amounted to $13,624.77.[50] The next year showed equally dismal losses.[51] From the ACM's

point of view, the mine at Southern Cross had been a poor investment. Recognizing the folly of operating a money-losing branch line handling only a few cars a week, the railroad abandoned it piecemeal. Service was suspended west of Dalton, and the westernmost 10 1/2 miles of track were pulled up in 1925.[52] A year later, service west of Browns was discontinued, and the track from there to Dalton was removed.[53] The fate of the Georgetown Lake extension was typical of many lightly trafficked branch lines in the West after World War I. The demise of the BA&P's mixed train to Southern Cross was mourned by few, if any, of its former passengers, who increasingly were turning to the convenience of automobiles.

The abandonment of the Southern Cross branch in 1925 and the stable level of business through the 1920s produced another surplus of steam locomotives on the BA&P. Only about four of the existing eight engines were required to service the branch line to the limestone quarry at Browns and to the slime pond spurs along the Stuart branch east of Anaconda.[54]

Below: A double-headed excursion train headed for Georgetown Lake on the Southern Cross branch, ca. 1915, pulled by Nos. 24 and 19. The automobile in the foreground is prophetic—branch line passenger trains like this one were doomed by improved roads and mass-produced automobiles. *Marcus Daly Historical Society of Anaconda, #18547*

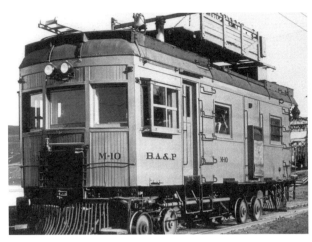

Line Car M-10, built by the BA&P shops in 1925. The work platform on top of the car could be raised or lowered pneumatically for access to the overhead. *World Museum of Mining, #6593*

Limestone quarried at Browns was moved by steam to Anaconda or East Anaconda; then the electrics hauled it to the smelter. Slime, the wet residual waste of powdered rock left by the concentrating process, was loaded into cars at the concentrator and hauled east along the Stuart branch to to be dumped. Because the track on the slime pond spurs was regularly shifted to allow room for the piles of waste material, electric operation would have been more costly. Slag from the smelter was also disposed of in a similar manner, creating a black mountain to the north and east of the Washoe Works.[55]

In late 1925 the Anaconda shops built a new self-propelled line car, which was placed in service in January, 1926. The converted Federal truck had proven adequate for much of the small line work, but was too small for jobs requiring a full-fledged work train consisting of a locomotive and one or two tower cars. In addition to the cost of the train and engine crews, a work train tied up a locomotive which could otherwise be engaged in revenue service. Line Car M-10 was an eight-wheeled, self-propelled unit equipped with a pneumatic work platform. It was capable of carrying enough men and equipment to perform most routine maintenance on the catenary.[56]

In the late 1920s the BA&P again became an industry innovator when it undertook an extensive field test of a new air hose coupling. Electrification had helped speed the movement of trains over the road, but switching cars at the mines and smelter had continued to be as time-consuming as ever. Unloading ore at the smelter was particularly inefficient, because each car had to be uncoupled from the rest of the cars in

Line car M-10 and crew making repairs in Silver Bow Canyon, April 1943. *Butte-Silver Bow Public Archives*

order to be emptied of its ore by the rotary car dumper at the concentrator. Air brakes and automatic couplers made the brakeman's job safer than had been the case in the 1880s, but they required two separate couplings, operated independently of each other. Uncoupling cars was easy. A brakeman stood at the side of the car and uncoupled the car by lifting a lever on the end of the car which unlocked the coupler. When the locomotive pulled ahead, the car would be left standing and the air hoses would uncouple as the cars pulled apart. Coupling up cars, however, was more time-consuming. The car couplers worked on impact, closing and locking, but the air hose couplings were not automatic. After the cars were coupled together, the brakeman had to step between the cars, and manually couple the air hoses together to allow the air brakes to function.

A faster way to couple cars and air lines, simultaneously if possible, was much desired. Combined car and air couplers were thought to be a promising solution to this problem, and were used by some rapid transit systems. Another solution was an automatic

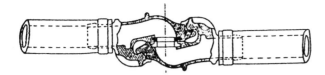

Standard air hose coupling, or "Gladhand." (*Railway Age,* January 29, 1927, p. 385.) *Simmons-Boardman Publishing Company*

coupling for air lines, which was introduced in the late '20s by the Consolidated Connector Corporation, a Cleveland, Ohio, firm. The company's automatic air line connector offered an automatic air hose coupling which would allow cars to be coupled and uncoupled on impact, automatically. While this faster, safer concept seemed promising, its success depended on its wholesale adoption, since interchangeability would be a principal issue; unless all railroads adopted the automatic air coupler, it would not be useful. If the BA&P could prove the viability of the automatic air coupler, the ICC might be moved to mandate its use on all equipment being interchanged. This was the manufacturer's hope. Discussions between Consolidated Connector and the BA&P in the spring of 1927 resulted in an agreement by the railroad to give the air connector a comprehensive trial. Underlying the decision was the claim by Consolidated Connector that the railroad could realize a 25 percent savings in operating costs through the use of the automatic connector.

As the first large-scale test of an automatic air line connector on freight cars, the BA&P was once again the proving ground for innovative railroad technology. Passenger Motor No. 66, one baggage car, and two coaches were the first rolling stock to receive the new air line couplings.[57] Next, one thousand ore cars were equipped with the Consolidated Connector Cor-

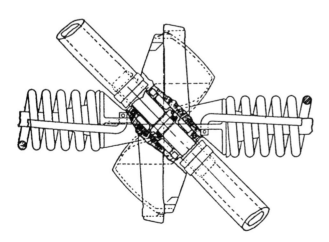

Automatic air connector (*Railway Age,* January 29, 1927, p. 385) *Simmons-Boardman Publishing Company*

poration's automatic air connector, at a cost of $40.00 per car for parts, with labor supplied by the railroad. Equipping the freight cars and the rest of the electrics took longer, and was not completed until 1928.[58]

Initial tests of the automatic air connector were promising enough to encourage the interest of several of the largest operating railroad brotherhoods. Seeking to improve safety for their members, the Brotherhood of Railway Trainmen and the Order of Railway Conductors obtained the support of the unions representing engineers and firemen to present a unified petition to the ICC for the adoption of the automatic air line connector on all equipment used in interstate service. After the petition was filed with the ICC in February 1929, the Commission approved an additional series of tests of the connector at Purdue University, in Indiana.[59]

Though Purdue offered laboratory conditions, the BA&P gave a rigorous full field test to the automatic air connector. The railroad's results indicated that the automatic air connector was an idea whose time had not yet come. After twelve years of extensive testing on 1,000 cars, the BA&P concluded that the automatic air connector was costing money, rather than saving

Brakeman helping to spot a load of ore in the rotary car dumper at the Washoe Works, ca. 1943. Electric spotter motor is in center background. *Montana Historical Society, Helena, #Lot 19.A57*

it. In a 1940 memorandum, the BA&P superintendent recommended reconsideration of the use of the automatic air connector, noting that no other railroads had adopted the design. Mechanically, the automatic air connector was inferior to the manually coupled air hoses used by other railroads, and the BA&P's mechanical department complained that the automatic air connector was costing money due to increased repairs.[60]

Specifically, rapid wear of the connectors caused air leakage, which reduced the efficiency of the air brake system on the cars. Providing a supply of jumper hoses to permit the interchange of freight cars from other railroads to operate on BA&P freight trains added to the expense and inefficiency. These short sections of air hose had the automatic connector on one end, and the standard air hose "glad hand" coupling at the other. In order to move cars received from other railroads in a train along with ore cars, the jumper hose had to be placed between the ore car and the other cars. Use of the jumper hoses required the brakemen switching to make additional air hose connections, which still required moving between cars. A supply of the jumper

hoses had to be carried on locomotives and cabooses, and the brakemen had to carry one or more around to wherever needed. Using the jumper hoses added time to the process of switching cars of supplies for the mines and smelter, which added to the expense of switching. Mechanically and economically, the automatic air connectors failed to deliver either promised economic rewards or increased safety for switching crews. Based on the test results, the ICC decided against requiring it on the nation's railroads. BA&P reconverted its locomotives and ore cars to "glad hand" air hose couplings, which to this day are used by the railroad industry for coupling air hoses between cars.

During the early 1930s, a very important improvement was made on the motive power fleet: roller current collectors were replaced by sliding contact shoes. General Electric had recognized the shortcomings of the roller contact for pantograph current collectors soon after the BA&P first electrified. All of the electrics built for the CM&StP in 1915 were delivered with sliding shoes. Between the fall of 1930 and the summer of

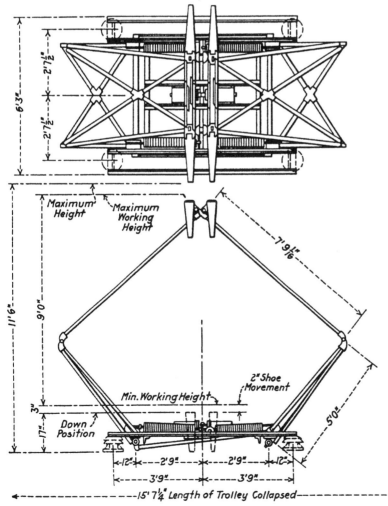

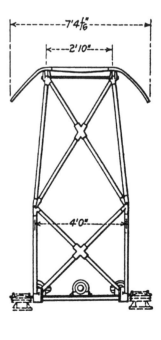

General Electric pantograph with double sliding contact shoe. (*Locomotive Cyclopedia*, 7th edition, p. 905.) *Simmons-Boardman Publishing Company*

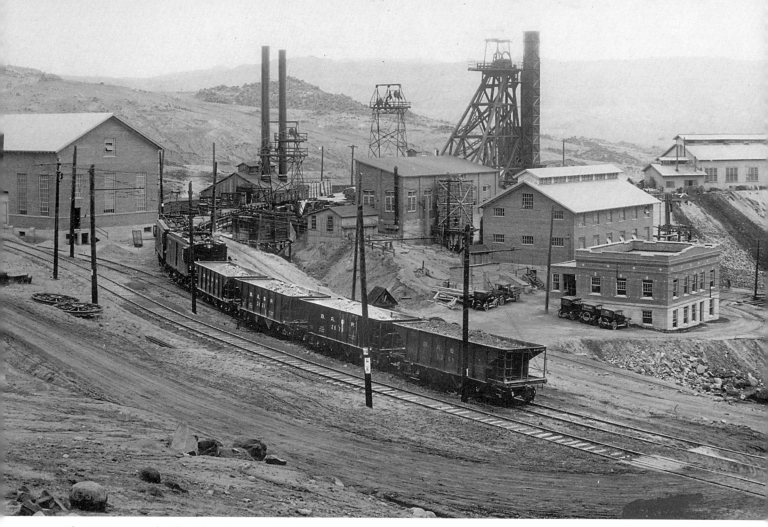

The BA&P spur to the Elm Orlu Mine. *Montana Historical Society, Helena, #PAc 98-95.57*

1931, the BA&P rebuilt the pantographs on its locomotives with sliding contact shoes similar to those used on the Milwaukee's electrics.[61]

At the time of electrification in 1913 the freight car fleet had been adequate for the volume of business being carried. To meet the war-time demand for copper, over 500 steel ore cars were added to the roster. After World War I ended, the rolling stock remained quite adequate for the foreseeable future. One reason for this was the gradual shift of low-volume local freight business away from railroads in general, and the BA&P in particular. As the BA&P freight car fleet aged, it became less acceptable in the general flow of commerce throughout the nation. However, this was of little or no consequence to the ACM, which was concerned solely with the movement of ore from mines to smelter. The aging hopper fleet was ample for the company's needs. First, the volume of ore being transported through the 1920s and early '30s remained below the levels of 1916 through 1918. Second, the BA&P cars were used almost exclusively for movement between Butte and Anaconda; shipment of finished copper products was accomplished in cars supplied by other railroads.

As regulations governing the interchange of cars changed after 1920, the railroad car technology of 1900 became less acceptable. All wood cars were obsolete by 1920, although some continued to be built as late as 1925.[62] The arch bar freight truck was rapidly becoming obsolete, as the structural superiority of one-piece cast truck sideframes became widely recognized. However, BA&P continued to operate a number of all-wood flat cars, and a vast majority of its freight cars rode on trucks with fabricated sideframes. Arch bar trucks predominated. Over 1,000 ore cars, and many of the flats, both steel and wood, were so equipped. Some of the flats and box cars were on Fox patent trucks, which used a built-up side frame of pressed steel shapes, riveted together.[63]

The Interstate Commerce Commission forced the railroads to phase out wooden car construction by ordering changes in what would be accepted for cars interchanged between railroads in interstate common-carrier service. New cars built from 1926 on were required to have steel underframes, and rebuilt wooden cars needed to have steel center sills installed as a minimum improvement during the overhaul.[64] Consequently, the BA&P retired some of its oldest all-wood cars after 1925, or sold them to the ACM for use on trackage inside its various plants. Cars used exclusively on the industrial trackage owned by the ACM would not be subject to interchange regulations, except if offered to the BA&P, which was not likely to reject them.[65]

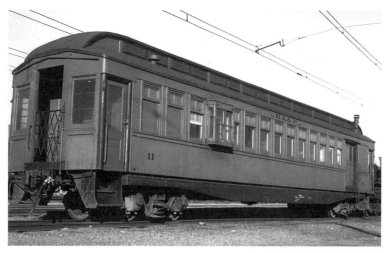

Combination car No. 11, after it was rebuilt with a steel underframe and freight car trucks by the Anaconda car shop. The bay window enabled the conductor to use the car as a caboose. *Robert K. Dowler*

Economic depression had an impact on the BA&P, as it did throughout the industrial sector of the U.S. economy following the stock market crash in the autumn of 1929. At the depth of the depression, for the years 1932 through 1934, an average of 650,000 tons of ore was hauled each year, roughly a third of the amount carried in 1931. But 1933 saw a new low, when only 627,322 tons of Butte ore—approximately 35 carloads a day—moved over the BA&P.[66] A protracted strike by miners and smelter men in 1934 kept traffic levels depressed.[67] Passenger ridership was even more dismal.

Both freight and passenger business dropped after the 1929 stock market crash. In 1936 the BA&P discontinued operating separate passenger trains, and offered only mixed train service to the public. In March of that year, Motor No. 66 was re-geared for freight service, and two more of the passenger cars were retired the following month.[68] Although the timetable continued to list Trains 1 and 3 and 2 and 4 as passenger trains, they actually had become mixed trains, as evidenced by the re-gearing of the last passenger motor. A pair of electrics would leave the Butte station with a single combination car, carrying the conductor, brakemen, and any passengers who might have purchased tickets. At Rocker the combination car was placed at the end of forty or fifty ore cars, and the train ran to East Anaconda, where the ore cars were set out on a siding. The motors and their lone combination car then proceeded west to the Anaconda station to deliver the passengers. The passenger trains were the only ones listed in the timetable.[69] If ore tonnage exceeded the amount that could be carried from Rocker to East Anaconda by two scheduled trains a day, an extra or unscheduled train would be operated.

Business picked up in 1935, and ore traffic exceeded the million tons-per-year mark again. Thereafter, it remained at or above two million tons-per-year through World War II. Still, the BA&P was more sufficiently equipped with motive power than it needed. Four of the oldest steam locomotives were retired in the summer of 1937, reducing the steam roster to three nearly identical Brooks-built 2-8-0's. The 4-6-0, kept as a spare passenger locomotive, was retired since it was unlikely that the BA&P would ever run passenger trains again. The pair of compound 4-8-0's were expensive to maintain, and the 0-6-0 was over forty years old, the smallest engine on the roster. At this retirement, unlike twenty years before, there was no market for used steam locomotives, since most railroads had lines of stored, outdated motive power. All four were cut up for scrap at the Anaconda shops in June.[70]

As the ACM's production gradually climbed after 1934, the BA&P upgraded its freight car fleet. Wooden flat cars were retired and replaced with steel cars built in company shops, using the trucks and couplers salvaged from the wooden cars.[71] In 1936 the BA&P began retiring box cars and using the trucks and steel underframes from them to build flat cars for hauling mine stulls.[72] There was little reason to maintain a large

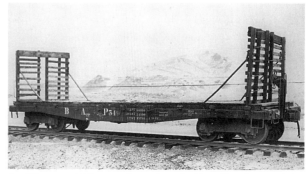

Steel flat car, with Fox trucks, equipped with stull racks at ends for handling mine stulls. *BA&P Records, Butte-Silver Bow Public Archives*

"Torching" a car to thaw the frozen ore before unloading it at the Washoe Works. *BA&P Records, Butte-Silver Bow Public Archives*

box car fleet for the small volume of local general merchandise business. Local freight, including less than carload lot (lcl) traffic, had been diminishing steadily since World War I,[73] as motor trucks increasingly filled local freight needs.

An issue that became more prominent after 1935 was wear and tear on the ore car fleet. Due to rough usage, cars frequently required repairs to offset damage in service, especially that caused by their unloading at the smelter. At the smelter, the entire car was turned upside down in a rotary car dumper, which emptied the ore out much more rapidly than it could flow out of the four hopper doors in the bottom of the car. The process of being turned upside down subjected the tops and sides of the cars to being banged against the car dumper, with resultant damage. Worse, however, was damage caused by thawing frozen loads of ore in the winter. Ore from the mines came up out of the shafts wet, and was deposited as such into the cars. When solidly frozen in the very cold Montana winter conditions, the entire load adhered to the

car body instead of tumbling out when the car was inverted. The car's hopper bottom gave the load even more surface to freeze to, making it harder to break loose and empty.

In Minnesota and Michigan iron country, also acquainted with bitter cold weather, steam points were used to thaw ore in the cars immediately before dumping during the cold months.[74] The BA&P, however, used a much more direct and destructive technique called "torching" to thaw frozen loads. Gas burners on a light pipe frame were placed against the hoppers and

Hopper underframe on the Anaconda repair track shows heat damage to center and side sills caused by torching. Warped sills were a result, requiring replacement more frequently than on cars not subjected to the process. *BA&P Records, Butte-Silver Bow Public Archives*

underframe of the car. Once ignited, the flames heated the steel, thawing the load sufficiently to be emptied. Though the process worked, it was extremely hard on the equipment.[75] By 1937 the BA&P was experimenting with baffles on the center sills of cars to reduce the damage to the underframe and confine the worst of the heat damage to the hoppers and side sheets; it was easier to replace these than the sills of the car's underframe.[76] Because torching frequently damaged cars, it was desirable to have a surplus of cars on hand. Thus, allowance could be made for torch-damaged cars which were out of service while being repaired by the car shop. Despite its obvious disadvantages, torching continued to be the ACM's standard method of thawing cars.

As demand increased again, the BA&P bought more ore cars in 1937. One of the ACM's managers investigated equipment needs, and recommended to ACM Vice President D. M. Kelley that the BA&P should purchase 200 new, 70-ton capacity hopper cars to begin modernizing its car fleet.[77] However, instead of buying new equipment, the railroad decided to buy 100 used 50-ton hopper cars from Westmoreland Coal Company.[78] These cars were virtually identical to those already in service, equipped with arch bar trucks. And, like those in service, they were already viewed as obsolete by the mainline railroad community and would soon be deemed unacceptable for interchange service.

Arch bar trucks were simple to construct, which appealed to railroad maintenance departments. The journal boxes (where the axle bearing, or journal, rode) were bolted to side frames consisting of bent steel bar stock. There was no need for large foundry work, just drilling, punching, and bending the flat bars that composed the side frames. However, fabricated truck side frames suffered from the inherent weakness of metal fatigue. The weakest points in an arch bar truck were where the bolts holding the journal boxes went through all the bars of the side frame. Nuts and bolts sometimes came loose, and metal fatigue was more likely where the bars were bent, which was also where some of the bolt holes passed through them. Failure of either a bolt or of one of the bars in the truck frame usually resulted in a derailment, which could be

Anaconda car shop, ca. 1965. Much of the work was done outside. The single stall brick building in the background was used to house wrecking crane No. D-2. *World Museum of Mining, #4941*

catastrophic if the truck came apart at any speed above a walk. As a result, the arch bar truck was banned from interchange service after December 31, 1939.[79]

Although most railroads were unwilling to accept equipment in interchange that did not meet current interchange standards, the BA&P was able to avoid the expense of re-trucking its cars. Most of its ore cars were used strictly in BA&P local service and on the spurs of the GN or NP serving mines on the Butte Hill.

The use of arch bar trucks in interchange service ended just as the world again entered a global war, and the demand for copper, as well as other metals, increased. A 1939 agreement between the GN and the BA&P allowed the BA&P to continue using the now obsolete arch bar trucks for service just between Anaconda and Great Falls.[80] This allowed the movement of calcine (roasted copper ore) and concentrates from the Anaconda smelter to the ACM's Black Eagle plant at Great Falls. The shipment involved interchanging the BA&P cars with the Great Northern at Butte for the trip to Great Falls. Shipping the material in BA&P cars saved the ACM money, because railroads pay for the use of cars from other railroads. By shipping from Anaconda to Great Falls in BA&P cars, the GN paid the BA&P for the use of the short line's cars during the time they were on GN rails. If the ACM had used cars supplied by the GN, then it would have been indirectly paying for car use as well as freight charges. By supplying its own cars for Anaconda to Great Falls service, the BA&P earned per diem for the use of the cars while they were off BA&P rails. The GN chose to accept obsolete BA&P cars in interchange and pay the per diem instead of committing a portion of its own car fleet to this service in a time of increasing traffic. However, the GN offset its costs by receiving a share of the freight charges. Both companies found the arrangement satisfactory and the agreement remained in effect for over 20 years after arch bar trucks had been excluded from general use in North America. Probably the presumption was that freight train speeds were slow on the GN between Butte and Great Falls, so the threat of serious accidents was minimized.

With the onset of World War II in September 1939, demand for copper increased. Tonnage hauled from Butte jumped from 2,600,000 tons in 1939 to just under 4 million tons in 1940. From 1941 through 1945, the volume of ore hauled from Butte to Anaconda was never less than 4 million tons per year, an annual average of over 4,250,000 tons.[81] Freight business boomed; by February 1942 the BA&P was running eight trains a day in each direction between Anaconda and Rocker. Four scheduled trains, which still appeared in the timetable as passenger trains, ran between Butte and Anaconda. Four daily freight trains between Rocker and East Anaconda were added to the schedule. The scheduled freights replaced the extra (unscheduled) trains that had been operating on an as-needed basis.[82]

The United States did not experience the same kind of railroad gridlock during World War II that had occurred in 1917, and federal regulation was less

Loading waste rock in Butte, ca. 1943. *Montana Historical Society, Helena, #Lot 19.B203*

intrusive. There was no 1942 version of the USRA, but railroads, like all other industries, had to function under the controls of the War Production Board. This agency regulated production and distribution of new rail, locomotives, cars, and other essential supplies. Rail replacement on ten miles of the main line, which was scheduled for the summer of 1942, was put off, as the War Production Board refused to allocate new rail to the BA&P. Tie replacement and ballasting went ahead, to keep the track sound for the heavy traffic operating on it, although even that project was disrupted by labor shortages due to the war.[83]

Only 381 passengers rode the BA&P in 1939, 376 in 1940, and 317 in 1941.[84] Mixed train service was more than adequate, as the train crew usually outnumbered passengers. In March 1942, General Manager Robert E. Brooks was optimistic that gasoline and rubber rationing might require the company to reintroduce passenger trains. "On account of war restrictions affecting automobiles and busses," Brooks remarked, "it is possible that we will have to establish regular passenger service in this territory."[85] People did ride the trains to a greater extent than in the previous two decades, but most carpooled or found other ways of traveling between Butte and Anaconda. Brooks' optimism was ill-placed; ridership never exceeded 700 for any year from 1942 through 1945. Paying passengers in-

creased from 428 in 1942 to 695 in 1945, but their numbers never reached the point of even filling the combination car on the daily mixed trains, let alone requiring a separate passenger run.[86] War-time rationing did give passenger trains across the United States a brief upsurge in patronage, but only temporarily disrupted the American love affair with the automobile.

Only one serious crisis occurred on the BA&P during the war years. In March 1943, Silver Bow Creek experienced record floods. All three railroads along Silver Bow Creek worked to shore up fills and protect bridges, but on March 28, 1943, the BA&P lost its contest with the swollen creek. Between Silver Bow and Durant, portions of the BA&P track washed out, including the bridge at milepost 11.87. Because movement of ore, fuel, and supplies to the smelter was critical—a shut-down of the smelter was an expensive and time-consuming process, to be avoided if at all possible—it was arranged to operate BA&P ore trains over the less damaged NP track between Silver Bow and Durant the next day, allowing the smelter to remain in operation.[87] General Manager Brooks succeeded in arranging for the use of a pile driver and bridge repair crew from Pocatello on the Union Pacific, which arrived at Silver Bow on March 31. Working around the clock, the UP and BA&P crews built a pile bridge across the creek, and opened the line to traffic again

Repairs to flood damage in Silver Bow Canyon, April 1943. The track has been cribbed up before replacing fill. *BA&P Records, Butte-Silver Bow Public Archives*

UP pile driver repairing flood damage to the BA&P bridge in Silver Bow Canyon, April 1943. The background provides a glimpse of an NP work train dumping new fill and ballast along the NP track. *BA&P Records, Butte-Silver Bow Public Archives*

on April 4, 1943. BA&P trains returned to their own rails, and the delivery of ore to the smelter continued without further interruption. Discussions between the BA&P and the NP culminated in a June 1945 agreement to allow NP trains to operate in an emergency over the BA&P between Butte and Durant. However, the agreement stipulated that the largest classes of NP steam locomotives could not be used, as they were too heavy for the BA&P bridges.[88]

The peak times of activity following electrification of the railroad were the two world wars, when demand for copper increased. Daily ore tonnage varied from 12,000 to 17,000 tons between 1915 and 1918, averaging 14,000 tons, or 282 car-loads.[89] After the armistice the demand dropped, and production was curtailed sharply the following year, and then dropped to 533,000 tons in 1921. Ore traffic increased to more than 2,334,000 tons in 1922. Butte's mines increased production in 1923, and the BA&P hauled 3,310,000 tons of ore to the smelter that year. Ore production and

BA&P ore tonnage remained at or above 1910 levels through 1929.

War again drove up the demand for copper after 1939. After the strike in 1934, mine output and smelter production gradually moved up from 1935 through 1941. A boom followed in 1942 through 1945, after the United States entered World War II. Although ore production in Butte did not reach the high of 1915, the amount hauled by the BA&P exceeded 4,000,000 tons per year for the period from 1942 through 1945.[90] With the end of the war, copper demand again dropped off, and the BA&P moved only 2,863,053 tons of ore from Butte to Anaconda in 1946.[91]

During the 1920s and '30s, while the transcontinental railroads struggled to combat the effects of increased highway competition and the depression with more efficient steam locomotives and larger freight cars, the BA&P quietly and conservatively went about its job of moving Butte Hill ore to the Anaconda smelter for the Anaconda Copper Mining Company.

NOTES

1. A. H. Armstrong, "Economies of Steam Railroad Electrification," General Electric Review, Vol. 17, No. 11 (November, 1914), p. 1003. Armstrong was listed as the assistant engineer in the Railway and Traction Engineering Department at GE.

2. BA&P Records. "Tonnage and Revenue," January–June, 1914, and July–December, 1914, XX, 1-1.

3. Ibid., January–June, 1916, and June–December, 1916, XX, 1-1.

4. Ibid., 1917–1918, XX, 1-1.

5. Ibid., January–June, 1916, XX, 1-1.

6. Ibid., January–June, 1917, XX, 1-1.

7. Cox, pp. 1054-1055.

8. BA&P Records. "Timetable No. 16," p. 21. Timetable No. 10, dated 1937, does not give engine ratings. However, the 1951 timetable, No. 16, does.

9. BA&P Records, "Tonnage and Revenue," 1914–1917, XX, 1-1.

10. Cox, p. 1058.

11. Tractive effort is the term railroaders use for the force exerted by the locomotive to pull itself and/or a train. In North American practice, it is usually expressed in pounds. A variant term, "tractive force," is also used. Wright, Locomotive Cyclopedia (Seventh Edition), p. 90.

12. A slug is the common term for a unit with traction motors but no power source of its own, that is controlled by a diesel-electric unit and draws current from it. Slugs provide the same added tractive effort for diesel-electric switching locomotives that the BA&P's tractor units provided for a single electric unit. Slugs are not commonly used for road freight service.

13. ICC Records, Bureau of Valuation, "Valuation of BA&P Ry, Account 534, Locomotives," 1919.

14. BA&P Records, "Tonnage and Revenue," 1913–1918, XX, 1-1. The railroad meticulously tracked tonnage of coal received for company use on its tonnage and revenue reports. In 1914 the BA&P received 12,343 tons of coal. The following year 23,339 tons of company coal were received, reflecting a significant increase in steam locomotive operation. A small quantity of coal was required for caboose stoves and heating depots and other buildings. The vast majority was for locomotive use.

15. BA&P Records, "Annual Report to the State Railroad Commission, Year Ending June 30, 1915," p. 9.

16. BA&P Records, "Steam Locomotives," I-4-3-A; ICC Records, Bureau of Valuation "Valuation of BA&P Ry, Account 534, Locomotives," 1919; "Valuation of Tooele Valley Railway Ry, Account 534, Locomotives," 1919.

17. BA&P Records, "Steam Locomotives," I-4-3-A.

18. BA&P Records, "Cars, Purchases," Pressed Steel Car Co. contract, January 4, 1916. VII-1.

19. ICC Records, Bureau of Valuation, "Valuation of BA&P Ry, Account 532, Service Equipment," 1919.

20. Ibid.

21. BA&P Records, "Cars, Purchases," Pressed Steel Car Co. contract, January 4, 1916. BA&P VII-1; ICC Records, Bureau of Valuation, "Valuation of BA&P Ry, Account 531, Freight, Express and Mail Cars," 1919.

22. ICC Records, Bureau of Valuation, "Valuation of BA&P Ry, Account 531, Freight, Express and Mail Cars," 1919.

23. Roy V. Wright, Ed., Car Builders Dictionary and Cyclopedia, Ninth Edition (New York: Simmons-Boardman Publishing Co., 1919), pp. 960-1008.

24. ICC, "Valuation of Tooele Valley Railway, Valuation Docket No. 9;" ICC Reports, Vol. 110, p. 310.

25. BA&P Records, "Steam Locomotives," I-4-3-A.

26. Ibid.

27. Ibid.

28. Ibid.

29. Ibid.

30. The problems leading up to the creation of the USRA and the experiment with government operation of the railroad network during World War I are covered in several sources, most of which are quite dated. Walker D. Hines, War History of American Railroads (New Haven, Connecticut: Yale University Press, 1928), and William G. McAdoo, Crowded Years: The Reminiscences of William G. McAdoo (Boston: Houghton Mifflin Company, 1931). Both wrote about the USRA, McAdoo in his autobiography, and Hines in a history of the agency. I. Leo Sharfman, The American Railroad Problem: A Study in War and Reconstruction (New York: Century Company, 1921), gave an overview immediately afterwards. Albro Martin argues in Enterprise Denied that the reason the nation's railroads failed in the hour of need was excessive regulation by the ICC.

31. A wreck train is comprised of railroad equipment used to clear wreckage after an accident, open the track, and restore service. A small railroad often only had a tool car with track tools and jacks as the sum total of its wreck train. Transcontinental railroads had larger wreck trains consisting of several tool and supply cars, a kitchen car, one or more cars of rail and ties, another car loaded with spare freight car trucks, and a rail-mounted crane stationed at strategic communities. The BA&P wrecking train included a steam crane or "wrecker" (Number D-2), accompanied by tool, supply, and bunk cars. BA&P Records, "Cars and Shop Equipment," and ICC Records, Valuation of BA&P, 1919. Since 1980 most railroads have relied more on bulldozers and highway cranes than on rail-mounted cranes for accident clean-up, because the work of clearing the wreckage can be done more rapidly when the crane is not restricted to moving only on rails.

32. W. T. Cheney photographs, in Cornelius W. Hauck, "Union Pacific, Montana Division," Colorado Rail Annual No. 15, pp. 138-139. Cheney was a UP employee at Lima, Montana, during World War I who took photographs of his work. Three published views show BA&P wrecker No. D-2 working to clean up a derailment near Lima.

33. BA&P Records, "USRA," United States Railroad Administration. Circular No. 5, October 10, 1918, XX, 1-5.

34. The United States Railroad Administration was arguably as close to fulfilling the old Populist dream of nationalizing railroads, telegraph, and telephone systems as the country has ever come.

35. BA&P Records, "Annual Report to the State Railroad Commission," 1918, p. 107.

36. Ibid., 1924, p. 107.

37. BA&P Records, "Contract Between Chicago Milwaukee & St. Paul Railway Company and Butte, Anaconda & Pacific Railway Company Governing Terminal Facilities," April 25, 1921; XIV-2-A 'Milwaukee—BA&P Joint Terminal.'

38. Ibid.

39. BA&P Records, "Tonnage and Revenue," 1913–1918, XX, 1-1.

40. Ibid., 1916–1921, XX, 1-1.

41. Ibid., 1921–1924, XX, 1-1.

42. BA&P Records, "Authority For Expenditure," AFE No. 12Eq, January 1, 1924, XV-1.

43. Ibid., AFE No. 14Eq, December 13, 1924; AFE No. 15Eq, January 20, 1925, XV-1.

44. BA&P Records, "Steam Locomotives;" I-4-3-A; "Authority For Expenditure," AFE No. 20 Eq, November 1925; AFE No. 21Eq, November, 1925, XV-1.

45. ICC, "Valuation of Butte, Anaconda & Pacific Railway, Valuation Docket No. 1018," *ICC Reports*, Vol. 141, p. 759.

46. BA&P Records, "Tonnage and Revenue," January–June, 1913, and July–December, 1913, XX, 1-1.

47. Ibid., January–June, 1914, and July–December, 1914, XX, 1-1.

48. Ibid., January–June, 1916, and July–December, 1916, XX, 1-1.

49. Ibid., 1918–1921, XX, 1-1.

50. BA&P Records, "Western Extension, Revenue and Expenses," VI.

51. Ibid.

52. BA&P Records, "Annual Report of the BA&P to the Montana Railroad Commission," 1925.

53. Ibid., 1926.

54. Also called tailings, the waste rock from the concentrating process was often allowed to remain liquefied, and was pumped into settling ponds where the water would evaporate or drain off, leaving a pile of fine, sand-like material. Because hauling slime by rail is much less efficient than pumping it as a slurry through a pipeline, most slime disposal in the precious metals industry was done by means of slurry. At Climax, Colorado, the Climax Molybdenum Co. used slurry disposal to fill an entire valley with the tailings from milling and concentrating its molybdenum ore. (Author's personal observations).

55. The slag piles from the original Anaconda Smelters, the Upper and Lower Works (not the Washoe Works) have become The Old Works Golf Course, designed by Jack Nicklaus. Spokane, Washington *Spokesman-Review*, June 5, 1999, "Inland Northwest" magazine, pp. 4-5, 11.

56. BA&P Records, "Electrical," XIX, 3-8-G.

57. BA&P Records, "Authority For Expenditure," AFE No. 39Eq, February 25, 1927, XV-1.

58. BA&P Records, "Automatic Air Connectors," H.A. Gallwey to Consolidated Connector Corporation, June 8, 1927; Consolidated Connector Corporation to H.A. Gallwey, June 11, 1927, I-3-4B; "Authority For Expenditure," AFE No. 45 Eq, August 4, 1927; AFE No. 57 Eq, November 6, 1928, XV-1.

59. ICC, *Interstate Commerce Commission Activities, 1887–1937*. (Washington, D.C.: GPO, 1937), p. 131.

60. BA&P Records, "Automatic Air Connectors," R. E. Brooks, Memorandum to File, June 15, 1940, I-3-4-B.

61. Don Roberts, Photograph Collection, Oregon Historical Society. Photographs of BA&P electric locomotives taken in November 1930 show roller contacts on the pantographs. Photographs taken in July and August of 1931 show sliding contact shoes on the pantographs.

62. White, *Freight Car*, p. 598.

63. Ibid., pp. 590-596 has a good capsule biography of Fox, stressing his role in steel car design.

64. ICC Interchange Rules, Rule 3, Section (r), quoted in: *Railway Age*, Vol. 76 No. 35 (June 18, 1924), p. 1673. The railroad which owned a car no longer considered interchangeable could use it on its own rails as long as it wished. However, no railroad had to accept a car classified as "illegal" for interchange under the freight car interchange rules. Such obsolete cars often were relegated to maintenance-of-way service, used only on the owning company's track.

65. BA&P Records, "Authority For Expenditure," AFE No. 35 Eq, October 8, 1926; AFE No. 43 Eq, July 22, 1927, XV-1.

66. BA&P Records, "Tonnage and Revenue," 1929–1934, XX, 1-1.

67. BA&P Records. "Annual Report of the BA&P to the State RR Commission," 1934.

68. BA&P Records, "Authority For Expenditure," AFE No. 2-36 Eq, March 18, 1936; AFE No. 8-36 Eq, April 22, 1936; AFE Nos. 8-36 Eq and 9-36 Eq, April 22, 1936, XV-1.

69. BA&P Records, "Timetable No. 10." Effective November 7, 1937.

70. BA&P Records, "Steam Locomotives," I-4-3-A.

71. BA&P Records, "Authority For Expenditure," AFE No. 7-36 Eq, April 22, 1936; AFE No. 12-36 Eq, August 10, 1936, XV-1.

72. Ibid., AFE No. 10-35 Eq, 11-36 Eq, 15-36 Eq, 19-36 Eq. August 12, 1936–September 9, 1936, XV-1.

73. BA&P Records, "Tonnage and Revenue," 1918–1935, XX, 1-1.

74. Hidy, et al., pp. 116, 217, 267.

75. BA&P Records, Administrative Correspondence, "AB Brakes," I-3-3-B.

76. BA&P Records, "Authority For Expenditure," AFE No. 25-37Eq, July 29, 1937, XV-1.

77. BA&P Records, Administrative Correspondence, "Ore Cars," C. D. Woodward to D. M. Kelley, May 24, 1937, I-3-4-A.

78. BA&P Records, "Authority For Expenditure," AFE No. 21-37 Eq, June 18, 1937, XV-1.

79. BA&P Records, "Arch Bar Trucks," ICC Interchange Rule 3, quoted in Memorandum of December 15, 1939. Administrative Correspondence, I-3-4-A. In fact, there were several railroads with agreements similar to that between the GN and BA&P. The Denver & Rio Grande Western and the Rio Grande Southern routinely interchanged narrow gauge freight cars with arch bar trucks until the abandonment of the RGS in 1952.

80. Ibid., Memorandum, R.E. Brooks to BA&P officials, December 15, 1939. Administrative Correspondence, I-3-4-A.

81. BA&P Records, "Tonnage and Revenue," 1939–1945, XX, 1-1.

82. BA&P Records, "Quarterly Reports," 1942, XIV-2-A.

83. Ibid., 1942, XIV-2-A.

84. BA&P Records, "Tonnage and Revenue," 1939–1941, XX, 1-1. The BA&P's records only list the total number of passengers

carried and revenue earned. Because the records do not supply specific details regarding passenger's travels, there is no way to determine how many were starting or completing long journeys which involved a change of trains at Butte. The annual report filed with the State Railroad Commission is equally non-specific.

85. BA&P Records, "Quarterly Reports," 1942, XIV-2-A.

86. BA&P Records, "Tonnage and Revenue," 1942–1945, XX, 1-1.

87. BA&P Records, Administrative Correspondence, "Silver Bow Canyon Flood, 1943," 5-3. The records do not indicate how the BA&P moved these trains over the NP, which was not electrified. The BA&P probably leased NP steam locomotives, since the BA&P owned only three steam locomotives itself.

88. BA&P Records, "Bridges," BA&P to NP, May 29, 1945, and NP to BA&P, June 1, 1945, I-3-3-B.

89. BA&P Records, "Tonnage and Revenue," 1914–1918, XX, 1-1.

90. Ibid., 1942–1945, XX, 1-1.

91. Ibid., 1946, XX, 1-1.

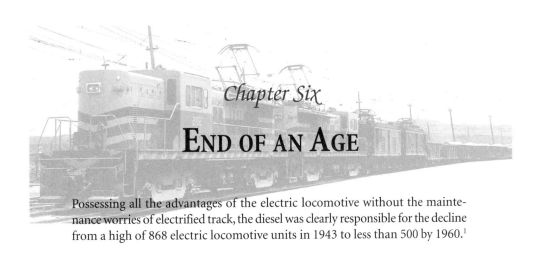

Chapter Six

END OF AN AGE

Possessing all the advantages of the electric locomotive without the maintenance worries of electrified track, the diesel was clearly responsible for the decline from a high of 868 electric locomotive units in 1943 to less than 500 by 1960.[1]

*A*T THE END OF WORLD WAR II, mining and railroad industries underwent profound changes. Steam locomotives vanished from most of the nation's railroad system by 1960. Diesel-electrics, which rendered steam obsolete, replaced electric traction in heavy freight service as well. Domestic mining and metal production became less lucrative than overseas sources, and U.S. mining companies either closed mines or adapted new technologies to reduce operating expenses. New technologies changed the way mining and railroading were conducted. The BA&P was itself transformed, leading to its demise and subsequent reincarnation as the Rarus Railway in 1985.

Though early twentieth-century advocates of electric power thought that cleaner, more efficient electricity would change railroading in America, the cost of building the electric infrastructure required was simply too high to be economical for most purposes. Further killing the use of electric motive power on a broad scale was the breakthrough of the diesel-electric locomotive in the 1930s. This machine proved to be a machine that the railroads could practically adopt. Diesel-electric technology exhibited genuine promise to bring railroading the mechanical efficiency of electric traction motors without the expensive electrical distribution system of catenary or third rail, substations, and transmission lines. The traction motors on the axles of a diesel-electric locomotive are powered by electric current, which is created by a diesel-powered generator on the locomotive. Because it has its own self-contained power source, a diesel-electric is a genuine *locomotive* in the sense that it is self-propelling, as compared to an electric unit, which requires current supplied from an external source.[2] First used extensively in streamlined passenger trains of the early to mid-1930s, the diesel-electric (which soon came to be called simply "diesel" in U.S. usage) became an accepted freight hauler by the end of the decade.

General Motors rolled out the first full-sized, mass-produced freight diesel in 1939, sending it on a cross-country demonstration trip over twenty different railroads. Called the "FT" for freight, the new locomotive offered the flexibility of multiple unit control, and the 24-hour availability that had heretofore been found only in electric motive power.[3]

Just as major railroads began fully to appreciate the financial savings offered by dieselization, the United States entered World War II, and government production controls made it impossible for many railroads to obtain diesels. Consequently, steam obtained a short-term lease on life, which lasted until 1945 when diesels began rapidly to replace steam on the nation's railroads. Like many small railroads, the BA&P was initially skeptical about the feasibility of dieselization, given the high cost of new locomotives. Furthermore, the majority of the BA&P's operations were conducted with a satisfactory, if aging, electric locomotive fleet. Steam locomotives were adequately performing the work on the small portion of nonelectrified trackage around Anaconda. An expensive change of motive power might not be practical unless there was a long period of operation ahead through which the potential savings of dieselization could be realized.

At the same time, the ACM was faced with a challenge. Butte's mines were becoming less productive as higher grades of ore were exhausted. Reaching depths of 4,000 feet below the surface, the mines were also becoming more expensive to maintain and operate. Water had to be pumped out, and the timber supporting the shafts and drifts[4] required regular inspection and maintenance. Maintenance costs were increasing as the mines deepened, as was the cost of getting the ore to the surface. Although improvements were made in ventilation and hoisting equipment, Butte's mines reached a point where ore production stagnated while mining costs continued to rise.[5]

An experiment which began in 1944 led to the post-war application of a new method of underground mining called block caving. The technique, developed in Arizona copper mines, allowed for less costly mining of low-grade ore than the traditional method of stoping out the ore body. In block caving, a large volume of ore, measuring 120 feet by 120 feet, is undermined and allowed to collapse into a broken mass by its own weight. The broken ore is removed from underneath, causing the subsidence and continued caving of the ore body through gravity.[6] Recognizing that extensive reserves of low-grade ore containing one percent copper or less existed in the Butte district, the ACM decided to try mass mining low-grade ore to supplement the expensive vein mining which had previously been the source of most of the copper extracted from Butte.

The Adams trial block caving project began in 1944 to test the concept. For three years, in addition to the Adams block caving work, exploration and development work was performed with traditional underground methods in four of Butte's mines. In three years the ACM was able to obtain information about the tonnage and boundaries of low grade ore that could be profitably exploited by mass mining methods.[7]

Implications for the railroad were immense. If mass mining proved successful, the BA&P would have to increase the amount of ore that it was hauling from Butte to the Washoe Works every day. In 1942 an average of 12,500 tons of ore shipped from Butte daily.

Theoretically, this could increase by fifty percent or more in the next few years. Once the Adams project was under way, however, the war ended and the price of copper dropped. The actual ore tonnage moved by the BA&P from 1944 through 1947 declined, dropping to just under 8,600 tons per day in 1947.[8]

Concluding the Adams block caving test in 1947, the ACM moved to a larger scale of operations, and commenced the Greater Butte Project that year. For five years, that operation continued to develop block caving practices and to conduct exploration work to determine the extent of the low-grade ore that could be mined economically with the new techniques.[9] A central component was the new Kelley Shaft, located in Dublin Gulch, approximately a third of a mile east of the Steward Mine. Unlike most of the earlier shafts, which were timbered to prevent caving, the Kelley Shaft was concrete-lined and much larger than previous shafts in the district. Designed to hoist 15,000 tons of ore per day from 2,000 feet below the surface, the Kelly Shaft promised to increase the volume of ore shipped to Anaconda when it attained maximum daily production. However, the tonnage of ore mined from underground veins declined as the volume of ore mined by block caving increased, so that the total tonnage being shipped to Anaconda remained under 12,500 tons per day through 1950.[10]

Movement of slime to the Anselmo shaft in Butte became an issue at this time.[11] Concern about subsidence of ground after ore was removed had led to the practice of backfilling empty stopes with waste rock. Then it was discovered that slime could be used, and could be pumped into the stope, which was easier than handling waste rock. Slime, or tailings, is the powdered waste rock and water left after the milling and concentrating process. Generally it was of no commercial value, but it had to be disposed of somewhere. For years, slime had been dumped in piles near the various concentrators. A pumping plant was installed at the Anselmo shaft. Slime movement from the Stuart branch line east of Washoe began in 1946, creating a backhaul for some of the cars which would otherwise have returned empty from Anaconda.[12] Cars of slime were spotted over an unloading bin, and emptied into

Subsidence due to block caving. *Silver Bow Public Archives, #210*

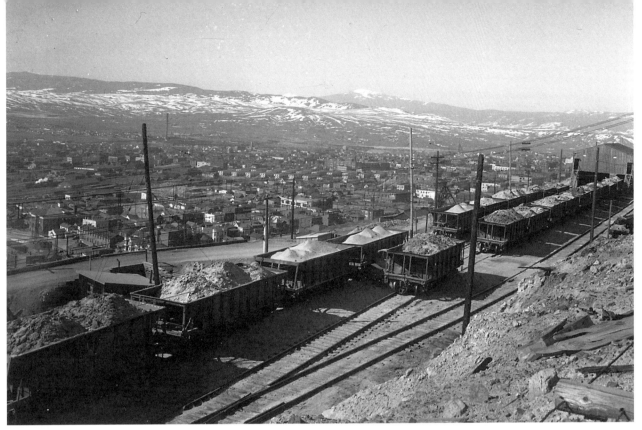

Cars of slime spotted for unloading at the slime plant (far right) at the St. Lawrence Mine. Butte sprawls below it in this view toward the southwest, ca. 1950. *World Museum of Mining, #3187*

the pumping plant. Pipes carried the liquid mixture of water and powdered rock from the pumping plant into the stopes.

Slime movement created its own special problems for the BA&P. Most of the company's cars were ill-suited to the transport of any semi-liquid, fine-ground product. After being thawed by torching a few times, and subjected to banging on the hoppers and sides to loosen any recalcitrant ore, the hopper doors generally did not close tightly enough to avoid leaking fine, sand-sized particles of material. A trickle of powdered rock and water seeping out of the doors would result in a gradual loss of part of the load. Annoying as this might be to the ACM, it caused added expenses to the BA&P. As the cars dripped a mixture of powdered rock and water while moving, some would splatter back onto car trucks, seep into the journals, and damage axles.[13] In addition, leaked slime clogged the ballast on the track. Ballast that has become fouled with sand or cinders does not drain effectively, which in turn accelerates tie decay. It can also cause the roadbed to become saturated with water, which can lead to soft track and possible derailments. As a solution, the railroad had to caulk the hopper

door openings of the slime cars with burlap to keep the contents from leaking. The necessity of checking and adjusting the caulking after the cars were emptied, and again before loading, adding significant labor costs to the process.

The process of slime movement also increased incidence of journal damage due to contamination during the unloading process. Maintenance of the caulking in the hopper doors was the railroad's responsibility, but protecting the journals from spills while

Emptying cars of slime at the St. Lawrence Mine slime plant, ca. 1950. A similar facility was operated at the Anselmo Mine. *World Museum of Mining, #5659*

emptying the car was the duty of the mine crew where the slime was received. A continuing battle between railroaders and mining company personnel ensued. Personnel at slime receiving points were instructed to place protective shields over the car trucks before unloading a car. This added time to their work, and was frequently ignored if no one from the railroad was watching. Train crews complained about hot boxes, and nursed damaged cars to the car shop for repair. Complaints by the railroad would cause some positive change temporarily, but the unloading crews would eventually resort again to not using the shields. Difficulties with hot boxes on cars used to haul slime, consequently, became a recurrent problem.[14]

Probably the most important issue for the railroad in the latter half of the 1940s was the aging of the ore cars and their suitability for continued service. As railroad management sought to upgrade equipment for handling an anticipated increase in ore tonnage, they were concerned about locating the most efficient car for ore service. All of the BA&P's existing cars were an early design of hopper-bottom car, intended to be a general purpose car for ore, coal, limestone or gravel loading. Rated at 50-ton capacity, the BA&P cars were smaller than the 70- and 75-ton cars on other railroads in 1945. BA&P's cars were also battered from hard use and "torching" in the winter. As an experiment, 22 cars were rebuilt by February 1946. The hopper bottom was replaced with a solid, flat floor. Results proved very positive as far as the railroad was concerned, as it cost less to fix damaged cars with flat bottoms than to repair hoppers and hopper doors.[15]

Car design became something of a political matter, with the railroad and the mining company both pushing for favorite ideas. The BA&P favored solid-floor, flat-bottom cars. Because some zinc ore was mined at Butte, the ACM wanted to be able to unload zinc ore from a dump car's hopper doors at separate receiving bins for zinc, instead of at the copper ore receiving bins served by the rotary car dumper.[16] Anaconda

Below: Box cabs Nos. 59 and 69 near the Anselmo Mine. *Photo #92-3229, Philip C. Johnson Collection, K. Ross Toole Archives, University of Montana, Missoula*

The Butte Hill yard. Four motors shuffle loads and empties. The railroad sorted loads and empties here, assembling cuts of loaded cars received from the mine spurs into short trains for Rocker. Trains of empties were broken up, and empty cars spotted on mine spurs for loading. *Photo #92-2976, Philip C. Johnson Collection, K. Ross Toole Archives, University of Montana, Missoula*

Copper Mining Company executives were impressed with the dumping characteristics of Ingoldsby cars in use on copper hauling railroads in Arizona and South America, which they thought might be the answer both for zinc ore and general copper loading.[17] While the mining company executives debated the matter, the railroad's general manager suspended converting any more hoppers to flat-bottomed cars. Though this satisfied protocol, it failed to address the BA&P's concern, which was having enough rebuilt cars on hand to give them a thorough testing in severe winter weather. In October ACM officials were still arguing for Ingoldsby cars, and requesting additional study of the matter.

Winter arrived, and finally, a decision was reached to rebuild one hopper car as an Ingoldsby dump, and road-test it under extreme conditions.[18] On January 8, 1947, the railroad's general manager dutifully informed the vice president of the ACM that the rebuilt

car was ready to be placed in service.[19] Five months later, the BA&P railroaders were satisfied that the Ingoldsby car was a failure, no matter how much the ACM's New York executives believed in its merits. At best, it took as long to empty as the old hoppers, and at worst, twice as long. The bottom of the car was sloped upwards at each end from the flat-floored mid-section of the car, where the doors were, but the slope was not steep enough to cause the ore at the end of the car to discharge of its own weight. In fact, even in ideal weather, the complete load would not empty through the bottom doors without manual assistance. Moreover, zinc ore froze to the car ends, requiring torching and loosening in the winter. In the summer, five tons of wet ore typically stuck to the ends of the car, requiring manual labor to shovel it out. After nine months, the ACM decided to discontinue the Ingoldsby experiment, and it dropped the matter.[20]

Motor 54 leading a train of empties into the Butte Hill Yard. *Photo #92-2978, Philip C. Johnson Collection, K. Ross Toole Archives, University of Montana, Missoula*

As a result of planning for the Greater Butte Project, it became apparent that additional motive power would be needed. Bringing the Kelley Shaft into production for hoisting block-caved ore could theoretically add 15,000 tons of ore per day to the quantity the railroad was expected to move from Butte to Anaconda. In addition to having to handle more ore, the BA&P would need to bring in more limestone from the Browns quarry, and handle larger amounts of slime from the concentrator and slag from the smelter. Neither of the two latter operations was on electrified track and the existing trio of steam locomotives was already worked to capacity. (With three operable steam locomotives, the BA&P could rotate one through the shops for regular repairs, keeping two under steam at any given time.) More motive power was mandatory, but the cost of the new diesel-electrics was prohibitive, and could not reasonably be considered an option. New steam locomotives were still a possibility, but few railroads wanted to invest much money in an obsolete technology.[21] Most of the major railroads began widespread dieselization after 1945, dumping their steam locomotives at bargain prices. Therefore, expecting that an increase in ore traffic from the Kelley Shaft would strain its existing steam power, the BA&P bought a 43-year-old 2-8-0 from the Union Pacific in November 1947.[22]

One of the largest manufacturers of diesel electric locomotives, the Electro-Motive Division of General Motors in La Grange, Illinois (better known to railroaders as EMD) soon cast its eye on the BA&P. The company was founded in the 1920s as the Electro-Motive Corporation, a pioneering firm in the manufacture of gas-electric railroad passenger cars as a replacement for steam passenger trains on branch lines. General Motors purchased Electro-Motive Corporation in 1930, and merged it into the parent company in 1941. After 1945, EMD marketed diesel-electrics so successfully that by 1960 it had become the nation's preeminent manufacturer of such locomotives.[23] One reason for GM's success was a dependable product; another was its highly efficient, hard-working sales force, typified by Corliss A. Bercaw. Based in San Francisco, Bercaw traveled widely, meeting with railroad executives, wining and dining them, and constantly extolling the merits of his product.[24] After departing from a visit to a prospective customer, the salesman adeptly

followed up with letters and telegrams, encouraging the client to think diesel, and think EMD.[25]

Bercaw visited Montana in early 1949, and received a thorough briefing on BA&P operations from Superintendent Frank W. Bellinger. Armed with this information, a team of EMD planners prepared a report for the BA&P, explaining how dieselization could save the railroad money. Proposing to replace steam locomotives with 1,000 hp switch engines, EMD calculated the new motive power would offer a 34 percent return on investment. Hoping to ink a sales contract, Bercaw promised to be in Butte on April 18th.[26] At that time, however, BA&P's general manager, Robert E. Brooks, was out of town, and unavailable to meet with the EMD sales representative.[27]

Upon his return to Anaconda, Brooks found that Superintendent Bellinger had been talking to motive power departments on the NP and GN about diesels. Although he doubted EMD's claim of thirty-four percent savings, Bellinger was eager to obtain a trio of diesel switchers. He was concerned about the fire potential due to steam operation, and complained, "it is not at all certain that our small Machine Shop force can keep four old Steamers operating."[28] Fire was always a possibility with coal-fired steam locomotives, and the labor-intensive nature of steam was one of the reasons EMD could forecast a savings of over 30 percent with diesel use.

How to reduce labor costs related to locomotive maintenance had long been a concern, and the diesel question brought renewed examination of the issue. Conversion of BA&P's remaining steam power to diesel would bring an end to using and maintaining water tanks and ash pits, washing and inspecting the boiler of each steam locomotive on a monthly basis, regular flue replacement in the boilers, and patching leaks in the tender water tanks. It was appealing to consider alleviating the need for a group of skilled craftsmen retained just to repair and adjust the steam-operated appliances on four steam locomotives.

Convincing the BA&P that diesels would save it money, however, did not guarantee that steam was finally being retired. Even though Bellinger was convinced that it was time to dieselize, approval for such a large expenditure had to be obtained from ACM. And ACM was not in the mood to spend any more money on railroad equipment than absolutely necessary. The mining company, as Brooks noted in a letter to Bercaw, repeatedly refused to approve the purchase of new diesels. Reasons given by the ACM were the declining price of copper and the increasing cost of mining in Butte—

Nos. 31 and 32, two of the three ex-UP 2-8-0's at Anaconda, ca. 1950. Diesels had replaced the elderly Consolidations on the UP, and would soon retire them from the BA&P. *Marcus Daly Historical Society of Anaconda, #18519*

partially due to the exploration work conducted as part of the Greater Butte Project.[29]

Consequently, instead of new diesels, the corporation authorized the purchase of two used Baldwin 2-8-0's. Purchased from the UP, one in 1949 and one in 1950,[30] these 2-8-0's were identical to the locomotive bought in 1947, built to the same standard design used by the UP in the early 1900s.[31] While that simplified the matter of parts inventory, there was no doubt that this was a stop-gap measure at best. Nonetheless, the ACM's managing vice president overseeing Montana operations, Ed S. McGlone, was not inclined to buy diesels yet—not until he was certain the cost could be justified. He believed the electrics, which were paid for, would continue to be operable for the foreseeable future. These decisions highlight ACM management's uncertainty about the future direction of its Butte operations.

By 1950 block caving for low-grade copper deposits, which had begun in 1948 as part of the Greater Butte Project, had not proved entirely satisfactory. Consequently, open pit mining was beginning to be considered by ACM. In Utah, Arizona, and Nevada, competitors were open-pit mining low grade copper ore, with railroad haulage from pit to concentrator and smelter. Anaconda was one of several mining companies examining the cost differential between using trucks or railroads in large open pit mines. Kennecott Copper operated open pit mines with rail transport of the ore at Bingham Canyon, Utah, and Ely, Nevada. Phelps-Dodge also used a railroad in its open pit mine at Morenci, Arizona, though some mining companies were becoming more interested in using large trucks, which eliminated the need to shift and extend the track as the pit expanded.[32]

As ACM and BA&P mulled over possible mining techniques and the impact on the railroad during the latter half of 1949, the EMD sales force prepared for another round of persuasive sales calls. On April 27, 1950, the indomitable salesman Bercaw returned to Anaconda with more information about the benefits of completely dieselizing the BA&P.[33] Failing to obtain a sale, EMD sent its eastern representative, P. A. McGee, to talk to the ACM executive vice president, R. E. Dwyer, in New York. There in corporate headquarters, the pressure was intensified, as McGee not only reemphasized that new diesels would save ACM money over the cost of electric operation, but pointedly remarked that GM was a major purchaser of copper. Not intimidated, Dwyer countered with McGlone's argument: because the motors were paid for, it would be difficult to cut operating costs below the cost of running the electrics.

Ultimately, however, Dwyer conceded to McGee that the decision was really McGlone's, as vice president over Montana operations. McGee then wrote Bercaw on June 18th: "My recommendation would be that you get Mr. McGlone to recommend the purchase of the equipment," implying that EMD was not ready to give up on the sale yet. Another visit by Bercaw was scheduled to influence BA&P management, and perhaps to apply more pressure on the ACM's McGlone.[34]

While Bercaw visited the BA&P in July 1950, he took the BA&P's general manager and superintendent to dinner, as well as meeting with McGlone and the ACM's resident mechanical engineer, R.J. Kennard. Bercaw kept hoping to convince the BA&P to trade in its nearly forty-year-old electrics for new diesels. How-

ever, McGlone, still unconvinced about diesel economy, wanted a second opinion. He directed Kennard to contact General Electric for a review of EMD's calculations, because GE possessed statistics comparing diesel and electric operating costs compiled by the Chicago, Milwaukee, St. Paul & Pacific (formerly the CM&StP). The information provided by GE indicated that it cost the Milwaukee $0.015 less per mile to run electrics than new diesel-electrics.[35] When McGlone heard GE's reply, he was satisfied with the decision that the BA&P had no need for diesels on its main line. After forwarding the information to ACM's chairman of the board,[36] McGlone's decision was accepted by the corporate office.

A few years later, the hardworking Bercaw finally got a sale—disappointingly, of only two diesels to replace branch-line steam power, rather than the twenty or more he had hoped for to replace the electrics. Two new, 1,500-hp GP-7 diesel electrics were delivered to the BA&P in 1952.

With the arrival of the diesel-electrics, the BA&P began to move back into the mainstream of common railroad practice. Steam exited swiftly on the BA&P, as on most of the nation's railroads. The railroad had planned to retain at least one steam locomotive for standby service until a third diesel unit could be obtained.[37] However, maintaining even one steam locomotive for standby service proved to be more expensive than anticipated. All of the steam locomotives were worn out, and even the one in the best mechanical

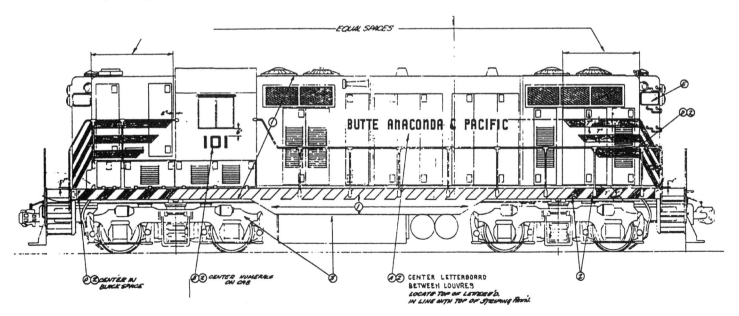

Diagram of an EMD GP-7 Diesel-electric locomotive (side elevation only, not reproduced to original scale). *BA&P Records, "Administrative—Locomotives—Diesel," 4-3-A, Butte-Silver Bow Public Archives*

condition required new flues and other expensive boiler work. After a year of diesel operations on the BA&P, General Manager Brooks was able to convince the ACM that a third GP-7 was a better investment than refueling a forty-year-old steam locomotive. Once the new diesel arrived in the summer of 1953, the remaining steam locomotives were scrapped.[38]

Diesel operations were initially restricted to the non-electrified lines around Anaconda, serving the slime ponds and the limestone quarry at Browns. Although the electrics were still performing main-line duties and switching the electrified trackage on the Butte Hill, there were reasons to reevaluate EMD's proposal to dieselize the entire railroad. While the BA&P had concluded electrics were less expensive to operate than either diesel or steam locomotives, the calculations had been made in light of existing operations. For any extension of electric operation, the cost of constructing the catenary had to be considered. Railways like the BA&P, the Great Northern, and the Milwaukee all faced new questions: Why should any railroad operate both electric and diesel motive power? Was the expense of extending electrification over more mileage justified? An additional component in the question for the BA&P was the considerable age of its fleet of electrics.

Extension of electrification was part of the overall consideration regarding open pit mining. As ACM planning focused on doubling the tonnage mined at Butte, BA&P planning addressed two issues: possible use of rail equipment in the Berkeley Pit, and the logistics of handling twice the previous maximum daily tonnage based on the projections that the Berkeley Pit would produce 12,000 tons of ore daily. Open-pit copper mining had historically been conducted using railroad equipment, but during the war some small open pit mines had been developed that used motor trucks because railroad supplies were difficult to obtain at that time.[39] The idea originated with west coast loggers, who used trucks to solve similar problems in the 1920s.[40] Although railroads could haul larger loads at a time, they cost more than trucks to install and maintain. In a short haul, such as the Berkeley Pit, the transfer from truck to rail might arguably be more economical than the cost of constantly moving track.

ACM spent from 1952–54 comparing the costs of rail and truck operation in the Berkeley Pit. Finally the company concluded that the flexibility of trucks and the savings from not moving track in the pit outweighed the convenience of loading ore directly into cars within the pit.[41] A one-mile extension from the BA&P's spur connecting to the Northern Pacific was built to loading bins at the edge of the Berkeley Pit in 1955 as part of the development work at the new mine. Off-road dump trucks moved ore from the pit to the loading bins, where the BA&P's cars were loaded for the trip to the smelter. The first car-load of ore from the Berkeley Pit was shipped to the Washoe Works in July, 1955. A year later, an average of 12,500 tons of ore per day moved to the smelter over the BA&P.[42]

While ACM executives assessed the feasibility of open pit mining at Butte, a study of the carrying capacity of the BA&P was occurring. The new pit mining methods under consideration would at least double the amount of ore sent to the Anaconda smelter. In late 1951 or early 1952, William E. Mitchell, the ACM's reduction (milling) department manager, contacted Bellinger, who had been promoted to BA&P general manager, asking how the BA&P would propose to handle 30,000 tons of ore daily.[43] Concerns addressed included the cycling time for cars and the possibility of using conveyor belts as a replacement for part of the rail haul.

Cycling is the time that it takes an empty car to be loaded, moved to the smelter, emptied, returned to Butte, and spotted at an ore bin for loading. Historically, the mines loaded only during the day shift, so the railroad was forced to move more cars to the smelter than would actually be emptied in an eight-hour shift, because the smelter needed to be employed around the clock. In the winter, the ore froze in the cars if it sat for more than eight to ten hours. Torching the cars to thaw the ore allowed it to be dumped, but at great damage to the cars. From the BA&P's perspective, an operating plan that cycled cars every eight hours instead of 16–24 hours was highly desirable.

Areas of inefficiency came under scrutiny at this time. Cuts of 25 cars at a time had to be made to move them from the East Anaconda yard over the Smelter Hill branch to be dumped at the concentrator tipple seven miles away. One solution proposed was to install a conveyor belt from a new rotary car dumping tipple in the East Anaconda yard to allow the cars to be unloaded there, eliminating the additional seven-mile journey. Such an improvement would require the railroad to spend $407,000 for equipment and track improvements; the cost of the tipple and conveyor belt would be the ACM's responsibility.[44]

Ore could be delivered to the concentrator more efficiently by expanding the yards at the concentrator, and double-tracking the Smelter Hill branch to allow more trains to operate on it. Bellinger initially

Nos. 53 and 39 bringing loads down Missoula Gulch to Rocker. The view is toward the northeast, with Orphan Girl Mine in the upper right, May 24, 1961. *Photo #92-2980, Philip C. Johnson Collection, K. Ross Toole Archives, University of Montana, Missoula*

estimated this would cost $845,000.[45] Another solution proposed was for the railroad to purchase new flat-bottom, 100-ton capacity ore cars, which would double the capacity of the cars in service.[46]

Basing his figures on use of existing fifty-ton capacity cars, Trainmaster A. A. Holland wrote Bellinger that an estimated eighteen trains a day would have to operate over the main line, nine in each direction, to handle 30,000 tons of ore daily. Seven ore trains would originate in Rocker, and two in Butte.[47]

After conducting further study, Bellinger was able to convince ACM that a new tipple at East Anaconda with a conveyor belt to the concentrator would save over $2,700,000.[48] Authorization to begin work on the conveyer was received from New York, and Bellinger was directed to make the necessary track changes to accommodate the new car dumper to be built by the mining company late in the year.[49] Although the mining company would not approve the acquisition of 100-ton ore cars, the new tipple and conveyor at East Anaconda would accelerate the unloading process enough

to allow the BA&P to handle the projected 30,000 tons of ore a day.

By September 1952, BA&P operating officials were formulating plans for switching crews to work around the clock to serve the mines and smelter, and planned to install three shifts of road crews to keep ore moving day and night in order to cycle cars in eight hours.[50]

The Butte, Anaconda & Pacific still maintained its legal status as a common carrier. As a common carrier, the short line was required by law to provide service to any and all members of the public who presented freight to carry, or sought transportation for themselves. Common carriers were highly regulated. State and federal regulatory agencies determined not only when common carrier railroads could provide new services, but how much they could charge for them. They also governed when service could be suspended. A way for ACM to avoid such regulation would be to get the BA&P officially removed from common carrier status.

Then, it could function as an industrial railroad, able to eliminate all business not directly related to carrying ore and local switching at the smelter. Ending the railroad's common carrier status would also terminate the need for extensive record-keeping as mandated by the ICC, plus mandatory compliance with ICC safety and interchange regulations.[51]

As ore traffic grew during the 1950s, passenger business dwindled. The combination car at the end of the four scheduled ore trains carried an average of one paying passenger a day most years from 1946 until the end of service in spring 1955.[52] Montana residents, like most Americans, had grown used to the convenience of automobile ownership. Mixed train service was a relic from a half-century before. The movement of the combination car not only cost money, it delayed the more important business of moving the ACM's ore. Therefore, the railroad applied to discontinue passenger service, a move which was readily approved by the Montana State Public Utility Commission. The mixed train was discontinued in 1955, and the BA&P was limited to carrying freight only—well ahead of its larger

neighbors, some of which continued to provide passenger service to Butte until the creation of Amtrak in 1971.

Though passenger traffic had always figured as an afterthought for the BA&P, local freight business had served a significant role from the 1890s until the 1950s. However, just as passenger business became a casualty of the automobile, the small-volume freight business was also vulnerable to motor transport competition. Much of the business was less-than-carload lots (lcl), which were more conveniently moved by truck than by rail, especially for short distances. Small freight shipments from Butte to Anaconda were easy pickings for trucks, as independent owner-operators could easily price their services lower than the railroad, which had to obtain approval for its tariffs from the Interstate Commerce Commission.

Although railroads were encountering increasing competition from trucks, cars, and aviation, the industry remained one of the most heavily regulated in the nation. In the 1950s they could not set their own rates and could not institute or suspend service of their

The beginning and end of an era. On the left, the crew of Motor No. 60 poses with the new electric soon after it was delivered by GE. On the right, the crew of No. 66 poses for the last passenger run at Butte, April 15, 1955. *Marcus Daly Historical Society of Anaconda, #18501*

own volition; for this they relied on the Interstate Commerce Commission (ICC). Federal regulation of the industry had its roots in the wretched excesses of the Gilded Age, and since its creation, the ICC had systematically increased the scope of its regulatory policies. The BA&P was simply one small section of a national transportation system whose rates were regulated for the public benefit by the commission. By the 1950s, however, the BA&P was much more concerned about moving the freight of its owner than the tiny amount of business offered it by the general public.

Therefore, abandonment of common carrier status was given serious consideration during the late 1950s. Converting the railroad from a common carrier to an industrial plant operation was investigated by the Anaconda Mining Company's Office of General Council. Revenue and expense figures for a five-year period starting in 1953 were gathered by the BA&P's office staff, and forwarded to the ACM legal office in the spring of 1958.[53] No further action was taken, however, so the BA&P remained a common carrier, even though the revenue generated by local freight service to non-ACM shippers accounted for only three-tenths of one percent of the total business in the year 1957.[54] The share of revenue from freight received from other railroads for freight shipped to or received by the ACM netted more than $1,224,000 of income, which would have been lost if the BA&P operated as an industrial railroad for the ACM.[55]

Increased ore loading from the new Berkeley Pit more than offset the gradual decline of ore being mined by the underground methods at Butte. In response to the issues raised by Bercaw and EMD, the BA&P evaluated the cost of dieselization compared with several degrees of modernization of the existing electric operation on the main line to permit the railroad to handle up to 50,000 tons of ore per day. General Manager Bellinger concluded that the least expensive option was to increase use of diesels, while retaining the electrics for as much of the work as they could handle. Bellinger estimated the purchase of five more GP-9's from EMD at a total cost of $891,760 would provide sufficient additional motive power to move up to 40,000 tons of ore per day by 1957.[56] Improvements to handle the increased tonnage with electrics alone would cost $1,789,000. This included the purchase of five new electrics and two additional substations.

General Electric had recommended rebuilding the existing 28 electrics, but Bellinger argued that he saw little point in spending $2,000,000 to rebuild the 43-year-old units, since that would raise the total cost of updating the electric operation of the railroad to nearly $4,000,000. Total dieselization, recommended by EMD, was rejected for reasons of cost, which was estimated to be $2,874,000.[57] A very conservative plan for new railroad equipment was developed in 1956, to retain the existing electric operation as long as possible. Improvements ultimately authorized included new locomotives and ore cars, and an electric substation, all placed in service in 1957.

The newest electrics, Nos. 202 and 201, pulling a train of ore with Nos. 57 and 39 at Rocker on June 22, 1960. *Photo #92-2817, Philip C. Johnson Collection, K. Ross Toole Archives, University of Montana, Missoula*

A westbound ore train pulled by electrics meets eastbound empties pulled by a pair of diesel-electrics at Durant on July 29, 1960. The empties are 75-ton flat-bottom cars built by Pullman-Standard in 1957. *Photo #92-2840, Philip C. Johnson Collection, K. Ross Toole Archives, University of Montana, Missoula*

Two new electric locomotives and the substation were ordered from GE. Shipped in July, 1957, the pair of 2,480 hp, 125-ton units had been specially designed for the BA&P. Initial discussions with GE in 1956 had started from the premise of building 2,400 volt versions of the units GE had recently built for Kennecott's main line operations between the Bingham Pit and the smelter.[58] However, Bellinger had decided that Kennecott's units were not suitable for conditions on the BA&P, and GE had to custom design a pair of units, which added $19,000 to the cost.[59] The new GE-built substation was installed at Dawson, near the mid-point of the main line, boosting the power available to match the increased electrical load when all of the electric units were in operation.[60]

Four new GP-9 diesels, improved and slightly more powerful versions of the GP-7 units the BA&P had bought originally, were ordered from EMD. Designed to run in multiple with other diesels, the 1,750 hp GP-9's could be used with each other or the GP-7's on the main line when needed. However, the diesels and the electrics were not equipped to run in multiple together, so mixing the two types of motive power was not possible unless two crews were employed, one for each type of motive power.[61]

Two hundred new, flat-bottomed, 75-ton capacity ore cars were ordered from Pullman-Standard in 1956.[62] These were state-of-the art freight cars, equipped with roller-bearing axles instead of the conventional brass journal bearings lubricated by oil-soaked cotton waste. Roller bearings were becoming more widely accepted, having been used under some of the early streamlined passenger trains in the 1930s. Although progressive railroads were beginning to order roller-bearing equipped freight cars, much of the nation's freight car fleet in 1957 still rested on the conventional journals.

New equipment purchases were only part of the strategy for moving 40,000 tons of ore per day. With their slow-speed gearing, the original electrics could not move trains as fast as the diesel-electrics. Negotiations with the Northern Pacific Railway in 1956 resulted in an agreement reached in January, 1957, to allow BA&P diesel-hauled freights to use the NP main line between Butte and Durant. For use of this section of the NP, the BA&P paid $2.30 per car. By careful dispatching, this strategy enabled the BA&P to move faster, diesel-powered ore trains between Durant and East Anaconda without encountering delays from the slower-moving electrics.[63]

Ore movement increased dramatically after 1956, as all elements required to process an average of 40,000 tons of ore per day were now in place. The time-consuming Smelter Hill operation had been eliminated by the new unloading tipple at East Anaconda feeding a conveyor belt to the mill and smelter. Cars were being cycled more rapidly than had been possible when the old unloading tipple at the concentrator had been in use. New cars and locomotives gave the BA&P additional carrying capacity. Operation of diesel-hauled trains over the NP further added to the carrying capacity of the railroad, so that by 1958 an average of over 30,000 tons of ore per day was being carried.[64]

Modernizing mining methods enabled the Anaconda Copper Mining Company to work low-grade ore deposits at Butte economically. However, the cost of transporting 30,000 tons of low-grade ore to Anaconda each day was a significant expense. Furthermore, the concentrator at the Washoe Works, though upgraded and modernized from its original 5,000-ton-per-day capacity, was now functioning at its maximum limit. The concentrator, which had been designed to handle higher grade ore using an alkaline flotation process, was not well suited for processing the low-grade copper sulfide ore from the Berkeley Pit. Efforts to treat 50,000 tons per day were impossible without major modernization and expansion, or a new concentrator. In the early 1960s, ACM studied the feasibility of upgrading the Washoe Works concentrator to handle ore from the Berkeley Pit, but chose instead to build a new

Diesel-electric units with Butte-bound empties at Durant on March 20, 1959. The connection to the Northern Pacific, visible at the upper right, allowed diesel-powered BA&P trains to use the NP from Durant to Butte. *Photo #92-2758, Philip C. Johnson Collection, K. Ross Toole Archives, University of Montana, Missoula*

concentrator at the mine, and thereby also reduce transportation costs.[65]

Originally, the Anaconda location had been chosen for Daly's copper smelter because of its nearby abundance of water, a resource which was not available in Butte. As ACM considered revamping the Washoe works concentrator to enable it to handle greater quantities of low-grade ore, the company had water needs in mind. But a cost study indicated that it would be less expensive to bring water to Butte than to move the ore to Anaconda. Therefore, a 34-inch diameter pipe was constructed to carry water from Anaconda to the new concentrator in Butte, by means of an intermediate pumping station at the low point of the pipe line.[66] Work on the Weed Concentrator (named for ACM official Clyde Weed) began in late 1961, and was completed in May 1963.[67] Designed to mill 50,000 tons of ore per day, the Weed Concentrator was located at the eastern edge of Butte, near the site of the former suburb of Meaderville.[68] Once the Weed Concentrator began functioning, BA&P's load to Washoe Works diminished, consisting of a much smaller tonnage of ore concentrates.

Because new rolling stock was needed for concentrate service, 20 new covered hoppers from the Shipper's Car division of American Car & Foundry (ACF) were purchased in 1963. This was state-of-the-art equipment, boasting a new "center flow" design for carrying all manner of bulk commodities requiring protection from weather and contamination. Each car consisted of three compartments and could carry 100 tons. Because of the density of copper concentrates, normal operating procedure involved filling two compartments with 50 tons each of concentrate, leaving one compartment empty to avoid exceeding the load limit of the car.[69] After these cars proved successful, another fifteen cars were obtained, giving the railroad thirty-five cars for concentrate service between Butte and the Washoe Works.[70] These changes signaled the end of BA&P's busi-

Three American Car & Foundry "center-flow" covered hoppers used for hauling concentrates from the Weed Concentrator to the Washoe Works at the Anaconda Yard, ca. 1964. *World Museum of Mining, #5096*

est years. The railroad continued to haul ore to Anaconda from underground mining, but the amount diminished appreciably after 1965.[71]

Shortly after the installation of the Weed Concentrator, effective June 8, 1964, the BA&P ended less-than-carload freight service by filing official notice to the public 30 days before discontinuing the service.[72] This move reflected the increased significance of trucks for short-haul transport. Other changes were also under way. Surplus equipment was disposed of, much of it slowly because it was obsolete and ineligible for use in interstate commerce; some of it, unsold, was still on the property fifteen years later, when the ACM closed its namesake operations in Montana.

Total dieselization of the BA&P, long sought by EMD, became a reality in 1967. The railroad ceased electric operation after it became evident that the aging box cabs and catenary maintenance were costing more than diesel operation would. Per mile operating and maintenance costs in 1964 for the electrics were $1.40 per mile, compared to $1.45 per mile for the diesel-electrics. However, the following year the figures were markedly different: the diesels cost $1.48 per mile to operate, while operating costs for the electrics had soared to $1.93 per mile.[73] The cost differential favored diesels consistently for the next year and a half. After 1965, with the volume of ore greatly reduced, the number of units required dropped so drastically that it was possible to store the newest electrics, which never turned a wheel in revenue service after the end of 1965.[74] In 1966 use of the aged electrics further diminished, as most of the freight was hauled behind the diesels. Before the electrics were taken out of service in mid-1967, they were accounting for a third of the locomotive miles, and were costing $.34 per mile more to operate than diesels.[75]

Fifty-three years of electric operation ended quietly. White coal had displaced coal-fired steam power in 1914, and in turn, hydro-generated electricity gave way to petroleum in the 1960s. After a year in storage, the electrics were all put up for sale, and the trolley wire was sold to the ACM in December 1968. Arrangements to salvage the copper were concluded, and the work completed in the summer of 1969, netting the BA&P nearly $250,000 from the scrap copper.[76] The electric locomotives remained in storage, pending sale, until 1973, when one was donated to the World Museum of Mining in Butte, and another 27 were sold for scrap. The newest electrics remained, while the company tried to find buyers for them. Finally they also were written off and junked in 1976.[77]

⚒

The end of electric freight operation on the BA&P was consistent with the universal trend away from electric freight operation by mainline railroads after 1950. The Great Northern concluded that it was more economical to install ventilating fans in the Cascade Tunnel and run diesels through it than to continue electric operation. Consequently, the GN went diesel in 1956.[78] Though the GN shared its 1956 study with the BA&P, the BA&P concluded that it would not realize savings by immediate dieselization.[79] On the neighboring Milwaukee, electrification was abandoned piecemeal. The electrified trackage in Washington State was converted to exclusively diesel-electric operation in 1971, and the Montana and Idaho section in 1974.[80] In both cases, the electrics were efficient, but limited to use only on lines under catenary. The diesels could run anywhere on the entire system, and could run from Chicago to Tacoma or Seattle without being uncoupled from the train. This versatility, coupled with low fuel costs for most of the century, gave diesel-electrics the ultimate edge over the conventional electric, which required an expensive power distribution system. For major railroads, electrification was simply not competitive with diesels.

In the late 1960s the ACM made plans to add a new crusher at the Weed Concentrator. This required the re-location of part of the Northern Pacific main line to the south of the concentrator. During 1969 arrangements were made by the mining company for the construction of a new line for the NP, which the ACM would then deed to that railroad. The contract specified that ACM would grade the roadbed and BA&P would lay the track. As part of the project, new spurs into the concentrator were built for the BA&P, with similar labor arrangements.[81]

Through the late 1960s and early 1970s, the tonnage of ore shipped over the BA&P declined. It increased beginning in November 1973 and remained strong through 1974.[82] Though ore loading exceeded

5 million tons, all other categories of freight, including copper concentrates for the smelter, were less than anticipated. Inflation, driven largely by the Organization of Petroleum Exporting Countries' (OPEC) oil embargo, hit the ACM and the railroad hard. The price of diesel fuel more than doubled between August 1973 and December 1974.[83] Though operating revenue was greater than the previous year, operating expenses had mushroomed, and the BA&P posted a net loss of over $57,000 for 1974.[84] Red ink flowed more freely the following year, and the railroad showed a loss of over $619,000 for 1975.[85]

Problems for the railroad were compounded by the difficulties the ACM was encountering. Mining costs were increasing in the United States, and the Montana operations were under pressure to comply with new, stricter pollution controls. Anaconda mines in Chile were nationalized by the government of Salvador Allende in 1970, eliminating some of the more profitable property from the company portfolio. Labor costs continued to climb, but copper prices were not climbing with them. Efforts to market the Butte mines in the early 1970s were unsuccessful, until the ACM itself became the target of a corporate take-over. In 1976 the Atlantic Richfield Corporation (ARCO) began its bid to acquire Anaconda, which was consummated in 1977.[86]

While ACM was attempting to find a corporate white knight to effect a financial rescue of its aging Montana operations, the BA&P rolled along as a modestly profitable short line, adjusting its services to meet the needs of its primary customer. Butte shipped its last carload of ore from underground mines to the Washoe Works in 1975, but copper concentrates continued to move to the smelter for another five years.[87] From 1976 through 1980, the BA&P remained modestly profitable, and made efforts to improve the rolling stock and physical plant while living within the spending limits imposed by its parent company. John W. Greene, the BA&P's superintendent of transportation, created a five-year capital plan in 1978, calling for the purchase of fifty new hoppers, forty flat cars, ten slurry cars, and two locomotives. He was still promoting the plan in 1980, but the project was dropped when ARCO bought ACM.[88]

Atlantic Richfield recognized that the long-term costs of making the ACM's Montana properties comply with new environmental regulations would be substantial. The Washoe Works was obsolete. The railroad connecting the mines to the smelter was gradually modernizing, but much remained to be done. Although the mineral reserves at Butte were considerable,

ARCO chose to shut down operations rather than risk becoming entangled in a protracted and expensive effort to make smelter and refinery operations comply with new environmental regulations.[89] Anaconda's Washoe Works was closed first, followed by the electrolytic refineries at Great Falls.[90] Finally, in 1982, the Berkeley Pit was closed and the pumps draining the pit's bottom were shut down. After the Washoe Works ceased operations, ARCO began dismantling the smelter and commenced environmental clean-up work at the site.

Closure of the mines and the smelter did not, however, mean an immediate end for the BA&P. Dismantling the smelter and environmental remediation required the movement of machinery and scrap out of the smelter site. Trains continued to run after the smelter closed, although seemingly on borrowed time. Scrapping the smelter logically should have resulted in the demise of the BA&P as the final act of the cleanup. Unlike most short lines owned by their major client, however, the BA&P survived the demise of its parent, albeit with a new identity. In May 1985 the Butte, Anaconda & Pacific was sold to local investors, beginning a new life as the Rarus Railway.[91]

Short lines often have a precarious existence attempting to attract business, but the Rarus was blessed with good fortune when the Berkeley Pit and the Weed Concentrator were sold to a new owner in 1986. Montana Resources, owned by Dennis Washington, acquired the Butte mining properties from ARCO, and resumed mining just east of the original Berkeley Pit, in the Continental Pit. With its connection to the Weed Concentrator, the Rarus Railway is a vital link in the transportation of Butte copper to market. Copper concentrates bound for smelting overseas begin their journey out of Butte over the rails formerly belonging to Marcus Daly's copper short line, now connected to the Burlington Northern-Santa Fe and the Union Pacific systems. The mine is currently (2002) in a maintained, mothballed status waiting for favorable economic conditions.

NOTES

1. John F. Stover, *American Railroads* (Chicago: University of Chicago Press, 1997), pp. 213–14.

2. Wright, *Locomotive Builder's Cyclopedia,* 1930, pp. 1065–68.

3. Jerry A. Pinkepank. *The Second Diesel Spotter's Guide.* (Milwaukee, Wisconsin: Kalmbach Publishing Co., 1973.), p. 25.

4. In mining terminology, shafts are vertical openings descending into the ground from the surface. Fay, p. 606. Drifts are horizontal passages driven underground. Fay, p. 231.

5. Shovers, et al., p. 13.

6. Block caving was first used for copper mining by the Inspiration Consolidated Copper Co. at Miami, Arizona in 1914. This is covered in an article by Alfred C. Stoddard, "History and Development of Block Caving at the Mines of the Inspiration Consolidated Copper Co.," *Transactions of the American Association of Mining Engineers,* Volume 163 (1945), pp. 96–120; and Shovers et al., p. 13.

7. Richard N. Miller, "Production History of the Butte District and Geological Function, Past and Present," in *Guidebook for the Butte Field Meeting of the Society of Economic Geologists, Butte, Montana August 18–21, 1978.* (n.p., n.d.), p. F-5.

8. BA&P Records, "Tonnage and Revenue Reports," 1943–47.

9. Miller, "Production History", p. F-5.

10. BA&P Records, "Tonnage and Revenue Reports," 1944–52; Miller, "Production History", pp. F-5–7.

11. Slime is the wet, crushed rock created by milling. Slime is the generally accepted term; however, much of the correspondence in the BA&P files uses the term "slum." This is especially evident in memoranda relating to the disposal areas around Anaconda. Both spellings are accepted as correct usage. Correspondence regarding slime disposal in Butte uses the more common spelling, i.e. "slime plant." See definitions in Fay, pp. 623, 626.

12. BA&P Records, "Tonnage and Revenue Reports," 1946.

13. White, *Freight Car*, pp. 483–87. White notes the conventional freight car journal, which remained virtually unchanged for over a century, was prone to damage from dirt contamination. Today, roller bearing axles, with the bearing surfaces of the axle secure in a sealed, lubricated bath, have eliminated most of the problems associated with the old cotton-waste lubricated brass journal.

14. Hot box is the railroad term for an overheated journal. Dirt or any kind of contaminant in the journal would score the bearing surface, leading to imperfect lubrication, followed by overheating, and a telling cloud of smoke issuing from the overheated journal box when it became hot enough to cause the oil and cotton waste to burn. Too much heat could break an axle, resulting in a wreck. White, *Freight Car*, pp. 483–87.

15. BA&P Records, Administrative Correspondence, "Cars–Flat Bottom," I-3-4-A, Memorandum of February 15, 1946.

16. Ibid., ACM Memorandum, cc to BA&P, October 15, 1946. I-3-4-A. A memorandum dated July 31, 1947 specifically references ACM's New York office wanting to try Ingoldsby cars. Zinc ore was shipped primarily from the Anselmo mine in Butte. Richard N. Miller, "Production History," p. F-4.

17. BA&P Records, Administrative Correspondence, "Cars, Flat Bottom," ACM Memorandum, cc to BA&P, July 31, 1947. I-3-4-A. Possibly the writer meant to include Mexico, as Ingoldsby pattern cars were in use on the Chihuahua Mineral Railway at Santa Eulalia, Chihuahua, and at Cananea, Sonora.

18. BA&P Records, Administrative Correspondence, "Cars, Flat Bottom," ACM Memorandum, cc to BA&P, October 5, 1946. I-3-4-A.

19. Ibid., January 9, 1947. I-3-4-A.

20. Ibid., ACM to BA&P, July 16, 1947, July 31, 1947, May 14, 1948. I-3-4-A.

21. *Railway Age* produced an annual review of new equipment purchases during these years. These show that virtually all U.S. railroads ceased ordering new steam locomotives by 1944, and that most locomotive orders after 1945 were for diesel-electrics.

22. BA&P Records, "Steam Locomotives," Roster. [n.d.]

23. Pinkepank, p. 25.

24. BA&P Records, Administrative Correspondence, "Locomotives, Diesel," C. A. Bercaw (EMD Regional Manager) to R. E. Brooks (BA&P General Manager) July 17, 1950. 4-3-A. The EMD correspondence regularly refers to visiting Butte, although the general offices of the BA&P were always located at West 300 Commercial Street, in Anaconda. The building is, as of 1999, the office for the Rarus Railway.

25. BA&P Records, Administrative Correspondence, "Locomotives, Diesel." The file contains correspondence, and telegrams between Bercaw and Robert E. Brooks, BA&P General Manager regarding dieselizing the BA&P. 4-3-A.

26. Ibid., C. A. Bercaw to R. E. Brooks, April 5, 1949. 4-3-A.

27. Ibid., Telegram, L. V. Kelly (Chief Clerk) to C. A. Bercaw, April 8, 1949. 4-3-A.

28. Ibid., Memorandum, Bellinger to Brooks, April 26, 1949. 4-3-A.

29. Ibid., Brooks to Bercaw, May 10, 1949. 4-3-A.

30. BA&P Records, "Steam Locomotives," Roster.

31. Union Pacific Railroad Company, "Locomotive Diagram Sheet No. L-3-15, Locomotives No. 560–622," issued October 5, 1945.

32. BA&P Records, Administrative Correspondence, "Locomotives, Diesel," 4-3-A. Walter C. Lawson, "Laying Panel Track at the Morenci Pit," American Institute of Mining Engineers *Transactions*, Volume 181 (1949), pp. 159–71.

33. BA&P Records, Administrative Correspondence, "Locomotives, Diesel," E. S. McGlone to R. E. Brooks, July 6, 1950. 4-3-A.

34. Ibid., P. A. McGee (EMD Eastern Sales Representative) to C. A. Bercaw, June 8, 1950. How the BA&P came into custody of a copy of McGee's report to Bercaw is not indicated in the records. Clearly it was before Bercaw's July 17, 1950, visit, as indicated by an exchange of letters between McGlone and Brooks a week earlier. 4-3-A.

35. Ibid., W. H. Mott (General Electric Co.) to R. J. Kennard, August 3, 1950. 4-3-A.

36. Ibid., E. S. McGlone to C. F. Kelly (Chairman of the Board, Anaconda Copper Mining Co.), September 20, 1950. 4-3-A.

37. BA&P Records, Administrative Correspondence, "Locomotives, Steam," Memorandum, F. W. Bellinger to W. F. Conroy (BA&P superintendent), April 13, 1953. 4-3-A.

38. Ibid., Memorandum, F. W. Bellinger to W. F. Conroy, May 4, 1953. 4-3-A.

39. Navin, p. 39.

40. [unsigned article] "Plans For Motor Truck Logging," *Timberman*, Volume 22:9 (July, 1921), pp. 97, 100. The *Timberman* was a trade journal for the west-coast logging industry. Railroad logging has been largely ignored by academic historians, although an extensive literature on the subject exists in the enthusiast press. An extremely thorough overview of the use of railroad technology for logging in the province of British Columbia is: Robert D. Turner, *Logging By Rail: The British Columbia Story* (Victoria: Sono Nis Press, 1990).

41. Miller, "Production History," p. F-6

42. Miller, "Production History," p. F-6.

43. BA&P Records, Administrative Correspondence, "East Anaconda Tipple, " Bellinger to Mitchell, January 14, 1952, I-5-4.

44. Ibid., Bellinger to Mitchell, March 20, 1952, I-5-4.

45. Ibid., Bellinger to Mitchell, January 14, 1952, I-5-4.

46. Ibid., A. A. Holland [BA&P Trainmaster] to F. W. Bellinger, March 1, 1952, I-5-4.

47. Ibid., A. A. Holland [BA&P Trainmaster] to F. W. Bellinger, March 7, 1952, I-5-4.

48. Ibid., F. W. Bellinger to W. E. Mitchell, June 4, 1952, I-5-4.

49. Ibid., C. H. Steele (ACM Vice President) to F. W. Bellinger, December 22, 1952, I-5-4.

50. Ibid., A. A. Holland [BA&P Trainmaster] to F. W. Bellinger, September 25, 1952, I-5-4.

51. The ACM was not alone in facing the challenges of modernizing its transportation and mining after World War II. One of its competitors, Kennecott Copper, faced identical problems with ore transportation at its Bingham, Utah, operations. Rail haulage in the open pit had been a given from the start of operations. Kennecott's subsidiary, the Utah Copper company, operated its own railroad within the pit, then turned the cars over to a Kennecott-owned subsidiary, the Bingham & Garfield (B&G) for the 20-mile haul to the mill and smelter. Just like the BA&P, the B&G had been built by the mining company because it was dissatisfied with the service received from main line railroads. Although the B&G handled very little freight except ore and company supplies, the road had been incorporated as a common carrier, and therefore was required to provide freight service to all shippers who offered business. Steam-operated from its inception, the B&G relied on a group of 0-8-8-0 Mallet articulateds for the ore trains, and smaller motive power for switching and local freight business. (ICC Records, Bureau of Valuation, "Valuation of Bingham and Garfield"; ICC "Valuation Docket 257," *ICC Reports*, p. 450.)

Kennecott arranged to abandon the B&G on August 1, 1948, eliminating the problems of common carrier operation. (ICC, *Statistics of Railways of the United States, 1948*, [Washington, D.C.: GPO, 1950], p. 584.) A new line parallel to the B&G was constructed and electrified at 3,000 volts DC, giving Kennecott a new, high-capacity industrial railroad in place of the steam-operated common carrier. Only involving a twenty-mile distance, the cost of hanging the catenary and operating a 3,000-volt DC electric railroad was deemed acceptable by Kennecott.

52. BA&P Records, "Tonnage and Revenue Reports," 1946–1952; Quarterly Reports, 1945–1955; Montana State Railroad Commission Annual Report of the BA&P, 1946–55.

53. Ibid., W. M. Kirkpatrick, Western General Counsel's Office, the Anaconda Company, to W. F. Conroy, BA&P General Manager, May 20, 1958.

54. Ibid., Memorandum, "Local Freight, 1957."

55. Ibid., Memorandum, "Local Freight, 1957."

56. BA&P Records, Administrative Correspondence, "Diesel Study," F. W. Bellinger, Memorandum of April 26, 1956. 4-3-A.

57. Ibid., F. W. Bellinger, Memorandum of April 26, 1956. 4-3-A.

58. BA&P Records, Administrative Correspondence, "Locomotives—New Electrics," General Electric Co. to BA&P, Proposal for 125 Ton, 2,400 volt DC Electric Locomotives," April 9, 1956. I-4-3-A

59. Ibid., F. W. Bellinger to Thomas Jenkins, Anaconda Company Purchasing Department, July 26, 1957. I-4-3-A

60. BA&P Records, Administrative Correspondence, "Diesel Study," F. W. Bellinger, Memorandum of April 26, 1956. 4-3-A.

61. Ibid., F. W. Bellinger, Memorandum of April 26, 1956. 4-3-A.

62. [unsigned article] "Freight Car Orders, 1956," *Railway Age*, Vol. 142:2 (January 16, 1957), p. 116.

63. BA&P Records, Administrative Correspondence, "Tonnage over NP," P. G. Ramswick, NP Accounting Department, to J. L. White, assistant treasurer and auditor, BA&P, May 16, 1958 (quoting agreement). XX-1-3.

64. BA&P Records, Administrative Correspondence, "Traffic Study, 1958," "Traffic Study, 1958." I-5-3.

65. Shovers, et al., p. 57.

66. Shovers, et al., p. 57.

67. Miller, "Production History," p. F-7. Note that Shovers, et al. gives 1964 as the date when the Weed Concentrator went into service; Shovers, et al., p. 57.

68. Much of Meaderville vanished into the Berkeley and Continental Pits. Meaderville was named for Charles Meader, an early Butte mining entrepreneur. Henry Campbell Freeman, *A Brief History of Butte, Montana: The World's Greatest Mining Camp* (Chicago: Henry O. Shepard Co., 1900), p. 17.

69. BA&P Records, Administrative Correspondence, "Slurry Cars," Press Release, August 6, 1963. I-3-4-A.

70. Ibid., W. F. Conroy (president and general manager, BA&P) to E. Davies, manager of operations, PEKO Mines, Australia, July 9, 1970 . I-3-4-A. The lack of extensive material on the slurry cars in the records held by the Butte-Silver Bow Public Archives reflects the retention of currently active records by the Rarus Railway, successor to the BA&P.

71. Miller, "Production History," Figure F-1.

72. BA&P Records, Administrative Correspondence, "LCL Service, Discontinuance of," W. C. Conroy to American Short Line Association, May 4, 1964. I-5-4.

73. BA&P Records, Administrative Correspondence, "Locomotives, Electric," Annual Operating Costs, 1960–67. I-4-3-A.

74. Ibid., Annual Operating Costs, 1960–1967. I-4-3-A.

75. Ibid., Annual Operating Costs, 1960–1967. I-4-3-A.

76. BA&P Records, Administrative Correspondence, "Trolley Dismantling," J. F. Harvey, ACM Purchasing Department, to W. F. Conroy, BA&P, July 8, 1969. I-5-4.

77. BA&P Records, Administrative Correspondence, "Capital Budget Plan, 1976," Authority to write off assets, May 20, 1976.

78. Hidy, et al., pp. 267–68.

79. BA&P Records, Administrative Correspondence, "Diesel Study," F. W. Bellinger, Memorandum of April 26, 1956. 4-3-A.

80. Noel Holley, *The Milwaukee Electrics* (Hicksville, New York: New Jersey International, 1987), provides an enthusiast's look at the entire history of the Milwaukee's electrified operations.

81. BA&P Records, Administrative Correspondence, "NP Line Relocation, 1969," R. D. Piper, Anaconda Co. Mining Engineer, to W. F. Conroy, BA&P President, September 22, 1969.

82. BA&P Records, Administrative Correspondence, "Operational Plan, 1974," Report on Operations, 1974.

83. Ibid., Report on Operations, 1974.

84. Ibid., Report on Operations, 1974.

85. BA&P Records, Administrative Correspondence, "Operational Plan, 1975," Report on Operations, 1975.

86. New York *Times*, July 3, 1976, pp. 1, 31; January 13, 1977, p. 49.

87. BA&P Records, Administrative Correspondence, "Operational Plan, 1976," Report on Operations, 1976; Operational Plans for 1975 through 1980.

88. BA&P Records, Administrative Correspondence, "Capital Expenditure Recommendations," 1978, 1979, 1980.

89. New York *Times*, September 30, 1980, p. D-5.

90. Shovers, et al., p. 61.

91. Donald B. Robertson, *Encyclopedia of Western Railroad History: Volume II, The Mountain States: Colorado, Idaho, Montana, Wyoming* (Dallas, Texas: Taylor Publishing, 1991), p. 343.

*W*AS THE BUTTE, ANACONDA & PACIFIC a success or a failure? Clearly, as a component in the efficient production of copper, the short line was a key element in the industrial plant that helped make the Anaconda Copper Mining Company one of the world's largest and most successful copper producers before World War I.

Transportation costs diminished significantly from the time the first lode mining took place in Butte. Shipping the highest grade silver ore from Butte to smelters in Colorado or New Jersey was seldom profitable when the shipments were transported by steamboat or wagon. After 1869, the richest silver ore could be shipped profitably by wagon to Corinne, and then by rail to smelters in Colorado. Daly's first copper production involved shipment of highest grade copper ore from Butte to Swansea, Wales. Once the Upper and Lower Works were built at Anaconda, lower grades of copper ore, averaging around five percent copper, could be economically mined, since the transportation cost was reduced to the twenty-six mile railroad haul from Butte to Anaconda. Another reduction in

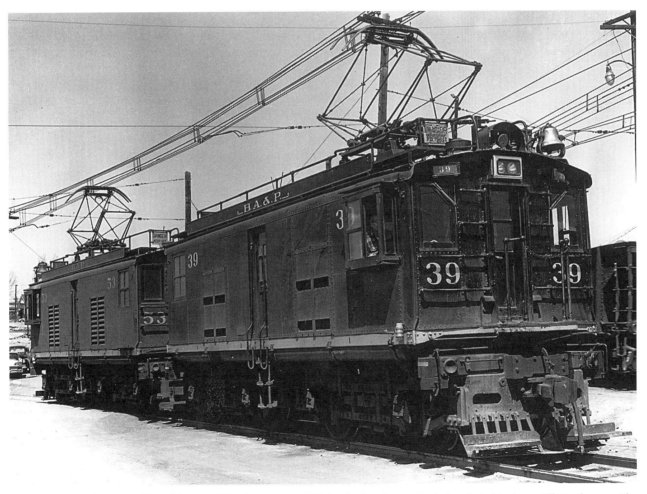

Nos. 53 and 39 at the Butte Hill yard in 1961. This view portrays differing body styles, particularly reflected in the ventillating louvers. The oldest units, typified by No. 53, had more louvers; the louver pattern of No. 39, one of the last motors built for the BA&P, was identical to those of the Milwaukee box cabs. *Photo #92-2975, Philip C. Johnson Collection, K. Ross Toole Archives, University of Montana, Missoula*

Nos. 59 and 62 at Rocker with ore loads bound for Anaconda, June 8, 1965. The near track is the Milwaukee, energized at 3000 volts DC.
Photo #92-3227, Philip C. Johnson Collection, K. Ross Toole Archives, University of Montana, Missoula

transportation costs occurred when ore as low as 0.5 percent copper began being concentrated at the Weed Concentrator in Butte. Over twenty years after closure of the Washoe smelter at Anaconda in 1980, it is still profitable for the concentrates to be shipped by rail and water to overseas smelters. For this reason, the Rarus Railway continues to serve the copper mining industry of Butte much the way the BA&P did a century ago when it opened for business.

From its first decade, those in charge of the BA&P showed a pioneering spirit in their willingness to employ new technologies—for better or worse. Though the railroad experienced decades of conservative management, the willingness to take calculated risks in order to promote efficiency was ever present.

- All-steel freight car construction was enthusiastically adopted by the BA&P after the first steel ore cars were road-tested in 1899.
- As a pioneer of electrification, the BA&P was undoubtedly a success story. Unfortunately, its suc-

cess was misunderstood by GE, the CM&StP, and other advocates of railroad electrification. The BA&P proved that electrification could be efficient for short, high-density traffic.
- BA&P's willingness to experiment saved time and money for the rest of the railroad industry when it tested the Automatic Car Connector and demonstrated that the invention, unfortunately, was a failure.
- In an efficient move in the 1950s, the company creatively combined its use of electric motors on electrified track and diesel-electric locomotives operating on a section of the neighboring NP to double its ore-carrying capacity without laying a second main track between Butte and Anaconda.

It must be unequivocally agreed that the BA&P succeeded, beyond Marcus Daly's dreams. That this short-line railroad has outlived its parent company is a testimony to over a century of efficient-minded planning and innovative thinking.

Appendix I

BUTTE, ANACONDA & PACIFIC RAILWAY
LOCOMOTIVE ROSTER, 1893–1898

Number	Type	Builder	Date	B/N	Specifications	Notes
1	0-6-0	Brooks	1892	2213	19x26, 49	Sold, 1917 (1)
2	0-6-0	Brooks	1892	2214	19x26, 49	Sold, 1918 (2)
3	0-6-0	Brooks	1892	2210	19x26, 49	Sold, 1912 (3)
4	0-6-0	Brooks	1892	2211	19x26, 49	Sold, 1917 (4)
5	0-6-0	Brooks	1892	2212	19x26, 49	Scrapped 1937 (5)
6	0-6-0	Brooks	1894	2444	19x26, 49	Sold, 1917 (6)
7	0-6-0	Brooks	1895	2529	19x26, 50	Sold, 1916 (7)
8	0-6-0	Brooks	1896	2653	19x26, 50	Sold, 1914 (8)
30	2-6-0	Brooks	1893	2408	19x24, 55	Renumbered 9. Sold. (30)
31	2-6-0	Brooks	1893	2409	19x24, 55	Renumbered 10. Sold, 1905. (31)
32	2-6-0	Brooks	1893	2410	19x24, 55	Renumbered 11. Sold, 1905. (32)
33	2-6-0	Brooks	1893	2443	19x24, 55	Renumbered 12. Sold, 1905. (33)
34	2-6-0	Brooks	1896	2632	19x24, 55	Renumbered 13. Sold, 1910. (34)
35	2-6-0	Brooks	1896	2724	19x24, 55	Renumbered 14. Sold, 1914. (35)
36	4-8-0	Schen.	1897	4504	23&34x32, 56	Renumbered 16. Sold, 1917. (36)
37	4-8-0	Schen.	1897	4595	23&34x32, 56	Renumbered 17. Sold, 1917. (37)
38	4-8-0	Schen.	1897	4596	23&34x32, 56	Renumbered 18. Sold, 1917. (38)
50	4-4-0	Rhd Is	1882	1195	17x24, 64	Sold by 1905? (50)
51	4-4-0	Rhd Is	1882	1200	17x24, 64	Sold by 1905? (51)

NOTES

Locomotives were re-numbered in 1898 by the BA&P. 2-6-0's No. 30–35 became Nos. 9–14. 4-8-0's No. 36–38 became Nos. 16–18.

Nos. 1–5 (Ex-GN Nos. 252–256) were GN class 7, later class A-7 0-6-0's, built by Brooks in 1892. The order included 10 locomotives, Builder's numbers 2206–2215. Two of these, B/N 2206 and 2207 were Montana Central No. 25 and 26.

Nos. 30–32 (Ex-GN Nos. 363, 364, 365) were GN class 37, later class D-4 2-6-0's, built by Brooks in 1893.

Nos. 50 - 51 (Ex-StPM&M 139, 134) were GN class 26, later class B-16 4-4-0's. Both were part of a group of six locomotives with consecutive builder's numbers (1195–1200) built in 1882 by the Rhode Island Locomotive Works for the StPM&M. One of the two was sold or disposed of by the BA&P before the 1898 locomotive renumbering. The entry for No. 15 in the BA&P's steam locomotive roster in its Administrative File is apparently for the surviving 4-4-0, and the information about the builder (given as Cooke) is in error. One of the 4-4-0's was gone from the roster by 1898, the other became No. 15, and was sold to the Yellowstone Park Ry. in 1906 as YP No. 1. The Yellowstone Park Ry. was reorganized as the Montana, Wyoming & Southern in 1909, YP No. 1 became MW&S No. 1.

The roster in the June, 1963 issue of *Trains* Magazine is incomplete, and does not explain the renumberings of steam locomotives in 1898 and 1905.

(1) Ex-GN 255, to BA&P 7-12-1893. Sold to General Equip't Co., New York City, Aug. 15, 1917.

(2) Ex-GN 256, to BA&P 7-10-1893. Sold to Central Iron & Steel, Harrisburg, Pennsylvania, January 1, 1918.

(3) Ex-GN 252, to BA&P 8-27-1893. Sold to Tooele Valley Ry., (No. 3?) February 16, 1912.

(4) Ex-GN 253, to BA&P 8-7-1893. Sold to General Equip't Co., New York City, July 24, 1917.

(5) Ex-GN 254, to BA&P 9-28-1893. Retired, scrapped June, 1937.

(6) Sold to Minneapolis Iron & Steel, January 1, 1917.

(7) Sold to Black Eagle Smelter, Great Falls, Montana June 2, 1916.

(8) Sold to Siems-Cary Co., March 10, 1914.

(15) BA&P administrative file roster identifies as a Cooke, but this presumably was actually either 50 or 51, which were built by Rhode Island. Sold to Yellowstone Park Ry., January 12, 1906 as YP No. 1. In 1909 to Montana Wyoming & Southern No. 1 (Company reorganized)

(30) Ex-GN 363, to BA&P No. 30, November 30, 1893. Renumbered 9 in 1898. Sold 1905.

(31) Ex-GN 364, to BA&P No. 31, November 30, 1893. Renumbered 10 in 1898; Sold to Columbia Southern in 1905. Sold to OR&N 1906; sold to Montana Western ca. 1928. Retired 1947. [Data from GN roster, R&LHS Bulletin 143]

(32) Ex-GN 365, to BA&P No. 32, November 30, 1893. Renumbered 11 in 1898. Brooks records indicate sale to Columbia Southern in 1905.

(33) Renumbered 12 in 1898. Sold to Kansas City, Mexico & Orient, March 3, 1905. [BA&P corr 1:9]

(34) Renumbered 13 in 1898. Sold to Tooele Valley Ry. (No. 2) July, 1910.

(35) Renumbered 14 in 1898. Sold to Siems-Cary Co., March 10, 1914.

(36) Renumbered 16 in 1898. Sold to Nashville, Chattanooga & St. Louis, October 10, 1917.

(37) Renumbered 17 in 1898. Sold to Nashville, Chattanooga & St. Louis, October 10, 1917.

(38) Renumbered 18 in 1898. Sold to Nashville, Chattanooga & St. Louis, October 10, 1917.

(50) Ex-StPM&M (GN) 139, to BA&P No. 50, November 17, 1893. See Note 15 above.

(51) Ex-StPM&M (GN) 134, to BA&P No. 51, January 1, 1894. See Note 15 above.

Sources: BA&P Administrative Files
           ICC valuation records
           Great Northern Railway All-Time Locomotive Roster, 1861–1970, R&LHS Bulletin No. 143
           Railway Age / Railway Gazette
           Notes on Brooks builder's records from: John B. Corns, Tim Diebert, Steve Delibert, and Ray Sauvy
           Trains Magazine, June 1963, BA&P Roster
           Doug Cummings

Compiled by C. V. Mutschler

BUTTE, ANACONDA & PACIFIC RAILWAY
LOCOMOTIVE ROSTER, 1898–1905

Number	Type	Builder	Date	B/N	Specifications	Notes
1	0-6-0	Brooks	1892	2213	19x26, 49	Sold, 1917 (1)
2	0-6-0	Brooks	1892	2214	19x26, 49	Sold, 1918 (2)
3	0-6-0	Brooks	1892	2210	19x26, 49	Sold, 1912 (3)
4	0-6-0	Brooks	1892	2211	19x26, 49	Sold, 1917 (4)
5	0-6-0	Brooks	1892	2212	19x26, 49	Scrapped 1937 (5)
6	0-6-0	Brooks	1894	2444	19x26, 49	Sold, 1917 (6)
7	0-6-0	Brooks	1895	2529	19x26, 50	Sold, 1916 (7)
8	0-6-0	Brooks	1896	2653	19x26, 50	Sold, 1914 (8)
9	2-6-0	Brooks	1893	2408	19x24, 55	Former 30. Sold, 1905. (9)
10	2-6-0	Brooks	1893	2409	19x24, 55	Former 31. Sold, 1906. (10)
11	2-6-0	Brooks	1893	2410	19x24, 55	Former 32. Sold, 1905. (11)
12	2-6-0	Brooks	1893	2443	19x24, 55	Former 33. Sold, 1905. (12)
13	2-6-0	Brooks	1896	2632	19x24, 55	Former 34. Sold, 1910. (13)
14	2-6-0	Brooks	1896	2724	19x24, 55	Former 35. Sold, 1914. (14)
15	4-4-0	Rh. Is.	1882		17x24, 64	Sold, 1906. (15)
16	4-8-0	Schen.	1897	4504	23&34x32, 56	Former 36. Sold, 1917 (16)
17	4-8-0	Schen.	1897	4595	23&34x32, 56	Former 37. Sold, 1917 (17)
18	4-8-0	Schen.	1897	4596	23&34x32, 56	Former 38. Sold, 1917 (18)
19	4-8-0	Schen.	1901	5634	23&34x32, 56	Sold, 1917 (19)
20	4-6-0	Baldwin	1901	19389	19x26, 67	Sold, 1917 (20)
21	4-8-0	Schen.	1903	28742	23&34x32, 56	Sold, 1917 (21)
22	4-6-0	Rogers	1905	37546	19x26, 66	Scrapped 1937 (22)

NOTES

The GN roster in R&LHS Bulletin No. 143 reports a renumbering of BA&P locomotives in 1898. The BA&P Administrative File locomotive roster (which appears to have been prepared as late as 1915, probably for valuation purposes) shows only two of the Brooks 2-6-0's, numbered 13 and 14. However, if the previous four were numbered starting at 9, the sequence fits for all locomotives on hand in 1898 and into the early 1900s. Builder's photos of 0-6-0 No. 6, 2-6-0 No. 35, and 4-8-0 No. 37 all are for locomotives delivered before 1898. Builder's photos for post-1898 delivered locomotives—4-8-0 No. 21, 4-6-0 No. 22, and 2-8-0 No. 29—all fit into the 1898 renumbering sequence. Retirement and sale of most of the moguls in 1905 is confirmed by correspondence in BA&P files, which allowed new 2-8-0's to assume numbers 9 and 10.

Nos. 1–5 (Ex-GN Nos. 252–256) were GN class 7, later class A-7 0-6-0's, built by Brooks in 1892. The order included 10 locomotives, Builder's numbers 2206–2215. Two of these, B/N 2206 and 2207, were Montana Central No. 25 and 26.

Nos. 9–11 (Ex-GN Nos. 363, 364, 365) were GN class 37, later class D-4 2-6-0's, built by Brooks in 1893. They became BA&P Nos. 30, 31, and 32, and were renumbered in 1898.

No. 15 Formerly either BA&P 50 or 51. These two (Ex-StPM&M 139, 134) were GN class 26, later class B-16 4-4-0's. Both were part of a group of six locomotives with consecutive builder's numbers (1195–1200), built in 1882 by the Rhode Island Locomotive Works for the StPM&M. The roster in the BA&P Administrative File lists No. 15 as being built by Cooke, but this appears to be an error. Apparently the surviving 4-4-0 was renumbered 15 in 1898, and was sold in 1906.

The roster in the June 1963 issue of *Trains* Magazine is incomplete, and does not explain the renumberings of steam locomotives in 1898 and 1905.

(1) Ex-GN 255, to BA&P 7-12-1893. Sold to General Equip't Co., New York City, August 15, 1917.

(2) Ex-GN 256, to BA&P 7-10-1893. Sold to Central Iron & Steel, Harrisburg, Pennsylvania, January 1, 1918.

(3) Ex-GN 252, to BA&P 8-27-1893. Sold to Tooele Valley Ry., (No. 3?) February 16, 1912.

(4) Ex-GN 253, to BA&P 8-7-1893. Sold to General Equip't Co., New York City, July 24, 1917.

(5) Ex-GN 254, to BA&P 9-28-1893. Retired, scrapped June 1937.

(6) Sold to Minneapolis Iron & Steel, January 1, 1917.

(7) Sold to Black Eagle Smelter, Great Falls, Montana June 2, 1916.

(8) Sold to Siems-Cary Co., March 10, 1914.

(9) Ex-GN 363. To BA&P 30 on Nov. 30, 1893. Renumbered from 30 in 1898. Sold 1905.

(10) Ex-GN 364. To BA&P 31 on Nov. 30, 1893. Renumbered from 31 in 1898. Sold to Columbia Southern No. 10 in 1905; to OR&N No. 10 July 1, 1906; to OWR&N No. 10 December 23, 1910; Sold to Montana Western No. 10 circa August 1929. Retired 1947.

(11) Ex-GN 365. To BA&P 32 on Nov. 30, 1893. Renumbered from 32 in 1898. Sold to Columbia Southern in 1905. [Brooks data indicates sale to CS.]

(12) Renumbered from 33 in 1898. Sold to Kansas City, Mexico & Orient, March 3, 1905.

(13) Renumbered from 34 in 1898. Sold to Tooele Valley Ry. (No. 2) July, 1910.

(14) Renumbered from 35 in 1898. Sold to Siems-Cary Co., March 10, 1914.

(15) BA&P administrative file roster identifies as a Cooke, but this presumably was either 50 or 51. Sold to Yellowstone Park Ry,. January 12, 1906 as YP No. 1. To MW&S No. 1 in 1909 (Corporate reorganization).

(16) Renumbered from 36 in 1898. Sold to Nashville, Chattanooga & St. Louis, October 10, 1917.

(17) Renumbered from 37 in 1898. Sold to Nashville, Chattanooga & St. Louis, October 10, 1917.

(18) Renumbered from 38 in 1898. Sold to Nashville, Chattanooga & St. Louis, October 10, 1917.

Sources: BA&P Administrative Files
ICC valuation records
Great Northern Railway All-Time Locomotive Roster, 1861–1970. R&LHS Bulletin No. 143
Railway Age / Railway Gazette
Trains Magazine, June 1963, BA&P roster
Notes on Brooks builder's records from: John B. Corns, Tim Diebert, Steve Delibert, and Ray Sauvy
Doug Cummings

Compiled by C. V. Mutschler

Appendix III

BUTTE, ANACONDA & PACIFIC RAILWAY
LOCOMOTIVE ROSTER, 1905–1985

Number	Type	Builder	Date	B/N	Specifications	Notes
STEAM LOCOMOTIVES						
1	0-6-0	Brooks	1892	2213	19x26, 49	Sold, 1917 (1)
2	0-6-0	Brooks	1892	2214	19x26, 49	Sold, 1918 (2)
3	0-6-0	Brooks	1892	2210	19x26, 49	Sold, 1912 (3)
4	0-6-0	Brooks	1892	2211	19x26, 49	Sold, 1917 (4)
5	0-6-0	Brooks	1892	2212	19x26, 49	Scrapped 1937 (5)
6	0-6-0	Brooks	1894	2444	19x26, 49	Sold, 1917 (6)
7	0-6-0	Brooks	1895	2529	19x26, 50	Sold, 1916 (7)
8	0-6-0	Brooks	1896	2653	19x26, 50	Sold, 1914 (8)
9	2-8-0	Brooks	1906	41221	21x28, 52	Scrapped 1953 (9)
10	2-8-0	Brooks	1906	41222	21x28, 52	Scrapped 1953 (10)
11	4-8-0	Schen.	1905	37942	23&34x32, 56	Scrapped 1937 (11)
12	4-8-0	Schen.	1905	37943	23&34x32, 56	Sold, 1917 (12)
13	2-6-0	Brooks	1896	2632	19x24, 55	Sold, 1910 (13)
14	2-6-0	Brooks	1896	2724	19x24, 55	Sold, 1914 (14)
15	4-4-0	Rh. Is?	1882		17x24, 64	Sold, 1906 (15)
16	4-8-0	Schen.	1897	4504	23&34x32, 56	Sold, 1917 (16)
17	4-8-0	Schen.	1897	4595	23&34x32, 56	Sold, 1917 (17)
18	4-8-0	Schen.	1897	4596	23&34x32, 56	Sold, 1917 (18)
19	4-8-0	Schen.	1901	5634	23&34x32, 56	Sold, 1917 (19)
20	4-6-0	Baldwin	1901	19389	19x26, 67	Sold, 1917 (20)
21	4-8-0	Schen.	1903	28742	23&34x32, 56	Sold, 1917 (21)
22	4-6-0	Rogers	1905	37546	19x26, 66	Scrapped 1937 (22)
23	4-8-0	Schen.	1906	41223	23&34x32, 56	Sold, 1917 (23)
24	4-8-0	Schen.	1906	41224	23&34x32, 56	Sold, 1917 (24)
25	2-8-0	Brooks	1907	44333	21x28, 52	Scrapped 1953 (25)
26	2-8-0	Brooks	1907	44334	21x28, 52	Sold, 1917 (26)
27	2-8-0	Brooks	1907	44335	21x28, 52	Sold, 1917 (27)
28	2-8-0	Brooks	1907	44336	21x28, 52	Sold, 1915 (28)
29	2-8-0	Brooks	1910	48884	21x28, 52	Sold, 1925 (29)
30	4-8-0	Brooks	1910	48885	23&34x32, 56	Scrapped 1937 (30)
31	2-8-0	BLW	1904	23668	22x30, 57	Scrapped 1953 (31)
32	2-8-0	BLW	1907	30228	22x30, 57	Scrapped 1953 (32)
33	2-8-0	BLW	1906	28776	22x30, 57	Scrapped 1953 (33)
ELECTRIC LOCOMOTIVES						
39	0-4-4-0	GE	1917	5763	2400 Volt DC	Retired 1968, Scrapped (39)
40	0-4-4-0	GE	1917	5764	2400 Volt DC	Retired 1968, Scrapped
41	0-4-4-0	GE	1917	5765	2400 Volt DC	Retired 1968, Scrapped
42	0-4-4-0	GE	1916	5540	2400 Volt DC	Retired 1968, Scrapped
43	0-4-4-0	GE	1916	5541	2400 Volt DC	Retired 1968, Scrapped
44	0-4-4-0	GE	1916	5542	2400 Volt DC	Retired 1968, Scrapped
45	0-4-4-0	GE	1916	4859	2400 Volt DC	Retired 1968, Scrapped
46	0-4-4-0	GE	1914	4879	2400 Volt DC	Retired 1968, Scrapped
47	0-4-4-0	GE	1914	4880	2400 Volt DC	Retired 1968, Preserved (47)
48	0-4-4-0	GE	1915	4881	2400 Volt DC	Retired 1968, Scrapped

Number	Type	Builder	Date	B/N	Specifications	Notes
49	0-4-4-0	GE	1915	4882	2400 Volt DC	Retired 1968, Scrapped
50	0-4-4-0	GE	1913	3817	2400 Volt DC	Retired 1968, Scrapped
51	0-4-4-0	GE	1913	3818	2400 Volt DC	Retired 1968, Scrapped
52	0-4-4-0	GE	1913	3819	2400 Volt DC	Retired 1968, Scrapped
53	0-4-4-0	GE	1913	3820	2400 Volt DC	Retired 1968, Scrapped
54	0-4-4-0	GE	1913	3821	2400 Volt DC	Retired 1968, Scrapped
55	0-4-4-0	GE	1913	3822	2400 Volt DC	Retired 1968, Scrapped
56	0-4-4-0	GE	1913	3823	2400 Volt DC	Retired 1968, Scrapped
57	0-4-4-0	GE	1913	3824	2400 Volt DC	Retired 1968, Scrapped
58	0-4-4-0	GE	1913	3825	2400 Volt DC	Retired 1968, Scrapped
59	0-4-4-0	GE	1913	3826	2400 Volt DC	Retired 1968, Scrapped
60	0-4-4-0	GE	1913	3827	2400 Volt DC	Retired 1968, Scrapped
61	0-4-4-0	GE	1913	3828	2400 Volt DC	Retired 1968, Scrapped
62	0-4-4-0	GE	1913	3829	2400 Volt DC	Retired 1968, Scrapped
63	0-4-4-0	GE	1913	3830	2400 Volt DC	Retired 1968, Scrapped
64	0-4-4-0	GE	1913	3831	2400 Volt DC	Retired 1968, Scrapped
65	0-4-4-0	GE	1913	3832	2400 Volt DC	Psgr. Retired 12968, Scrapped
66	0-4-4-0	GE	1913	3833	2400 Volt DC	Psgr. Retired 1968, Scrapped
T-1	0-4-0	GE	1914	4883	2400 Volt DC	Retired 1968, Preserved (T-1)
T-2	0-4-0	GE	1914	4884	2400 Volt DC	Retired 1968, Scrapped (T-2)
T-3	0-4-0	GE	1915	4885	2400 Volt DC	Retired 1968, Scrapped
201	0-4-4-0	GE	1957	32882	2400 Volt DC	Retired 1968, Scrapped (201)
202	0-4-4-0	GE	1957	32882	2400 Volt DC	Retired 1968, Scrapped (202)

DIESEL-ELECTRIC LOCOMOTIVES

Number	Type	Builder	Date	B/N	Specifications	Notes
100	SW-7	EMD	1952			Ex-TV 100. (100)
101	GP-7	EMD	1952			To Rarus Ry, 1985. (101)
102	GP-7	EMD	1952			To Rarus Ry. 1985. (102)
103	GP-7	EMD	1953			To Rarus Ry. 1985. (103)
104	GP-9	EMD	1957			To Rarus Ry. 1985. (104)
105	GP-9	EMD	1957			To Rarus Ry. 1985. (105)
106	GP-9	EMD	1957			To Rarus Ry. 1985. (106)
107	GP-9	EMD	1957			To Rarus Ry. 1985. (107)
108	GP-38-2	EMD	1977			To Rarus Ry. 1985. (108)
109	GP-38-2	EMD	1978			To Rarus Ry. 1985. (109)

NOTES

Renumbering or retirement to permit re-use of Numbers 9 through 12, inclusive. Retirement by means of sale of moguls 9–12 occurred in 1905, opening those numbers for new locomotives being received in 1905 and 1906.

Nos. 1–5 (Ex GN Nos. 252–256) were GN class 7, later class A-7 0-6-0's, built by Brooks in 1892. The order included 10 locomotives, Builder's numbers 2206–2215. Two of these, B/N 2206 and 2207 were Montana Central No. 25 and 26.

On May 1, 1995 the BA&P was sold to the new Rarus Railway Company, which took over the property and equipment of the BA&P.

(1)   Ex-GN 255, to BA&P July 12, 1893. Sold to General Equip't Co., New York City, Aug. 15, 1917.

(2)   Ex-GN 256, to BA&P July 10, 1893. Sold to Central Iron & Steel, Harrisburg, Pennsylvaina, January 1, 1918.

(3)   Ex-GN 252, to BA&P Aug. 27, 1893. Sold to Tooele Valley Ry. No. 3, February 16, 1912.

(4)   Ex-GN 253, to BA&P Aug. 7, 1893. Sold to General Equip't Co., New York City, July 24, 1917.

(5)   Ex-GN 254, to BA&P Sept. 28, 1893. Retired, scrapped June, 1937.

(6)   Sold to Minneapolis Iron & Steel, January 1, 1917.

(7)   Sold to Black Eagle Smelter, Great Falls, Montana June 2, 1916.

(8)   Sold to Siems-Cary Co., March 10, 1914.

(9)   Second No. 9. Retired 1953. Scrapped at Anaconda, 1953.

(10)   Second No. 10. Retired 1953. Scrapped at Anaconda, 1953.

(11) Second No. 11. Retired and scrapped, 1937.

(12) Second No. 12. Sold to General Equipt Co., New York City, July 21, 1917.

(13) Renumbered from 34 in 1898. Sold to Tooele Valley Ry. (No. 2) July, 1910.

(14) Renumbered from 35 in 1898. Sold to Siems-Cary Co., March 10, 1914.

(15) Sold to Yellowstone Park Ry., January 12, 1906.

(16) Renumbered from 36 in 1898. Sold to NC&StL, October 10, 1917.

(17) Renumbered from 37 in 1898. Sold to NC&StL, October 10, 1917.

(18) Renumbered from 38 in 1898. Sold to NC&StL, October 10, 1917.

(19) Sold to General Equip't. Co, New York City, July 24, 1917.

(20) Sold to Central Tuiucu Chucho, Cuba, August 18, 1917.

(21) Sold to General Equip't Co., New York City, July 24, 1917.

(22) Scrapped, June 1937.

(23) Sold to General Equip't Co., New York City, July 24, 1917.

(24) Sold to General Equip't Co., New York City, July 24, 1917.

(25) Retired, scrapped, October 1953.

(26) Sold to Great Northern Ry., February 19, 1917. GN No. 1326, scrapped, July 1948.

(27) Sold to Great Northern Ry., February 19, 1917. GN No. 1327, scrapped, May 1947.

(28) Sold to Tooele Valley Ry., No. ?? January 8, 1915.

(29) Sold to Tooele Valley Ry., No. 29, October 20, 1925.

(30) Second No. 30. Retired, scrapped, June 1937.

(31) Second No. 31. Ex-UP No. 566, to BA&P No. 31 November, 1947. Retired, 1953. Scrapped at Anaconda, 1953.

(32) Second No. 32. Ex-UP No. 595, to BA&P No. 32 May, 1949. Retired, 1953. Scrapped at Anaconda, 1953.

(33) Second No. 33. Ex-UP No. 591, to BA&P No. 33 April, 1950. Retired, 1953. Scrapped at Anaconda, 1953.

(39) Electrics retired in 1968, held for sale. After no sale, all scrapped except No. 47, donated for display at the World Museum of Mining. Now (2002) on display at the Anselmo Mine.

(47) Preserved for display, first at World Museum of Mining, then at Anselmo Mine in Butte.

(T-1) Preserved with No. 47. Nos. T-2 and T-3 scrapped.

(201) Retired 1968. Scrapped ca. 1977 after parts sold to Canadian National.

(202) Retired 1968. Scrapped ca. 1977 after parts sold to Canadian National.

(100) Ex-Tooele Valley Ry. No. 100, to BA&P 100 in 1972. Sold 1981 to Anaconda Aluminum Co.

(101) To Rarus Ry. No. 101, May 1, 1985.

(102) To Rarus Ry. No. 102, May 1, 1985.

(103) To Rarus Ry. No. 103, May 1, 1985.

(104) To Rarus Ry. No. 104, May 1, 1985.

(105) To Rarus Ry. No. 105, May 1, 1985.

(106) To Rarus Ry. No. 106, May 1, 1985.

(107) To Rarus Ry. No. 107, May 1, 1985.

(108) To Rarus Ry. No. 108, May 1, 1985. Sold 1986 to Alaska RR No. 2001.

(109) To Rarus Ry. No. 109, May 1, 1985. Sold 1986 to Alaska RR No. 2002.

Sources: BA&P Administrative Files
          Union Pacific RR Co. Locomotive Folios
          Interstate Commerce Commission, valuation records, BA&P Ry.
          Notes on Brooks builder's records from: John B. Corns, Tim Diebert, Steve Delibert, and Ray Sauvy
          Great Northern Railway All-Time Locomotive Roster, 1861–1970, R&LHS *Bulletin* No. 143
          Railway Age / Railway Gazette
          Trains Magazine, June 1963, BA&P Roster
          Donald B. Robertson, *Encyclopedia of Western Railroad History,* Volume II
          Doug Cummings. Locomotive roster information, BA&P, GN, UP
          Pete Kovanda, BA&P Roster at: http://mypage:direct.ca/o/onward/BAP.html

Compiled by C. V. Mutschler

Bibliography

PRIMARY SOURCES

American Locomotive Company. Records. Brooks Locomotive Works Order Book. ALCO Historic Photos, Mohawk & Hudson Chapter of the National Railway Historical Society, Schenectady, New York.

American Locomotive Company. Records. Photographs. ALCO Historic Photos, Mohawk and Hudson Chapter of the National Railway Historical Society, Schenectady, New York.

Anaconda Copper Mining Company. Records. Photograph Collection. Marcus Daly Historical Society of Anaconda. Anaconda, Montana.

Anaconda Copper Mining Company. Records. Photograph Collection. Montana Historical Society. Helena, Montana.

Anaconda Copper Mining Company. Records. Photograph Collection. World Museum of Mining. Butte, Montana.

Butte, Anaconda & Pacific Railway Company. Records. Butte–Silver Bow Public Archives. Butte, Montana.

Butte, Anaconda & Pacific Railway. Records. Correspondence, Photographs, and Time Tables. Eugene T. Hawk Collection. Eugene T. Hawk.

Butte, Anaconda & Pacific Railway Company. Records. Maps. Montana Historical Society. Helena, Montana.

Butte, Anaconda & Pacific Railway Company. Records. Rarus Railway Co. Offices. Anaconda, Montana.

Chicago, Milwaukee & Puget Sound Railway Company. Records. Third Annual Report (1912). Bill and Jan Taylor Collection. Bill and Jan Taylor.

Chicago, Milwaukee, Saint Paul & Pacific Railway Company. Records. Rocky Mountain Division Right of Way Maps, Station Plats, and Profiles. Montana Historical Society. Helena, Montana.

Denuty, Michael J. Photographs. Michael J. Denuty.

Dowler, Robert K. Photographs. Robert K. Dowler.

Great Northern Railway Company. Records. Annual Reports of the Great Northern Railway Company and its Predecessors. Minnesota Historical Society. Microfilm.

Great Northern Railway Company. Records. Engineering Drawings. Montana Historical Society. Helena, Montana.

Hill, James J. Papers. James J. Hill Library. Saint Paul, Minnesota.

Holloway, Theodore J. Photographs. Theodore J. Holloway.

Interstate Commerce Commission. Valuation Records. National Archives and Records Administration, Suitland, Maryland.

Johnson, Phillip C. Photographs. K. Ross Toole Archives, Maureen and Mike Mansfield Library, University of Montana.

Montana Board of Railroad Commissioners. Records. Montana Historical Society, Helena, Montana.

Montana Central Railway Company. Records. Maps. Montana Historical Society. Helena, Montana.

Roberts, Donald. Papers. Photograph Collection. Oregon Historical Society. Portland, Oregon.

Union Pacific Railroad Company. Records. Locomotive Diagram Sheets, Author's Collection.

U.S. GOVERNMENT DOCUMENTS

Becker, George F. *Geology of the Comstock Lode and the Washoe District*. U.S. Geological Survey, Monograph No. 4. Washington, D.C.: GPO. 1882.

Boutwell, John, Arthur Keith and Samuel Franklin Emmons. *Economic Geology of the Bingham Mining District, Utah*. U.S. Geological Survey, Professional Paper No. 38. Washington, D.C.: GPO, 1904.

Campbell, Marius R. et al. *Guidebook of the Western United States: Northern Pacific Route*. U.S. Geological Survey, Bulletin No. 611. Washington, D.C.: GPO, 1916.

Emmons, Samuel Franklin, and George W. Tower. *Geological Atlas of the United States*, Special Folio No. 38. U.S. Geological Survey. Washington, D.C.: GPO, 1897.

Fay, Albert H. *A Glossary of the Mining and Metal Industry*. U. S. Bureau of Mines, Bulletin No. 95. Washington, D.C.: GPO, 1920.

Interstate Commerce Commission. *Annual Report of the Interstate Commerce Commission*. Washington, D.C.: GPO. 1888–1980.

Interstate Commerce Commission. *Interstate Commerce Commission Activities, 1887–1937*. Washington, D.C.: GPO, 1937.

Interstate Commerce Commission. *Interstate Commerce Commission Reports*. Washington, D.C.: GPO.

Interstate Commerce Commission. *Statistics of Railways in the United States*. Washington, D.C.: GPO. 1892–1965.

Interstate Commerce Commission. *Valuation Reports*. Washington, D.C.: GPO.

Koschmann, A. H. and M. H. Bergendahl. *Principal Gold-Producing Districts of the United States*. U.S. Geological Survey, Professional Paper No. 610. Washington, D. C.: GPO, 1968.

Lord, Eliot. *Comstock Mining and Miners*. U.S. Geological Survey, Monograph No. 4, Washington, D.C.: GPO, 1883.

Spencer, Arthur C. *The Geology and Ore Deposits of Ely, Nevada*. U.S. Geological Survey, Professional Paper No. 96. Washington, D.C.: GPO, 1917.

U.S. Department of Transportation. Federal Railroad Administration. *United States Safety Appliance Standards and Power Brake Requirements*. Washington, D.C.: GPO, September, 1977.

U.S. Geological Survey. *Mineral Resources of the United States*. Washington, D.C.: GPO, 1881–1915.

Weed, Walter H. *Geology and Ore Deposits of the Butte District, Montana*. U.S. Geological Survey, Professional Paper No. 74. Washington, D.C.: GPO, 1912.

Weed, Walter H. "Ore Deposits at Butte, Montana," *Contributions to Economic Geology, 1902*. U.S. Geological Survey Bulletin No. 213, pp. 170–180. Washington, D.C.: GPO, 1903.

TRADE AND TECHNICAL PUBLICATIONS

Books

Buell, D. C. *Basic Steam Locomotive Maintenance*. Omaha, Nebraska: Rail Heritage Publications, 1980.

Forney, Matthias N. *The Railroad Car Builder's Pictorial Dictionary*. New York: The Railroad Gazette, 1879; reprint, with a new introduction by John F. Stover, New York: Dover Publications, 1974.

General Electric Co. *The Electric Divisions of the Chicago Milwaukee & Saint Paul Railway*. Schenectady, New York: General Electric Co., 1920.

Gray, Alexander. *Principles and Practice of Electrical Engineering*. New York: McGraw-Hill, 1947.

International Textbook Company. *Electric Railway Systems*. Scranton, Pennsylvania: International Textbook Company, 1908.

International Textbook Company. *Line and Track*. Scranton, Pennsylvania: International Textbook Company, 1908.

International Textbook Company. *Single Phase Railway Systems*. Scranton, Pennsylvania: International Textbook Company, 1908.

Mason, Arthur J. *Railroad Electrification and the Electric Locomotive*. New York: Simmons-Boardman, 1923.

Unified Industries. *A Report on U.S. Railroad Electrification*. Alexandria, Virginia: Unified Industries, 1977.

Wright, Roy V. (Ed.) *Car Builders Dictionary and Cyclopedia*. (9th Edition) New York: Simmons-Boardman, 1919.

Wright, Roy V. (Ed.) *Locomotive Cyclopedia of American Practice*. (7th Edition) New York: Simmons-Boardman, 1925.

Wright, Roy V. (Ed.) *Locomotive Cyclopedia of American Practice*. (9th Edition) New York: Simmons-Boardman, 1930.

Trade Journals

Electric Railway Journal. 1900–1920.
Engineering and Mining Journal. 1884.
General Electric Review. 1910–1930.
Mining and Scientific Press. 1884–1915.
Official Railway Equipment Register. 1895–1968.
Railroad Gazette. 1890–1907.
Railway Age. 1890–1998.

Timberman. 1910–1925.
Transactions of the American Institute of Mining Engineers. 1890–1920

Trade Journal Articles

Armstrong, A. H. "Economies of Steam Railroad Electrification," [Editorial], *General Electric Review*, Vol. 17, No. 1 (November 1914), p. 1033.

Armstrong, A. H. "The Last Stand of the Reciprocating Steam Engine," *General Electric Review*, Vol. 23, No. 4 (April, 1920), pp. 249–262.

Beeuwkes, Reiner. "Operating Results From the Electrification of the Trunk Line of the CM&St.P Ry.," *General Electric Review*, Vol. 20, No. 5 (May, 1917), pp. 340–347.

Bellinger, F. W. "Electric Operations—Butte, Anaconda & Pacific," *Railway Age*, Vol. 68, No. 24. pp. 1657–1658.

Burns, Willis T. "Notes on the Great Falls Electrolytic Plant," *Transactions of the American Institute of Mining Engineers*, Vol. 46 (1913), pp. 703–741.

Cox, J. B. "The Contact System of the Butte, Anaconda & Pacific Railway," *General Electric Review*, Vol. 18, No. 8 (August, 1915), pp. 842–859.

Cox, J. B. "The Electrical Operation of the Butte, Anaconda & Pacific Railway," *General Electric Review*, Vol. 17, No. 11 (November, 1914), pp. 1047–1065.

Dewhurst, John A. "A Review of American Steam Road Electrifications," *General Electric Review*, Vol. 17, No. 11 (November, 1914), pp. 1144–1147.

Dunshee, B. H. "Timbering in the Butte Mines," *Transactions of the American Institute of Mining Engineers*, Vol. 46 (1913), pp. 137–150.

Goodale, Charles W. "The Concentration of Ores in the Butte district, Montana," *Transactions of the American Institute of Mining Engineers*, Vol. 26 (1896), pp. 599–639.

Hare, K. R. "St. Paul to Electrify Over Cascade Mountains," *General Electric Review*, Vol. 20, No. 5 (May, 1917), pp. 348–351.

Hebgen, Max. "Hydro-Electric Development in Montana," *Transactions of the American Institute of Mining Engineers*, Vol. 46 (1913), pp. 789–816.

Hofman, H. O. "Notes on the Metallurgy of Copper in Montana," *Transactions of the American Institute of Mining Engineers*, Vol. 34. (1904) pp. 258–316.

Lawson, Walter C. "Laying Panel Track at the Morenci Pit," *Transactions of the American Institute of Mining Engineers*, Vol. 181 (1949), pp. 159–171.

Miller, Richard N. "Production History of the Butte District, and Geological Function Past and Present," in: Richard N. Miller (Ed.) *Guidebook for the Butte Field Meeting of the Society of Economic Geologists*, Butte, Montana: Anaconda Company, 1973.

Sales, Reno H. "Ore Deposits at Butte, Montana," *Transactions of the American Institute of Mining Engineers*, Vol. 46. (1913) pp. 3–109.

Smedes, Harry W., Montis R. Klepper, and Robert I. Tilling, "The Boulder Batholith, Montana," in: Richard N. Miller (Ed.) *Guidebook for the Butte Field Meeting of the Society of Economic Geologists*, Butte, Montana: Anaconda Company, 1973.

Stoddard, Alfred C. "History and Development of Block Caving at the Mines of the Inspiration Consolidated Copper Co.," *Transactions of the American Institute of Mining Engineers*, Vol. 163 (1945), pp. 96–120.

Tilling, Robert I. "The Boulder Batholith, Montana: Product of Two Contemporaneous But Chemically and Isotopically Distinct Magma Series," in: Richard N. Miller (Ed.) *Guidebook for the Butte Field Meeting of the Society of Economic Geologists*, Butte, Montana: The Anaconda Company, 1973.

[Unattributed] "Direct-Current 2400–Volt Electric Locomotive, Butte, Anaconda & Pacific Ry," *Railway and Engineering Review*, Vol. 53 (1913): 560–651.

[Unattributed] "Electrical Operation of the Butte, Anaconda & Pacific Ry," *Railway and Engineering Review*, Vol. 54 (1914): 640–645.

Wade, R. E. "The Electrification of the Butte, Anaconda & Pacific Railway," *Transactions of the American Institute of Mining Engineers*, Vol. 46. (1913) pp. 820–825.

Walker, Glen H. "Electric Locomotives for Mexican Railway," *Railway Age*, Vol. 75:22 [December 1, 1923], pp. 1021–1023.

Wheeler, Archer E. and Milo W. Krejci. "Great Falls Converter Practice," *Transactions of the American Institute of Mining Engineers*, Vol. 46. (1913) pp. 486–561.

SECONDARY SOURCES

Books

Albi, Charles and Kenton Forrest. *The Moffat Tunnel: A Brief History*. Golden, Colorado: Colorado Railroad Museum, 1986.

American Society of Mechanical Engineers. *George Westinghouse Commemoration*. New York: American Society of Mechanical Engineers, 1937.

Athearn, Robert G. *Union Pacific Country*. Chicago: Rand McNally & Company, 1971.

Bain, David Haward. *Empire Express: Building the First Transcontinental Railroad*. New York: Viking, 1999.

Bancroft, Hubert H. *The Works of Hubert Howe Bancroft, Volume 31: History of Utah, 1540–1886*. San Francisco, California: The History Company, 1889.

Bancroft, Hubert H. *The Works of Hubert Howe Bancroft: History of Washington, Idaho and Montana, 1845–1889*. San Francisco, California: The History Company, 1890.

Beal, Merril D. *Intermountain Railroads: Standard and Narrow Gauge*. Caldwell, Idaho: Caxton Printers, 1962.

Cash, Joseph. *Working the Homestake*. Ames, Iowa: Iowa State University Press, 1973.

Chandler, Alfred D. Jr. *Strategy and Structure: Chapters in the History of the Industrial Enterprise*. Cambridge, Massachusetts: MIT Press, 1962.

Cheney, Roberta C. *Names on the Face of Montana: the Story of Montana's Place Names*. Missoula, Montana: University of Montana Publications in History, 1971.

Conot, Robert. *A Streak of Luck*. New York: Seaview Books, 1979.

Derleth, August. *The Milwaukee Road: Its First Hundred Years*. New York: Creative Age Press, 1948.

Fahey, John R. *Inland Empire: D. C. Corbin and Spokane*. Seattle, Washington: University of Washington Press, 1965.

Fahey, John R. *Shaping Spokane: Jay P. Graves and His Times*. Seattle, Washington: University of Washington Press, 1994.

Fairlie, Robert F. *Railways or No Railways*. London: Effingham Wilson, 1872; reprint, Canton, Ohio: Railhead Publications, n.d.

Fogel, Robert W. *Railroads and American Economic Growth*. Baltimore, Maryland: Johns Hopkins University Press, 1964.

Fogel, Robert W. *The Union Pacific Railroad: A Case in Premature Enterprise*. Baltimore, Maryland: Johns Hopkins University Press, 1962.

Freeman, Harry Campbell. *A Brief History of Butte, Montana: The World's Greatest Mining Camp*. Chicago: H. O. Shepard Co., 1900.

Greever, William S. *The Bonanza West: The Story of the Western Mining Rushes, 1848–1900*. Norman, Oklahoma: University of Oklahoma Press, 1963.

Grodinsky, Julius. *Transcontinental Railway Strategy, 1869–1893: A Study of Businessmen*. Philadelphia: University of Pennsylvania Press, 1962.

Hays, Samuel P. *Conservation and the Gospel of Efficiency: The Progressive Conservation Movement, 1890–1920*. Cambridge, Massachusetts: Harvard University Press, 1959.

Hidy, Ralph W, Muriel E. Hidy, Roy V. Scott and Don L. Hofsommer. *The Great Northern Railway: A History*. Boston, Massachusetts: Harvard Business School Press, 1988.

Hilton, George W. *American Narrow Gauge Railroads*. Stanford, California: Stanford University Press, 1990.

Hilton, George W. *The Cable Car in America*. Berkeley, California: Howell-North Books, 1971.

Hilton, George W. and John F. Due. *The Electric Interurban Railways in America*. Stanford, California: Stanford University Press, 1964.

Hines, Walker D. *War History of American Railroads*. New Haven, Connecticut: Yale University Press, 1928.

Holley, Noel. *The Milwaukee Electrics*. Hicksville, New York: New Jersey International, 1987.

Hyde, Charles K. *Copper for America: The United States Copper Industry from Colonial Times to the 1990's*. Tucson, Arizona: University of Arizona Press, 1998.

Jackson, W. Turrentine. *Wagon Roads West: A Study of Federal Road Surveys and Construction in the Transmississippi West, 1846–1869*. New Haven: Yale University Press, 1965.

James, Don. *Butte's Memory Book*, Caldwell, Idaho: Caxton Printers, 1975.

Josephson. Matthew. *Edison*. New York: McGraw Hill, 1959.

Kerr, K. Austin. *American Railroad Politics 1914–1920: Rates, Wages and Efficiency*. Pittsburgh, Pennsylvania: University of Pittsburgh Press, 1968.

Kolko, Gabriel. *Railroads and Regulation, 1877–1916*. Princeton, New Jersey: Princeton University Press, 1965.

Lewis, Sinclair. *Babbitt*. New York: Grosset & Dunlap, 1922.

Limerick, Patricia N. *The Legacy of Conquest: the Unbroken Past of the American West*. New York: W.W. Norton, 1987.

Lewis, Sharon E. *Butte—Under the Hill*. Montana Bureau of Mines and Geology Information Pamphlet No. 1. Butte, Montana: Montana Bureau of Mines and Geology, 1989.

Lewty, Peter J. *Across the Columbia Plain: Railroad Expansion in the Interior Northwest, 1885 – 1893*. Pullman, Washington: Washington State University Press, 1995.

Lowenthal, Max. *The Investor Pays*. New York: Alfred A. Knopf, 1933.

Malone, Michael P. *The Battle for Butte: Mining and Politics on the Northern Frontier, 1864–1906*. Helena, Montana: Montana Historical Society Press, 1995.

Malone, Michael P. *James J. Hill: Empire Builder of the Northwest*. Norman, Oklahoma: University of Oklahoma Press, 1996.

Malone, Michael P. and Richard B. Roeder. (Eds.) *Montana's Past: Selected Essays*. Missoula, Montana: University of Montana Press, 1973.

Marcosson, Isaac F. *Anaconda*. New York: Dodd, Mead & Company, 1957.

Martin, Albro. *Enterprise Denied: Origins of the Decline of American Railroads, 1897–1917*. New York: Columbia University Press, 1971.

Martin, Albro. *James J. Hill and the Opening of the Northwest*. New York: Oxford University Press, 1976.

Mayer, Lynne R., and Kenneth E. Vose. *Makin' Tracks*. New York: Prager, 1975.

McAdoo, William G. *Crowded Years: The Reminiscences of William G. McAdoo*. Boston: Houghton Mifflin Company, 1931.

Middleton, William D. *The Time of the Trolley*. Milwaukee, Wisconsin: Kalmbach Publishing Company, 1967.

Middleton, William D. *When the Steam Railroads Electrified*. Milwaukee, Wisconsin: Kalmbach Books, 1974.

Miller, Richard N. (Editor). *Guidebook for the Butte Field Meeting of the Society of Economic Geologists*. Butte, Montana: Ananconda Company, 1978.

Morris, Patrick F. *Ananconda Montana: Copper Smelting Boom Town on the Western Frontier*. Bethesda, Maryland: Swann Publishing, 1997.

Myers, Rex C. and Harry W. Fritz. *Montana and the West: Essays in Honor of K. Ross Toole*. Boulder, Colorado: Pruett Publishing Co., 1984.

Myrick, David F. *Railroads of Arizona*, Volume 1. Berkeley, California: Howell North Books, 1975.

Myrick, David F. *Railroads of Nevada and Eastern California*, Volume 2. Berkeley, California: Howell North Books, 1963.

Navin, Thomas R. *Copper Mining and Management*. Tucson, Arizona: University of Arizona Press, 1978.

Paul, Rodman W. *Mining Frontiers of the Far West, 1848–1880*. New York: Holt, Rinehart & Winston, 1963.

Peterson, Richard H. *The Bonanza Kings: The Social Origins and Business Behavior of Western Mining Entrepreneurs, 1870–1900*. Norman, Oklahoma: University of Oklahoma Press, 1991.

Pinkepank, Jerry. *The Second Diesel Spotter's Guide*. Milwaukee, Wisconsin: Kalmbach Publishing Co., 1973.

Ploss, Thomas H. *The Nation Pays Again*. Chicago: Thomas H. Ploss, 1984.

Renz, Louis T. *Northern Pacific Data Tables*. Walla Walla, Washington: Louis T. Renz, 1974.

Richardson, Elmo. *Dams, Parks and Politics*. Lexington, Kentucky: University Press of Kentucky, 1973.

Rickard, T. A. *A History of American Mining*. New York: McGraw-Hill, 1932.

Riegal, Robert E. *The Story of the Western Railroads*. New York: MacMillan, 1926.

Robertson, Donald B. *Encyclopedia of Western Railroad History: Volume II, The Mountain States: Colorado, Idaho, Montana, Wyoming*. Dallas, Texas: Taylor Publishing, 1991.

Sandford, Barrie. *McCulloch's Wonder: The Story of the Kettle Valley Railway*. West Vancouver, B. C.: Whitecap Books, 1977.

Schwantes, Carlos A. *Coxey's Army: An American Odyssey*. Lincoln, Nebraska: University of Nebraska Press, 1985.

Schwantes, Carlos A. *Long Day's Journey: The Steamboat and Stagecoach Era in the Northern West*. Seattle: University of Washington Press, 1999.

Schwantes, Carlos A. *Railroad Signatures Across the Pacific Northwest*. Seattle: University of Washington Press, 1993.

Sharfman, I. Leo. *The American Railroad Problem: A Study in War and Reconstruction*. New York: Century Company, 1921.

Shovers, Brian, Mark Fiege, Dale Martin, and Fred Quivik. *Butte and Anaconda Revisited: An Overview of Early-Day Mining and Smelting in Montana*. Montana Bureau of Mines and Geology Special Publication Number 99. Butte, Montana: Montana College of Mineral Science and Technology, 1991.

Smalley, Eugene V. *History of the Northern Pacific Railroad*. New York: G. P. Putnam's Sons, 1883.

Smith, Duane A. *Rocky Mountain Mining Camps: The Urban Frontier*. Bloomington, Indiana: Indiana University Press, 1967.

Smith, Grant H. *The History of the Comstock Lode*. Reno, Nevada: Nevada Bureau of Mines and Geology, 1998.

Spence, Clark C. *Mining Engineers and the American West: The Lace-Boot Brigade, 1849–1933*. Moscow, Idaho: University of Idaho Press, 1993.

Stover, John F. *American Railroads*. Chicago, Illinois: University of Chicago Press, 1997.

Stover, John F. *The Life and Decline of the American Railroad*. New York: Oxford University Press, 1971.

Taylor, Bill, and Jan Taylor. *The Northern Pacific's Rails to Gold and Silver: Lines to Montana's Mining Camps, Volume I: 1883–1887*. Missoula, Montana: Pictorial Histories Publishing Company, 1999.

Taylor, Bill and Jan Taylor. *Over Homestake Pass on The Butte Short Line: the Construction Era, 1888–1929*. Missoula, Montana: Pictorial Histories Publishing Company, 1998.

Toole, K. Ross. *Montana: An Uncommon Land*. Norman, Oklahoma: University of Oklahoma Press, 1959.

Toole, K. Ross. *Twentieth Century Montana: A State of Extremes*. Norman, Oklahoma: University of Oklahoma Press, 1972.

Turner, Robert D. *Logging by Rail: The British Columbia Story*. Victoria, BC: Sono Nis Press, 1990.

Wahmann, Russell. *Narrow Gauge to Jerome: The United Verde & Pacific Railway*. Boulder, Colorado: Pruett Publishing, 1988.

Warne, Colston E. *The Pullman Boycott of 1894: The Problems of Federal Intervention*. Boston: D. C. Heath, 1955.

White, John H. *The American Railroad Freight Car: From the Wood Car Era to the Coming of Steel*. Baltimore, Maryland: Johns Hopkins University Press, 1993.

White, John H. *The American Railroad Passenger Car*. Baltimore, Maryland: Johns Hopkins University Press, 1971.

White, Richard. *"It's Your Misfortune and None of My Own": A History of the American West*. Norman, Oklahoma: University of Oklahoma Press, 1991.

Winks, Robin W. *Frederick Billings: A Life*. New York: Oxford University Press, 1991.

Wood, Frances and Dorothy. *I Hauled These Mountains in Here*. Caldwell, Idaho: Caxton Printers, Ltd, 1977.

Wyman, Mark. *Hard Rock Epic: Western Miners and the Industrial Revolution, 1860–1910*. Berkeley, California: University of California Press, 1979.

Yergin, Daniel. *The Prize: The Epic Quest for Oil, Money, and Power*. New York: Simon and Schuster, 1991.

Young, Otis E., Jr. *Western Mining*. Norman, Oklahoma: University of Oklahoma Press, 1970.

Articles

Dictionary of American Biography. Vol. 4. S. v. "Clark, William A."

Dictionary of American Biography. Vol. 5. S. v. "Daly, Marcus."

Dictionary of American Biography. Vol. 8. S. v. "Haggin, James Ben Ali."

Dictionary of American Biography. Vol. 8. S. v. "Hearst, George."

Dictionary of American Biography. Vol. 8. S. v. "Heinze, F. Augustus."

Dictionary of American Biography. Vol. 16. S. v. "Rogers, Henry H."

Dictionary of American Biography. Vol. 16. S. v. "Ryan, John D."

Dictionary of American Biography. Vol. 18. S. v. "Tevis, Lloyd."

Dictionary of American Biography. Vol. 20. S. v. "Westinghouse, George."

Doyle, Susan Badger. "Indian Perspectives of the Bozeman Trail," *Montana: The Magazine of Western History*, 40 No. 1 (Winter, 1990), pp. 56–57.

Dusenberry, Verne. "The Northern Cheyenne: All They Have Asked is to Live in Montana," *Montana: The Magazine of Western History*, 5 No. 1 (Winter, 1955), pp. 23–40.

Ferrell, Mallory H. "Utah and Northern: The Narrow Gauge that Opened a Frontier," *Colorado Rail Annual* No. 15, pp. 9–81. Golden, Colorado: Colorado Railroad Museum, 1981.

Gressley, Gene M. "Historical Commentary—Colonialism: The Perpetual Pendulum?," *Montana: The Magazine of Western History*, 38 No. 4 (Autumn, 1988), pp. 70–73.

Hauck, Cornelius W. "OSL&UN: The Oregon Short Line Era," *Colorado Rail Annual* No. 15, pp. 82–92. Golden, Colorado: Colorado Railroad Museum, 1981.

Hauck, Cornelius W. "Union Pacific, Montana Division," *Colorado Rail Annual* No. 15, pp. 93–160. Golden, Colorado: Colorado Railroad Museum, 1981.

Havard, Jack. "No Fleet Angle," *Montana: The Magazine of Western History*, 44 No. 3 (Summer, 1994), pp. 46–55.

Jackson, W. Turrentine. "Wells Fargo Stagecoaching in Montana: Trials and Triumphs," *Montana: The Magazine of Western History*, 29 No. 2 (April, 1979), pp. 38–53.

Johnson, Carrie. "Electrical Power, Copper, and John D. Ryan," *Montana: The Magazine of Western History*, 38 No. 4 (Autumn, 1988), pp. 24–37.

Keyes, Norman C. and Kenneth R. Middleton. "The Great Northern Railway, All-Time Locomotive Roster, 1861–1970," *Railway & Locomotive Historical Society Bulletin* No. 143 (Autumn, 1980), pp. 20–123.

Malone, Michael P. and Richard B. Roeder. "Mining," *Montana: The Magazine of Western History*, 25 No. 2 (Spring, 1975) pp. 21–35.

Martin, Mark W., J. H. Dilles, and J. M. Proffett. "U-Pb Geochronologic Constraints for the Butte Porphyry System," *Geologic Society of America Abstracts with Programs*, 31 No. 7 (1999), p. A-380.

Quivik, Frederic L. "Historical Landscapes—Early Steel Transmission Towers and Energy for Montana's Copper Industry," *Montana: The Magazine of Western History*, 38 No. 4 (Autumn, 1988), pp 67–69.

Rogers, Gordon W. "Where Electrification First Made Good: Butte, Anaconda & Pacific, Laboratory Under Catenary," *Trains* Magazine, Vol. 23 No. 9 (July, 1963) pp. 16–28.

Toole, K. Ross. "Anaconda Copper Mining Company: A Price War and a Copper Corner," *Pacific Northwest Quarterly*, Vol. 41 (October, 1950) pp. 312–329.

Toole, K. Ross. "When Big Money Came to Butte," *Pacific Northwest Quarterly*, 44 (January, 1953) pp. 23–29.

Wells, Merle W. "The Western Federation of Miners." *Journal of the West*, Vol. 12 No. (1973) pp. 18–35.

White, W. Thomas. "Boycott: The Pullman Strike in Montana," *Montana: The Magazine of Western History*, 29 No. 4 (October, 1979) pp. 2–13.

Newspapers

Anaconda *Standard*. Anaconda, Montana. 1884–1901.
Butte *Daily Miner*. Butte, Montana. 1884–1897.
Butte *Semi-Weekly Miner*. Butte, Montana. 1889.
Helena *Independent Record*. Helena, Montana 1889.
Missoula *Gazette*, Missoula, Montana. 1889.
Montana *Standard*. 1954–1980.
New York *Times*. New York, New York. 1885–1985.
Spokane *Spokesman-Review*. Spokane, Washington. 1999.

Unpublished Material

Leighton, Douglas Frank. "The Corporate History of the Montana Power Company, 1882–1913." M.A. thesis, University of Montana, 1951.

McCarthy, Thomas B. "From West Cork to Butte: The Irish Immigration to Montana, 1860–1900." M.A. thesis, Washington State University, 1987.

McNelis, Sarah. "The Life of F. Augustus Heinze." M.A. thesis, Montana State University, 1947.

Mercier, Laurie Kay. "Smelter City: Labor, Gender and Cultural Politics in Anaconda, Montana, 1934–1980." Ph.D. dissertation, University of Oregon, 1995.

Meyers, Rex C. "Montana: A State and Its Relationship with Railroads, 1854–1970." Ph.D. dissertation, University of Montana, 1972.

Tabor, Thomas T. "Short Lines of the Treasure State." Typescript, Madison, New Jersey, 1960. Copy in Montana Historical Society, Helena, Montana.

Toole, K. Ross. "A History of the Anaconda Copper Mining Company: A Study in the Relationship Between a State and Its People and a Corporation, 1880–1950." Ph.D. dissertation, University of California, Los Angeles, 1954.

Toole, K. Ross. "Marcus Daly: A Study of Business in Politics." M.A. thesis, University of Montana, 1948.

INDEX

Asterisk (*) indicates an illustration.

A

Acquisition claim, 9
air hose couplings, 85–87
Alder Gulch, Montana, 20–21
Alice Mine, 9–10
alternating current, 57–60, 63
Amalgamated Copper Co., 2, 12–15
amalgamation (ore processing), 6–7
American Car & Foundry (ACF) (car builder), 49, 114
American Locomotive Co., Schenectady, NY (ALCO)
    locomotives built, 45, 50
American Railway Union (ARU), 41
Anaconda Copper Mining Co. (ACM), 1, 5, 7, 14, 19, 24–25, 29, 33–34, 43, 63, 77–78, 81–82, 102–3, 109, 111, 113, 115, 119
    lumber department, 26
Anaconda (business car), 49*
Anaconda Mine, 2, 10, 10*, 11, 15, 24
Anaconda electrolytic refinery, 14
Anaconda, Montana, 5, 12–13, 25, 28–29, 35, 37*, 41, 114, 119–20
Anselmo Mine, 5, 100–1, 102*
Argo smelter, 13
Asteroid claim, 6
Atlantic Cable Mine, 69
Atlantic Richfield Co. (ARCO), 2, 115–16
Avery, Idaho, 69

B

Baldwin Locomotive Works
    locomotives built, 50, 64, 106
Baltimore & Ohio (B&O), 59–60
Bannack, Montana, 20–21
Bell Mine, 15
Bellinger, Frank W., 105, 108–9, 111–12
Bercaw, Corliss A., 105, 107, 111
Berkeley Pit (mine), 5, 108, 113
Bingham Pit (mine), 12, 106, 112
Bitterroot Valley, Montana, 34
Black Eagle smelter, 80, 92
Blackfeet Indian Reserve, 27
block caving (mining), 99–100
bonds (electrical), 65, 65*
Bonner, E. L., 26
Bonner, Montana, 28, 30
Boston & Colorado smelter, 12
Boston & Montana Consolidated Copper & Silver Mining Co. (B&M), 12–13, 15
Bozeman Trail, 20
brakes (railroad), 46–47
Broadwater, Charles A., 27, 35
Brooks Locomotive Works
    locomotives built, 37–38, 43–44, 61
Brooks, Robert E., 93, 108
Browns, Montana (quarry), 83–85, 108
Burlington Northern-Santa Fe (BNSF), 116
Butte, Montana, 5, 10*, 19–29 *passim*, 36, 44*, 101*, 111, 115, 119–20
Butte, Anaconda & Pacific (BA&P), 19, 33–34, 36, 42–43, 77–78, 116
    incorporated, 34
    begins service, 36
    surveys extensions, 42–43, 77–78
    sold, 116

(BA&P) electric operations begun, 65–66
(BP&P) freight cars, 39–40, 47*, 48*, 79, 88–89, 89*, 90*, 90–91, 93*, 112, 114*
(BP&P), Georgetown Extension (Southern Cross Branch), 66, 66*, 69, 83–84, 83*, 84*
(BP&P) labor relations, 41
(BP&P) line cars, 79, 79*, 85, 85*
(BP&P) locomotives, diesel-electric, 107, 107*, 108, 112*, 113*, 114
(BP&P) locomotives, electric, 62*, 64*, 65, 66*, 67–69, 68*, 69*, 70*, 71*, 77–78, 78*, 79, 80*, 88*, 102*, 103*, 104*, 107–8, 110*, 111*, 114, 119*, 120*
(BP&P), locomotives, steam, 37, 37*, 38*, 43, 44*, 45, 45*, 50, 50*, 58*, 61*, 64*, 66*, 67, 67*, 78, 78*, 79, 83, 83*, 89, 105–6, 106*
    retirement of, 107–8
(BP&P) Missoula Gulch Branch, 35, 41, 58*, 109*
(BP&P) passenger service, begins, 36, 40, 50*, 52, 62*, 66*
    electrified, 69, 69*, 70*, 82*, 83, 89
    mixed service, 89, 93, 110
    ended, 110, 110*
(BP&P) shops, 40*, 91*
(BP&P) Smelter Hill Branch, 66–67, 68*, 80*, 108, 113
(BP&P) wrecking crane, 81, 81*
Butte & Boston Consolidated Mining Co. (B&B), 12
Butte Hill, 5–6, 10*, 35, 41–42, 48*, 66, 92*, 108
Butte Hill Yard (BA&P), 42, 65*, 68, 103*, 104, 119*

C

Canadian National Railway (CN), 73
Cascade Tunnel , 60, 72
catenary (current distribution system), 60, 64–65, 85
Central Pacific (CP), 19
Chicago, Milwaukee & St. Paul (CM&St.P), 19, 29, 51, 63, 70, 70*, 71, 71*, 78, 82
    reaches Butte, 51
    use of BA&P trackage, 51, 63
Chicago, Milwaukee, St. Paul & Pacific (CMSt.P&P), 107–8
chloridization (ore processing), 7
Clark, William A., 1–3, 3*, 7, 12, 15
Cleveland, Grover, 27
Cliff Junction, Montana, 51
coal (fuel), 23–25
coal mines, 24–25, 28, 30
Colorado & Montana smelter, 12, 25
Colorado Junction, Montana, 30, 51, 71
Colusa Mine, 10, 15
Colusa smelter, 13
common carrier status, 109–11
Comstock Lode (Nevada), 6–9, 21
concentration (ore processing), 13
Consolidated Connector Corporation, 86
Continental Pit (mine), 5, 116
copper mining, 5
    Arizona, 9, 106
    Michigan, 9
    Montana, 9
    Nevada, 106
    Utah, 106
Corrine, Utah, 21
couplers (car), 46

D

Daly, Marcus, 1–2, 2*, 3, 5, 7, 9–10, 13, 15, 27–29, 33–36, 63, 119–20
    arrives in Butte, 9

ABOUT THE AUTHOR

Photo by Carol Raczykowski

CHARLES V. MUTSCHLER was born in Albuquerque, New Mexico, and spent much of his childhood in Colorado, New Mexico, and Utah. As a young boy he became fascinated with steam locomotives, railroads in general, and the mining camps of the American West. Following these interests in his academic work, he earned two master of arts degrees and a Ph.D. through research in the history of business, technology, and industry in the western United States. Charles Mutschler is currently employed as a university archivist and adjunct professor of history at Eastern Washington University in Cheney, Washington. His hobbies include bicycling, hiking, model railroading, and photography.